Punishment

A Philosophical and Criminological Inquiry

PHILIP BEAN

Martin Robertson · Oxford

© Philip Bean, 1981

First published in 1981 by
Martin Robertson & Company Ltd.,
108 Cowley Road, Oxford OX4 1JF.

British Library Cataloguing in Publication Data

Bean, Philip
  Punishment.
  1. Punishment
  I. Title
  364.6'01   HV8675

  ISBN 0-85520-391-9

Typeset in 10 on 12 pt Vladimir
by Pioneer, East Sussex.

Printed and bound in Great Britain by
Book Plan, Worcester.

Punishment

Contents

For Cynthia, Elizabeth, Gilbert and Vic

Preface

In 1976 I wrote *Rehabilitation and Deviance* as an intended polemic against the then prevailing view that rehabilitation was the only acceptable and humanitarian means of dealing with offenders. It brought forth from those who supported rehabilitation a considerable amount of hostility but no real debate. It was almost as if rehabilitation had become a belief system which was open to challenge only from the non-believers. However, in the last four years the subject matter has moved on a great deal, and it seems now as if the time is right to produce a less polemical and wider view of the issues involved in punishment. What follows therefore is an attempt to examine the major arguments relating to punishment, to show how those arguments relate to justice, and to show how a penal system would operate if any of those arguments dominated. There is also a concluding chapter on the punishment of children — an area neglected by traditional forms of philosophical inquiry but now assuming increasing importance. The book is written mainly from a philosophical standpoint, for it seemed to me that criminology must draw on its philosophical foundations if it is to continue its development. It also seemed as if the argument about punishment was a moral one requiring constant justification.

The most pleasurable part of the whole exercise is to thank those who gave their time to read the drafts and make comments, I would like to thank Professor John Smith at the University of Nottingham and Sister Patricia C.S.J., at the Good Shepherd School for the care taken to read the drafts and for the comments they made, all of which were considered and warmly appreciated. To Professor David Marsh and to my colleagues in the Department of Applied Social Science, University of Nottingham, I wish to record sincere thanks, and particularly to Stewart MacPherson, who bore the brunt of the discussions. As too did my wife Valerie and son Ian.

Ann Hodson typed the drafts in her usual efficient manner. To all

who assisted I acknowledge their help. Needless to say, the errors
that remain are mine.

Philip Bean
Department of Applied Social Science
University of Nottingham
September 1980

1

Overview and Definition

In 1974 Nils Christie said an air of coolness pervaded the concept and practice of punishment. He thought that punishment was not the type of activity that fitted the spirit of the times (Christie, 1974). He also noted that there were subtle attempts to conceal the nature of punishment by substituting terms such as 'sanctions', 'treatment' or perhaps 'training'. He could have added that attempts at disguise are seldom wholly successful particularly from those at the receiving end, yet disguises remain none the less.

It is not my intention here to examine the forms of those disguises, except and in so far as they affect the central issue, which is the nature and justification for punishment. Contrary to some accepted views, I do not believe we punish less than before. We may punish in different ways, and occasionally be more humane in our application, but we still punish. We punish offenders in the courts, we punish our children, and we punish countless others who break social rules. I do not think a great deal can be achieved by ignoring these simple facts. Few of us would, I think, be opposed to all forms of punishment for all people at all times. There may be a small number who can honestly claim that they have never punished their children (nor would never) and an equally small number who oppose the punishment of all offenders. Most of us find that the desire to punish is deeply ingrained within us and accept it as such. We may, like Bentham, say it is regrettable; and like Bentham we may regard other means that secure compliance as being more to our liking, yet accept punishment as a measure of last resort. For most of us it would be dishonest to say otherwise. Again with Bentham, we might say that all punishment is evil and ought to be admitted only in as far as it promises to exclude some greater evil (Bentham, 1948, p. 281). I do not want to suggest that most of us are, or should be, utilitarians; I only wish to extract from Bentham the sentiments that punishment may be regrettable.

The essence of punishment is that it involves suffering, or, in Grotius's terms, 'The infliction of an ill suffered for an ill done'. The suffering created by punishment is not incidental but the deliberate work of persons who claim the right to inflict it. Perhaps this explains why coolness surrounds the debate and why Nils Christie did not think punishment fitted the spirit of the times, for few of us may wish to be associated with the deliberate infliction of suffering. Inevitably strong emotions tend to be aroused by the nature of the subject matter. We cannot escape these, nor should we try; for they are integral to our inquiry and occasionally they provide the major thrust behind the debate. The aim here is to understand that debate and in later chapters to try to point to areas that are likely to assume importance in the immediate future.

Since punishment involves suffering it has led to strenuous attempts to justify it. In general terms some would justify punishment as being deserved for an offence, that is, as retribution; others would regard it as a means of controlling action, that is as deterrence or prevention. Still others would see it as a means of producing some form of moral or psycho-social regeneration, that is, as reform or rehabilitation. Within these general areas there are numerous divisions and subdivisions depending on the positions adopted by various writers. A supporter of rehabilitation, for example, may have little in common with a Hegelian, yet both in their way could be said to support a reformist position. Furthermore, supporters of one theory are committed by their theory not to the support of the practice of punishment generally, but only to aspects that satisfy requirements that they stipulate. Neither would supporters of one theory be necessarily influenced by the empirical evidence that was produced to promote their position. It may be satisfying to know that empirical studies show the effectiveness of (say) deterrence over (say) reform, but that of itself cannot provide the justification for the theory. Justifications have to be found in the quality of the argument, which in this case is a moral one, and we cannot derive a moral position from empirical data. The position adopted depends therefore on the type of questions to be asked. "How can punishment be justified?' is a moral question. 'How effective are punishments?' is a different question altogether. Here we shall be concerned primarily with the moral question.

To the practitioner, such as the judge or magistrate, these distinctions may not matter; or, rather, they may matter less than to the theoretician engaged in evaluating the merits of the theory. The judge or magistrate is faced with different demands, some of which are dictated by law, some of which are dictated by the conventions appropriate to his office. The judge may sentence the first person for retributive reasons, the second for deterrence and the third for reform, believing that his duty in the latter case is to help the offender rather than (say) to protect society. We accept these apparent inconsistencies as a feature of modern life, knowing that institutions such as the courts or the penal system are rarely theoretically pure or devoted to one theory to the exclusion of others. And perhaps it ought not to be otherwise, for the domination of a single theory may stultify development in the penal system and lead to a position where the purity of the theory becomes the prime consideration. Yet while the theoretician claims to support only those practices that satisfy his theory, the practitioner, in this case the judge or magistrate, has less opportunity to be selective.

When we talk therefore of punishment within the penal system we are often talking about questions of emphasis. We can ask if a magistrate or judge is more of a retributivist than a reformist or is more committed to deterrence than to retribution. We can also talk of a question of emphasis at the institutional level. In juvenile justice, for example, we can note that the juvenile courts place emphasis on the value of rehabilitation. They do not do so to the exclusion of retribution or deterrence — the emphasis means that juvenile courts are more likely to pass reformist sentences than others. Often our assessments of sentencing practices or legal punishments are derived from trends in sentencing, or from the emphasis placed on one punishment rather than another. Inevitably we must operate within the limits of these generalizations.

I am not suggesting that the practitioner has a limited role, merely that he has a different one. The theoretician's task is to evaluate the merits of the arguments and examine competing claims. In doing so he ought not forget the restrictions imposed on the practitioner, some of which lie outside the merits of any theoretical argument. For example, the decision to send an offender to a detention centre may be frustrated by a shortage of places, so instead of passing a retributive sentence the court decides to place the offender on probation. Or the court may substitute a probation order for a fine if the judge is persuaded that the probation service is over-worked and unable to cope with an additional case. The judge's decision may appear to lack consistency, but without knowing the limitations placed upon him we may be too quick to condemn. Justifications that are practical sometimes have to be assessed in a different way from those that are theoretical.

In one sense, of course, most of us resemble practitioners. Like the judges, although for different reasons, we may operate according to one theory and change when circumstances change. We may be committed to reformist measures with our children but are retributive occasionally and sometimes act for deterrent reasons. We may also punish our children for reasons largely to do with our inability to reason further with them, perhaps because they have reduced us to the position where we have become exasperated. It is a matter neither of pride nor of condemnation to recognize this; nor is it of help to be told that other societies have a more 'positive' approach to children than our own. It is only necessary to recognize that there are parallels with the practitioners in the courts, and that, while non-theoretical considerations ought not to be overwhelming, they can at least reduce our fanaticism and point to our shortcomings.

One should not I think be pessimistic about such limitations. Recently a committee of American Friends attempted to review modern methods of punishment and make recommendations (von Hirsch, 1976). One committee member found himself agreeing with a report that criticized rehabilitation and supported deterrence. He said he could not, or rather he would not, accept it as a declaration of desirable policy: it was merely less unacceptable than others considered at that time (p. 187). I do not see why he should have been led to such pessimism, but that is because I do not believe that any approach can do more than recognize the strength of competing claims. Neither do I believe that there are definite answers to the problems surrounding the justifications for punishment. The most that can be done is to assess the arguments.

A WORKING DEFINITION OF PUNISHMENT

Grotius defined punishment as 'The infliction of an ill suffered for an ill done'. His definition encapsulates some essential features which provide a useful starting point for our inquiry, although the definition itself is not entirely adequate. This does not matter at this stage, for we are concerned only with the broad outline.

First, Grotius wishes to see punishment as an inflicted ill, and by doing so he makes a link between the punishment and the deed. (In all remaining aspects of this and other definitions the terms are used in a neutral sense; the link between punishment and crime does not imply retribution, for example.) Second, he shows that punishment is intentionally inflicted, and not a random imposition of pain. Third, Grotius implies, although he does not say so, that punishment is given to someone who is supposedly answerable for his wrongdoings, that is as opposed to someone not fully in possession of his reason. Finally, Grotius implies that punishment is a social act produced by those claiming the right to punish and imposed on those deemed to deserve it. Punishment is therefore the work of personal agencies and not an act of Providence or imposed by a Deity.

Grotius's definition needs enlarging and refining. That provided by Professor Flew (1954) is much more comprehensive. Punishment in Flew's terms consists of five criteria.

(1) It must involve an evil, an unpleasantness to the victim. This is self-explanatory, although Flew, following Hobbes, prefers terms like 'evil' and 'unpleasantness' to the more stark words such as 'pain'; the former avoids suggestion of flogging or forms of torture.

(2) It must be for an offence, actual or supposed. This too is self-explanatory, although Flew is careful to tie down his definition by emphasizing the offence. So, for example, he says that a term spent in an old-fashioned public school, although doubtless far less agreeable than a spell in a modern prison, is not punishment — unless, of course, the child was sent there as a result of his offending behaviour.

(3) It must be of an offender, actual or supposed. By insisting that punishment is directed to an offender, Flew makes a logical connection between the evil, the offence and the sufferer. In his view we cannot then logically punish the innocent; for this would suggest a logical shift in syntax, in that the word would carry different implications from that which it would convey in a standard case of its primary sense.

(4) It must be the work of personal agencies. Put another way, punishment must not be the natural consequences of an action, for Flew wants to argue that evils occurring to people as the result of misbehaviour but not by human actions are not punishments but penalties. Thus unwanted children and venereal disease are penalties of, but not the punishment for, sexual promiscuity.

(5) It must be imposed by authority conferred through or by the institutions against the rules of which the offence has been committed. Here Flew is following Hobbes, who argued that evil inflicted by anyone, even a public authority acting without preceding condemnation, is not to be styled by the name of punishment but as a hostile act (Hobbes, 1973,* pp. 224-5). Similarly, direct action by an aggrieved person with no pretentions to special authority is not properly called punishment. It may be revenge, as in vendetta, or it may, in Hobbes's terms, be an act of hostility, but it is not punishment.

To these five criteria Benn and Peters (1959) add another: that the unpleasantness should be an essential part of what is intended and not merely coincidental to some other area. This additional criterion adds tightness to the definition by fixing punishments to the intentions of the work of the personal agencies who impose it.

Defined in this way, punishment as used in its primary sense precludes self-imposed forms of unpleasantness as suggested in psychoanalysis, and the punishment of scapegoats. So, for example, when the National Socialists issued a decree that, for distributing illegal pamphlets or for actions abroad that damaged Germany's reputation, and for which the perpetrators could not be arrested, certain people in concentration camps were 'punished', this was a use of the term in its secondary sense (Moberly, 1968, p. 79). Furthermore, while it may not be a misuse of the term to talk of sportsmen having a 'punishing game', this usage disregards one or more of the criteria listed above and should be treated as an extended use of the term.

The value of Flew's definition over Grotius's is that Flew forces us to see punishment in terms of a system of rules. So a parent, a principal of a college — even perhaps an umpire — can be said to impose punishment in the same way as a court of law. Punishment is not the prerogative of the judiciary, although we tend often to use the term as if it were. Parents punish their children and do so by conforming to the criteria mentioned above, although unlike the courts parental punishment involves different methods of determining guilt and has different aims. We shall concentrate mainly on judicial punishment here, but reference will be made to other forms,

---

* References will be based on the edition used and not necessarily the original edition.

albeit obliquely, on some occasions. When parents punish children we can, following Bradley (1927, p. 31), call this pedagogic punishment.

Definitions provide a boundary and shape to the subject matter. They do not provide arguments about justifications, for these involve normative relationships which require separate analysis. None the less, some philosophers have wanted to show that the justification for punishment rests on its definition. For example, some retributionists suggest that definitions of punishments imply desserts (Mabbott, 1939). Others view punishment as implying unpleasantness based on a certain fitness and propriety in the nature of things that renders suffering a suitable concomitant of vice (Godwin, 1971). Retributionists are not alone in arguing that definitions of punishment relate to the justification. Utilitarians* such as Rawls have argued on similar lines (Rawls, 1955). We shall deal with these arguments in much greater detail in the following chapter. For these purposes the definition provided by Flew is reasonably satisfactory because it provides the right emphasis by concentrating on the nature of rules and the actions resulting from breaking those rules. It is not complete; offences of strict and vicarious liability present obvious difficulties (i.e. offences of strict liability that occur where, say, a shop owner unintentionally sells adulterated goods, and of vicarious liability, where, say, a shop owner is legally responsible for certain activities of his employees). Even if it is possible to show that certain types of punishments fit uneasily into our definition, nothing of a substantial nature follows this. All that is needed at this stage is to delineate the emphasis of our inquiry.

THE SPECIAL RELATIONSHIPS IN PUNISHMENT

We tend to speak of punishment in a generalized way, perhaps forgetting that there are certain groups exempt from punishment and others where the method of punishment is less severe. The former are governed by legal requirements, the latter by social conventions.

---

* The term 'utilitarian' will be used throughout to describe all who support a deterrent position. It is used as a shorthand way of describing one philosophical approach to punishment, and may or may not be connected to the wider requirements of utility.

In law children (or 'infants', to use the legal term) under the prosecutable age are exempt from legal punishment; those over the prosecutable age (now 10 years) are divided into age categories where punishment is dependent on the fulfilment of certain conditions; for example, for children over 10 and under 14 years they are exempt from punishment unless it is proved not only that they caused an *actus reus* with *mens rea* but did so with 'mischievous discretion'.[1] The insane are similarly placed, being able to claim the insanity defence, which may operate at one of two stages: either before the trial or before the verdict. We shall be concerned with the punishment of children in Chapter 4 but not with the insane or with other legal requirements relating to this particular defence.[2]

Social conventions affect the methods of punishment although not of course the justifications. As a general rule, girls are punished less severely than boys and probably less often. The sentencing practices of the courts and the penal system reflects these assumptions. While it is true that there are fewer female offenders than males (about 8 per cent of boys in the 14- 18-year age bracket come before the courts in England and Wales compared with 2 per cent of girls), there are correspondingly fewer provisions for the female offenders. There are no detention centres for girls (one was started but quickly closed); there is only one closed borstal, and here the range of training activities is severely restricted. There are only three districts in England and Wales where a girl may be ordered to spend twelve or up to twenty-four hours, usually on Saturday afternoons at an attendance centre[3] (*The Times,* 9 July 1980). To some extent the lack of provisions reflects the lower numbers of offenders, but there is, I suggest, a marked reluctance by the courts to punish women or girls as severely as men, or to punish them in the same manner. Girls in schools are rarely given corporal punishment, nor is there any debate or any proposals that suggest it should be otherwise. The impression created by most writers, philosophers and criminologists alike is that punishment is given by males to males. Little or no discussion exists that attempts to discuss punishment in relation to gender. I think this would be a worthwhile area of study for social science generally and criminology in particular, although I would expect to see this rectified in the near future anyway. Unfortunately, a discussion of this nature requires much more than could be achieved within the scope of this book, although some references will be made throughout.

In spite of these conventions, the debate about punishment has always been concerned with the justifications for imposing suffering — and I suppose it always will. But while the arguments may not change, at least in their essential features, the way in which they are approached and the emphasis placed on certain aspects of the discussion need to be sifted over. Criminology has tended to ignore punishment, being somewhat over-concerned with the social and personal characteristics of the offenders, and more recently with the nature of penal institutions or the nature of the methods of control. My reasons for resurrecting the arguments are this: that punishment is central to the criminologists' subject matter, and without a close examination of punishment we shall ignore this simple but important point; second, that unless we recognize this we shall no longer be aware of its influence. (For the fact remains that punishment continues irrespective of the attention given to it by criminologists.)

A re-examination of the argument allows us to keep pace with events and hopefully to point to new areas of interest and doubt. That is to be the main aim throughout. In the next chapter the major arguments will be examined in order to show the boundaries of the subject matter. These boundaries have been called 'the great debate', if only to imply that certain areas are strongly disputed. Here the three major theories of punishment, retribution deterrence and rehabilitation will be examined, and their strengths and weaknesses determined. In the remaining chapters questions relating to justice, a justice decision, the punishment of juveniles, and trends in the modern penal system will be asked in respect of these theories in order to show that each has its own unique contribution to make. While I have tried to represent the merits of each theory, I have also tried to show that retribution has more merits than it is usually credited with — a somewhat unfashionable position to adopt.

NOTES

1. An excellent review of the law relating to children can be found in Smith, and Hogan, (1978), Chapter 9, entitled 'General Defences'. Smith and Hogan say that, where D has caused an *actus reus* with the appropriate *mens rea*, he will generally be held liable. But this is not invariably so, for there are certain defences that may still be available even in this situation. As well as special defences that apply in the case of particular crimes, there are certain defences that apply in the case of crimes generally (p. 155). Infancy and insanity are those discussed in detail by the authors.

2. The insanity defence and the issues surrounding it are complex. For a review and some recent proposals see HMSO (1975a).

3. Those not familiar with terms such as 'detention centre', 'borstal' or 'attendance centre' are advised to consult HMSO (1969) or Cross (1975). Briefly, detention centres are custodial centres, mainly for three months, for young people under the age of 21 where the regime is 'brisk and firm'. Borstals are medium-term training sentences for a similar age group, and attendance centres are non-custodial sentences for young offenders which operate on Saturday afternoons for periods of three hours at a time.

2

The Great Debate

The great theories of punishment, retribution, deterrence and reform stand in open and flagrant contradiction. Each side has arguments that are used to demonstrate the consequences of the rival theories. Supporters of retribution accuse the utilitarians of opportunism and the reformists of vicious paternalism. The utilitarians accuse the retributivists of vindictiveness and the reformists of failing to justify punishment by an insistence on treatment. The reformists see the retributivists as cruel, and utilitarians as inadequate when they attempt to control action. To complicate matters further, each theory has splinter groups offering rival or amended arguments. It is no easy task to pick one's way through the variety of positions adopted in this debate.

And yet the debate is important because it involves grave consequences for penal policy, for penal reform, and for all offenders who are punished each day in the courts. Although we may know or think we know more about the causes of crime, punishment is no less important now than hitherto. We may one day be able to use our knowledge of 'causes' to eradicate crime or to direct antisocial people into more socially approved activities, but that day is still far off. Nor do I know if the use of such knowledge would be desirable. In the meantime, punishment remains with us and requires justification.

In this and the following chapter the discussion on punishment will be confined to those areas that have direct relevance to the penal system. It is not therefore the intention to make an exhaustive review of punishment *per se*, for this has been done numerous times elsewhere. For these purposes the overall aim is to confine attention to the study of punishment in order that a greater understanding can be gained of the penal system generally.

RETRIBUTION

The theory of retribution has had a long and distinguished history. Recently it has fallen into disrepute, and some philosophers have gone so far as to predict its ultimate demise. In almost desperate tones one philosopher entitled his paper 'The retributionist hits back' (Armstrong, 1961), almost as if he feared that retribution was being swamped or neglected, and felt the need to keep the argument to the fore. He need not have worried; retribution has retained, and I suspect always will retain, its place in the philosophical debate on punishment. Yet those retributivists who believe they are reduced to a minority will also know how unpopular is their doctrine. In Britain, Professor McTaggart always called it 'vindictive retribution', and Professor Nowell-Smith argues that the retributive theory has a logical justification if a certain theological view is accepted; that view having been abandoned, the justification no longer exists. We are then forced back to the position, says Nowell-Smith, that punishment is fitting (1948, p. 230). I do not dispute that retribution involves a form of intuition, or that it is an appeal to arguments about natural law; but for Nowell-Smith to dismiss it on a crude socio-historical analysis is somewhat surprising. On that basis, deterrence could easily be linked to superstitions and rehabilitation to the witch-doctor. And what if they were? It would not affect the logical or philosophical merits of the argument.[1]

We find similar attempts to discredit retribution in the United States. The 1972 edition of the Model Sentencing Act states that 'Sentences should not be based on revenge and retribution'. The link with revenge is undoubtedly a slur and intentionally so, and a deliberate attempt to convince others that retribution was somehow barbaric. And yet I do not believe that retribution is intrinsically more barbaric than any other philosophy of punishment, and it is a good deal more honest than most, and more worthy of consideration for that reason alone. The Model Sentencing Act provides no reason why retribution should be so readily dismissed or why it should be linked to revenge for 'revenge' is unrestrained hostility, whereas retribution is entirely different.

RULES AND MORALS

There is no single theory of retribution, although Kant and Bradley provide the clearest examples with Bradley being the fiercest retributionist of modern times.

> Punishment is punishment only where it is deserved. We pay the penalty because we owe it and for no other reason; and if punishment is inflicted for any other reason whatever than because it is merited by wrong, it is a gross immorality, a crying injustice, an abominable crime and not what it pretends to be.[Bradley, 1927, pp. 26-7]

Bradley insists that there is a necessary connection between punishment and guilt. No person is to be punished unless he deserves it, and he deserves punishment because he has been guilty of doing wrong. 'Punishment is the denial of wrong by the assertion of right,' says Bradley (p. 27); or 'punishment is the complement of criminal desert; it is justifiable only so far as deserved and further is an end in itself'. Bradley's position contrasts with the utilitarians, who see punishment as a means to an end and not an end in itself. John Stuart Mill, for example, said 'there are two ends of punishment: the benefit of the offender himself, and the protection of others'. Bradley would not agree, for Mill would be seen as using punishment to secure another ethical system whereby the offender becomes a means to that attainment.

Now when Bradley insists on a necessary connection between punishment and guilt, he is stating one of the strongest arguments in favour of retribution, because he is arguing that only the guilty are to be punished and that guilt is a necessary condition of punishment. A similar argument has been provided by Kant.

> Punishment can never be administered merely as a means for promoting another good, either with regard to the criminal himself or to civil society, but must in all cases by imposed only because the individual on whom it is inflicted has committed a crime. For a man ought never to be dealt with merely as a means subservient to the purpose of another, nor be mixed up with the subjects of real right. Against such treatment his inborn personality has a right to protect him, even although he may be condemned to lose his civil personality. He must first be found guilty and punishable before there can be any thought of drawing from his punishment any benefit for himself or his fellow citizens. [Kant, 1897]

The link between punishment and guilt can be interpreted in one of two ways. First, it can be taken as a logical connection, for example as Anthony Quinton suggests when he says that if a man says to another 'I am going to punish you' and is asked 'What for?' he cannot reply 'nothing at all' or 'something you have not done'.

Quinton says that when we say 'punishment implies guilt' it is the same sort of assertion as 'ought implies can'. It is not, therefore, pointless to blame the innocent as some have argued, for it is often very useful; rather, the very conditions of punishment do not obtain in these circumstances (Quinton, 1954, pp. 137-8).

Retributionists, such as Bradley or Kant, are not content to see a logical connection but claim a moral one also. The link is established by making punishment a question of responsibility, for 'responsibility means punishment and punishment is the same as accountability' (Bradley, 1927, p. 32). 'Responsibility' can be interpreted in a number of ways: Bradley seems to use it in the sense of accountability, or of there being no compulsion and no defect of reason on the part of the offender. (A more detailed discussion on this follows in Chapter 4.) Bradley assumes that punishment can follow only when men can see the consequences of their actions and learn to avoid those that have punishment included. Or in Aristotelion terms, it is not a man's passions that are judged but his ability to control or fail to control them. Bradley, like Aristotle, would point to the responsibility man has towards his passions and show that praise or blame follows according to the extent of control.

Central to the retributive position is the connection between punishment and guilt — and, of course, the connection between punishment and moral guilt. This may appear at first sight to be a truism, but if it is then it is one of some importance, for no such truism exists in the utilitarian and rehabilitative theory. Kant argued that the right to punish contained in the criminal law is the right that the magistrate has to inflict pain on a subject in consequence of his having committed a crime (1965, p. 99). So it is with all rules. J. D. Mabbott shows how, as a warden of a university hall, he enforced the rules and punished those who broke them. He had no intention of reforming the offenders, or of deterring others, but was merely acting to enforce rules which he as warden was duty bound to do (Mabbott, 1939).

The second link is more contentious. Bradley wants to argue that there is a close connection between guilt and morality. So, punishment is imposed not because someone by chance unhappily and unintentionally breaks the law (unless for offences of strict liability), but because the offender is responsible and the law reflects moral sentiments. To a retributivist such as Bradley utilitarian views are unrealistic, for the criminal law is seen as resting on considerations of policy and utilitarianism discounts all moral indignation against wrongdoers. Bradley would therefore agree with Dr Ewing, who said: 'If our punishments were merely deterrent and not also disgraces they would not do their deterring work adequately', or, again, 'A theory which does not take account of the moral side of punishment can hardly . . . be complete, for an essential feature of crime is that it is morally wrong, and a theory of punishment which is wholly expressed in terms of pain can hardly be adequate to the moral issues involved' (Ewing, 1929, pp. 61, 60).

We find a similar argument stated by Kant, who said that punishment must at all times be inflicted on a person for no other reason than because he has acted criminally. Kant was linking punishment to the law, and the law in Kant's terms is a categorical imperative; 'and woe to the man who crawls through the serpentine windings of the happiness doctrine to find out some consideration which by its promise of advantage should free the criminal from his penalty, or even from any degree thereof' (Kant, 1965, p. 100). For Kant, punishment, guilt, the law and even justice are all theoretically linked.

Now it is questionable whether there is a direct link between law and morality. Law may be equated with morality in some instances but not in others; and there are many examples where morality is not equated with law. All this is well known and needs no further elaboration. However, the link between guilt and punishment opens up the argument to include the justification for punishments generally. Here the retributivist is on less sure ground, for he refuses to look at the consequences of punishment for its justification. It is virtually impossible for him to answer the question, 'What justification can there be for rules requiring that those who break them should be made to suffer?' Retributivists in general do not see that they have to justify the existence of rules except and in so far as they equate rule-breaking with wickedness. They might appeal to some ethic which has provided rules to preserve life and property, or justify them as Kant does as a means of preserving freedom, or perhaps dismiss the question by saying it is not a matter for concern. Alternatively, they might say that law represents the decision of democratic society and ought to be respected for that reason alone. However, once legal rules have been provided the retributivist accepts that they represent and reflect the moral order. But if all wrongdoing is wrong, ought there not to be a law to punish all wickedness?

Clearly there isn't, and retributivists are hard put to show why. Often they do nothing more than fall back on the position that law self-evidently represents rules that prevent wrongdoing.

What if it doesn't? What can the retributivist do about bad law? Presumably he can say that bad laws ought not to be obeyed and those who break them have not acted wickedly. How can he make such an assertion, for on what basis does he decide which are good and which are bad? He begins to be faced with insurmountable difficulties. This problem has led some retributivists such as Sir Ernest Barker and Professor Mabbott to avoid the debate altogether and see punishment as a natural corollory of law-breaking. 'The mental rule of law which pays back a violation of itself by a violent return, much as the natural rules of health pay back a violation of itself by a violent return' (Barker, 1952, p. 182). Or in Professor Mabbott's terms, 'punishment is not a corollary of law but of law breaking. Legislators do not choose to punish. They hope that no punishment will be needed . . . The criminal makes the essential choice he brings it on himself' (Mabbott, 1939, p. 161). So punishment remains associated with guilt, and it becomes no part of the debate to extend the argument to include the nature of law and law-making. That, say the retributivists, is utilitarian.

In one sense, of course, Mabbott is right. The essential force of the retributive position is that it does not concern itself with matters outside the direct connection between the offence and the punishment. Utilitarians and rehabilitativists have done so, and the overall effect on the modern penal system has not always been of value. Retributivists have been criticized because they support the *status quo* — a supremely naive assumption, as Nigel Walker says, based on the view that social change always produces improvement — and of course they do so when they, like Mundle, argue that 'the retributive theory implies that punishment of a person by the State is morally justifiable, if and only if he has done something which is both a legal and moral offence and only if the penalty is proportionate to the moral gravity of his offence' (Mundle, 1954, p. 227). In general terms, therefore, and particularly for judicial forms of punishment, it is probably true that retribution is essentially conservative.

Having acknowledged this we are no nearer solving the basic problem of the retributivist position, what do we do about bad law? Retributivists have no answer to this question, and this is acknowledged as such by Mabbott in his example of the punishment he gave as warden. He did not agree with the rules but punished none the less, and did not see his duty as otherwise. The courts are faced with similar dilemmas, where judges and magistrates may not agree with the law but still punish. Here the retributivist would wish to go no further, presumably arguing that questions about 'bad law' lie outside the range of his inquiry.

We can reasonably say this is a defect in the retributivist position. It is also a defect in the claims that law becomes equated with morality. Retribution accepts the rules whatever they are. It also accepts that those who make the rules are justified in doing so, and thereby accepts the claim that the rule-makers are able to provide the moral ethics under which others must live. Retributivists cannot do otherwise, for as Bradley says, 'we pay the penalty because we deserve it and for no other reason'. Retribution offers no debate about whether those who have to obey accept the legitimacy of the regime.

Essentially, then, retribution operates from a consensus model of society where the community, through the law or through a system of rules, is acting in the right. Conversely, the criminal is acting in the wrong. There are no possibilities within the retributivist position to permit and account for social change, nor are there radical elements, for retribution looks only to the crime. It offers, of course, no more nor less than other theories of punishment. The utilitarian may be able to account for social change, but he is still concerned with the offence, as is the rehabilitationist. All theories of punishment must operate from the basic position derived from Hegel — that crime or rule-breaking is wrong — for to reject this is to admit that crime is valid, i.e. not in conflict with rules. Mabbott sums up the position well:

> X is a citizen of a state. About his citizenship, whether willing or unwilling I have asked no questions. About the government, whether good or bad I do not enquire. X has broken a law. Concerning the law, whether it is well devised or not I have not asked . . . It is the essence of my position that none of these questions is relevant to whether a particular punishment is just. [Mabbott, 1939, p. 160]

But whose retribution are we talking about? If it is of no concern to Mabbott to question citizenship, the quality of government or the law, where does he find the justification to obey the rules? I do not think he finds it anywhere other than in the assertion that law is law and rules are rules and all are meant to be obeyed. He does not encompass a wider philosophy of the state, nor does he necessarily involve the link with morality so forcefully stated by Bradley. Mabbott offers a more restricted form of retribution.

Not so with Kant. The retributivist argument presented by Kant takes on a wider dimension, which involves the free will of the criminal and the relationship between the offender and the State. Kant views the criminal as exercising his own choice in such a way as to make the punishment necessary. 'The undeserved evil which anyone commits on another is to be regarded as perpetrated on himself', or, again, 'His own evil deed draws the punishment upon himself' (Kant, 1965, p. 133).

But what happens if the criminal wishes to argue that the punishment is not warranted; or perhaps that his crime is due to the associations or relationships established in childhood; or that the punishment will not be effective? Kant sees these questions either as irrelevant, or as entering the 'serpent windings of utilitarianism'. The criminal cannot argue that punishment is not warranted, for that would involve a debate about the value of law; neither can he claim that his acts are the products of early relationships, for that uses the defence of determinism and Kant wishes to treat everyone as a rational agent. Nor is it possible for the criminal to argue that punishments will not be effective, for that is utilitarianism.

Kant is still left with the question, 'whose retribution?' To tell the criminal that he 'draws the punishment upon himself' is all very well, but who is inflicting the punishment? Not the victim but, in the case of legal punishment, the State — an apparently disinterested party. So inevitably, Kant's theory of punishment is political, encompassing a wider theory of state powers. We find the same argument presented by Bosanquet, who holds that judicial punishment is not personal revenge, for general or social indignation is not the same as revenge. 'It is the offspring of a rough notion of law and humanity and of the feeling that a striking aggression demands to be strikingly put down. Such a statement is part of the conciousness which maintains the system of rights and can hardly be absent when the consciousness is strong' (Bosanquet, 1965, p. 211). We see in Bosanquet a strong resemblance to Durkheim's argument, freely acknowledged, who saw punishment as a means of reinforcing the collective sentiments that had been hurt by the crime. We see in Kant the same arguments when he says crime is compulsion or constraint of some kind, 'a hindrance to freedom'. If it is wrong that freedoms should be hindered it is right to block this hindrance, and to block the constraint of freedom is to apply constraint. Punishment is a 'hindering of a hindrance of freedom'. It is justified only to the extent that it hinders the compulsion of another (Pincoffs, 1975, p. 20).

To ask 'whose retribution?' is to seek an answer then in the philosophical theory of the State. To justify punishment of the criminal is to show that the compulsion the State uses on him operates by the same rule that he himself has operated, that is, by showing the criminal what he has willed. His deserts stem from his operations, which deny others freedom and by which he has benefited. It is clearly not the injured person who retributes or 'pays back'. As far as Sir Ernest Barker is concerned, it is not even the whole community of persons; 'it is the mental rule of law which pays back a violation of itself by a violent return' (Barker, 1952, p. 182), but we may think this argument too obscure to be of value. Kant wants to show that the community through the rule of law pays back to the criminal what he has willed.

We could argue then that retributivists are right to make the link between punishment and rule-breaking even if this leads to certain doubtful conclusions related to the types of law (and rules) that people are expected to obey. The link between punishment and rule-breaking is of its very nature retributive; or, as Quinton says, 'To say "I am punishing you for something you have not done" is as absurd as saying "I promise to do something which is not in my power".' Punishment implies deserts and deserts occur where laws are broken. Retributivists claim this theory provides an important check against tyranny, for a person is punished only when he deserves it; and the opposite is also true — that he is not punished if he does not deserve it ('deserts' are defined here as acting criminally.)

The link between punishment and guilt provides the retributivists with their strongest weapon to attack the utilitarians. Retributivists claim that utilitarians would permit the punishment of the innocent in order to achieve what Bradley calls 'social surgery'. Now in one sense 'punishing the innocent' becomes a logical impossibility, for it follows from our definition of punishment that suffering inflicted on the innocent cannot be punishment. It may still be unpleasant, but is more akin to the act of hostility described by Hobbes. And 'punishing the innocent' is of course different from punishing a person who claims his innocence but who we believe is guilty; for 'punishing the innocent' implies manufacturing evidence and imputing guilt while knowing he was innocent. Utilitarians have never justified this. It could however be argued that, unlike retributivists, utilitarians could inflict collective punishments which, while not strictly punishment in terms of the definition given in Chapter 1, none the less serve the same purpose. Would utilitarians justify this by their philosophy? Retributivists would certainly not.

Benn and Peters (1959) think that, on a crude understanding of utilitarianism, they could (p. 183), although they think it would leave out considerations of moral worth and respect for persons which they argue are necessary to the idea of utilitarian morality. But consider the example of a schoolmaster punishing a whole class of boys because the actual offender could not be found. The schoolteacher might argue that the method was justified on the grounds that it was vital for discipline to be maintained. The utilitarian weakness is evident, for unlike retributivists utilitarians can and have justified punishment of this nature in order to preserve discipline. Their justification for so doing stems from the initial assumptions of their theory, that the aim of punishment is to control action. When we said earlier that retribution provided a check against tyranny, it does so by insisting that the offenders are the guilty ones and none others. And supporters of utilitarianism find little assistance from Bentham, who thought that vicarious punishments were objectionable; not because they were unjust — a term that Bentham regarded as vague and meaningless — but because they were unlikely to be effective.

JUSTIFICATIONS OF PUNISHMENTS

It will be clear from what has been said earlier that the retributivist justifies punishment only in terms of rules. Here we must distinguish between a rule or an institution constituted by rules: the former Hart calls the General Justifying Aim and the latter he calls Distribution (1968, p. 4).[2] We can ask what is the justification of punishment in terms of its general justifying aims; that is to say, how can we justify rules that provide that offenders should suffer, and also how can we justify punishment for a certain individual? Benn and Peters (1959) observe that the retributivist and utilitarian have tried to answer both questions, each in their own terms, and that the strength of the former's case rests on his answer to the latter, while that of the latter rests on his answer to the former. Their difficulties arise from their trying to make one answer do for both questions (Benn, and Peters, 1959, p. 175).

Dealing first with the general justifying aim, the retributivist finds great difficulty in answering the question, 'What justification can there be for rules requiring that those who break them should be made to suffer?' Mabbott was unable to do so; neither did he try, for he like other retributivists refused to look at the consequences of punishment for its justification. Rules exist, laws exist; therefore those who break them should be punished. But this is hardly satisfactory for more is required to justify inflicting suffering than the breaking of rules. One could of course justify punishment generally in terms of the 'denunciation of the crime'. This argument was most recently stated by Lord Devlin, who opposed the conclusion of the Wolfenden Committee 'that there must be a realm of morality which is not the law's business', and argued that 'the suppression of vice is as much the law's business as the suppression of subversive activities' (Devlin, 1965; Hart, 1963; HMSO, 1957).

I do not intend to spend a great deal of time examining this argument, as it stands outside the main area of discussion, being more closely linked to legal theory than to the penal system. Briefly, the argument of retributive reprobation was firmly established by the nineteenth-century jurist James Fitzjames Stephen, who wished, in his chapter entitled 'Of crimes in general and of punishments', to establish what he called 'a close alliance between criminal law and moral sentiments', this being 'in all ways healthy and advantageous to the community'. He goes on to say:

> I think it highly desirable that criminals should be hated, and that punishments inflicted upon them should be so contrived as to give expression to that hatred, and to justify it so far as the public provisions of means for expressing and gratifying a healthy natural sentiment can justify and encourage it. [Stephen, 1883]

Stephen's arguments are classical expressions of reprobation where punishment is used as a means by which the State shows its disapproval of law-breaking. The modern version is provided by Lord Justice Denning in evidence to the Royal Commission on Capital Punishment — a position that incidentally led him to support the death penalty.

> The punishment for grave crimes should adequately reflect the revulsion

felt by the great majority of citizens for them. It is a mistake to consider the objects of punishment as being deterrent or reformative or preventive and nothing else . . . The ultimate justification of any punishment is not that it is a deterrent, but that it is the emphatic denunciation by the community of a crime. [HMSO, 1953, para. 53]

The aspect I regard as most disturbing about the comment by Fitzjames Stephen is the way that hatred is celebrated and held almost to be a virtue — a view that I think underpins his thinking throughout. No one can, or ought to, deny the extent of hatred one may feel for certain criminals when contempt for human wellbeing is deliberate and where there is an apparent liking for cruelty. (This applies to governments who commit crimes as well as to individuals.) But it is a long way from that to say 'it is highly desirable that criminals should be hated' or 'that punishments should be so contrived to give expressions to that hatred'. This is not the dark side of retribution but a different philosophy, which institutionalizes hatred. The weaker version of the argument put forward by Lord Denning, and weakened further by Lord Devlin, suffers from a different defect. While it is certainly true that there is a strong link between morality and the law (as Lord Devlin claims), Professor Hart suggests that the mere expression of moral condemnation is not a value to be pushed at all costs. Lords Denning and Devlin fail to answer two other questions that are important: first, how to justify punishments when some laws contain little or no moral force; and, second, how mere dislike can be justified as punishment without turning to vulgar prejudice.

But to return to the main argument: it is possible, I suppose, for the retributivist to justify punishment in general by regarding it as self-evident, or by maintaining that the wicked ought not to prosper, or even by appealing to some higher authority. If the justification is said to be self-evident then this is to deny the need for justification. But some people have felt the need to justify it, and it is by no means clear that to say it is self-evident, or even 'fitting that the guilty should be punished', is sufficient. To say that the wicked ought not to prosper is no justification either. 'Wickedness' can only be established by reference to rule-breaking, and to say the wicked ought not to prosper is only another way of saying those who break rules ought not to benefit from their actions. Similarly, to appeal to a higher authority, such as the law, is no justification, for the existence of the law requires justification in its own right. We could, as with Kant, accept the law as a categorical imperative, but this is dangerously close to making it self-evident again. And yet without a general justification, retribution can appear as an excuse for inflicting suffering on those who have broken rules. It can also appear as if retributivists do not see punishment as a *prima facie* evil and so by default grant this part of the argument to the utilitarians.

Often then retributivists are left justifying the practice of punishment as being self-evident that offenders should be punished, or on the grounds of intuition. Are they on more certain grounds when they attempt to answer the question of distribution, or of how much punishment is appropriate to a given offence? The answer must be equivocal; the strength of retribution is that it provides a rough and ready guide to the amount of punishment; the weakness is that the guide must remain rough and ready.

To ask how much punishment is appropriate to a given offence is ambiguous. We need to distinguish between the punishment allocated to a particular class of acts and a punishment within that class (Benn and Peters, 1959, p. 186). Penal laws generally state a maximum penalty, or even a fixed penalty. The judge or magistrate has to decide the appropriate sentence for a particular offence.

Dealing first with the punishment provided by the law; a major advantage of the retributive argument is that it demands a maximum penalty which is stated by law and known in advance of an offence being committed. The security provided by the knowledge of a maximum penalty seems to me essential in modern penal systems. That an offence under the Road Traffic Acts should (say) carry a punishment of a maximum of £10 distinguishes it sharply from an offence of (say) robbery, which carries a maximum penalty of life in prison. Utilitarians and rehabilitationists provide no such security; indeed, under a rehabilitative system it is impossible to fix a penalty in advance, for there is no way of knowing how long treatment will take. Under a utilitarian system the extent of punishment would depend on the degree of social disruption caused by this and similar offences, or on the degree of mischief caused, or both. Neither of these theories produces that sense of security so necessary to those who live in modern society with its profession of laws and professionalism of law-enforcers.

But this does not show the criterion by which punishments are fixed. To see the problem at its most acute, consider the position where the retributivist tries to determine the amount of punishment to be imposed by the judges for each offence. To Kant it is the right of requital (the Gleichheit) or *jus talionis* that fits the quality and quantity of the punishment. Other retributivists offer similar if less extreme arguments to relate the offence to the punishment. But the retaliatory principle of *jus talionis* will work literally in only a few special cases, the death penalty for murder being the oft quoted example — and even then it is doubtful — or perhaps financial penalties for stealing. Even so, there is still no guarantee that the loss of income imposed by a fine will affect offenders in the same way. It is essential to the retributivist case that suffering be equivalent to the guilt. But Benn and Peters say that suffering of one sort cannot be equated with another, and to attempt to do so involves something more than a preference but a quasi-quantitative comparison of the sufferings of two different people treated as objective fact.

Critics of retribution have always made great play of this weakness in the retributive position. Bosanquet speaks of the 'superstition' that punishment should be equivalent to offence (1965, p. 212). While in one sense punishments may be identical, i.e. a return of the offender's act upon himself, or in Bradley's terms as an annihilation of wrongdoing and a manifestation of a right, this is different from equivalence. Bosanquet insists that the State knows nothing of moral guilt nor has any means of securing it, and punishment cannot be adapted to factors that cannot be known. Now, of course he is right, but we ought not single out the retributive position for attack. Utilitarians following Bentham attempted a hedonistic calculus, and modern utilitarians still speak of punishment being adjusted according to the level of social mischief involved. Similarly, rehabilitationists adjust their treatments to the extent of social or psychological disease and yet are singularly unable to identify the symptoms or the disease condition itself. They also maintain that release from institutions is to be decided according to the extent to which the offender is cured, yet are unable to show what are the criteria for that decision.

I do not want to avoid answering the question by pointing to the defects of other theories, except to say that retributivists have been, in my view, unfairly singled out for attack by others whose own theories show similar weaknesses; for Godwin was surely right when he noted how often men deceive themselves in the notions for their own conduct and assign to one principle what in reality proceeded from another. Speaking of the position of judges and magistrates generally, Godwin saw judges as mere spectators attempting to form judgements, when the offender knows more about himself, and his offence, than any others (1971, p. 256). Godwin was agreeing with Bosanquet, but also showing how philosophical and psychological theories concerned with motives, or personality assessments, or degrees of social harm, face similar problems. Yet retributivists, it seems to me, have one point in their favour: people have a general scale of punishments related to the offences which provide a rough and ready guide as to what is considered fair. We may not as Hegel hoped produce an answer to the question of equivalence, but we can with Mabbott recognize that a general scale exists. 'We can grade crimes in a rough scale and penalties in a rough scale and keep our heaviest penalties for what are socially the most serious wrongs regardless of whether these penalties will reform the criminal or whether they are exactly what deterrence would require' (Mabbott, 1939, p. 162). Indeed, such a system already exists, although why Mabbott should reduce the value of his argument by inserting the phrase 'socially the most *serious* wrongs' when he should have said 'moral' is something of a mystery; by doing so he has inadvertently introduced a utilitarian argument.

We can accept a rough scale of penalties but it can be nothing more than that. By most standards murder is more serious than attempted murder, which is more serious than shoplifting, which is again more serious than speeding. But is rape more serious than robbery, or indecent exposure more serious than careless driving? And how do we allocate crimes that are intended to be temporary measures, as (say) in the Defence of the Realm Regulations introduced in the 1914-18 war? It is difficult to believe that an equivalent punishment could be decided for this type of offence. Or to give another example: attempted suicide was an offence until 1961, but the Home Office had stated as far back as 1928 that police prosecutions ought to be restricted to certain cases involving suicide pacts. How are judges to decide here? We also know from studies in the sociology of law that laws are often made for administrative convenience, and sometimes to fit in with international conventions (Bean, 1974). They become less and less expressions of pure moral thought. Much modern legislation nowadays is by statutory instrument. All these new developments make the views of Kant and Bradley seem inappropriate in their way. The *jus talionis* advocated by Kant may be more applicable to the traditional offences against the person or property, but they become less and less so in the wake of new legislation and new methods of making laws.

And yet a rough and ready guide still exists, and even Beccaria recognized the value of the retributive position when he said that punishment should be chosen in due proportion to the crime (1964, p. 63). It may not be possible to do more than provide a rough and ready scale, but its existence provides the basis by which offenders appeal against 'excessive punishments'. These scales may not be as rational as Hegel demanded, but they provide security against an intemperate judiciary.

The old arguments against retribution with its attempts to equate punishments with the crime are still valid. Modern retributivists such as Mabbott have not extricated retribution from those criticisms — except to point to a scale that is too general to meet detailed criticisms. Bosanquet is right: equivalence *is* a meaningless superstition, although he could have added that an *approximation* to it was well worth preserving.

THE WORTH OF THE OFFENDER

The retributivist is on firmer ground when he argues that punishment ought only to be inflicted on a person because he has committed a crime; in Kant's terms, 'for one man ought never to be dealt with merely as a means subservient to the purpose of another, nor to be mixed up with the subjects of real right'. Kant, who disliked many things, disliked paternalism above all else and saw in the utilitarian position a method of treating people as means to an end rather than as ends in themselves. Kant saw crime as an *'intentional transgression* — that is an act accompanied with the consciousness that it is a transgression'. In another passage that is worth quoting in full he makes a related point:

> Now the notion of punishment, as such, cannot be united with that becoming a particular of happiness; for he who inflicts the punishment may at the same time have the benevolent purpose of directing this punishment to this end, yet it must be justified in itself as punishment, that is, as mere harm, so that if it stopped there, and the person punished could get no glimpse of kindness hidden behind this harshness he must yet admit that justice was done him, and that his reward was perfectly suitable to his conduct. In every punishment as such there

must first be justice, and this constitutes the essence of the notion. Benevolence may indeed be united with it, but the man who has deserved punishment has not the least reason to reckon upon this. [Kant, 1949, p. 149]

This passage is remarkable in many respects, not the least in the link with justice. The phrase 'get no glimpse of kindness hidden behind the harshness' may have contributed to the belief that retribution was vindictive, but to Kant it is a way of restating the point that punishment is deserved. It is also a way of stating that the criminal is not being punished for his own good. If he does not deserve it we have no right to inflict it and, according to Kant, no right to inflict it in the name of some good of which the criminal may or may not approve. The criminal must be treated as a rational being, and rationality bestows dignity. We cannot force our judgements upon him or appeal to good consequences, for among other things the criminal may reject the means and the ends of those judgements.

Kant's argument is not without its difficulties, but consider first its merits. Modern penal systems have recently entered the 'serpent-windings of utilitarianism' and of rehabilitation also and ignored Kant's warnings. Those 'windings' have done little to restore the dignity to the criminal and under rehabilitation have often reduced him to the level of a child. Numerous schemes have been introduced, some under the name of therapy, which have been undignified displays of gross paternalism, or have led the criminal to play the game to secure early release. This is not what I think Kant would want when he talks of dignity and rationality, but is the price we have paid for ignoring his warnings.

But what is this dignity that the offender receives for being seen as rational? Is this a euphemism or an opportunity to inflict suffering because we hate criminals? And how can dignity be bestowed on the punished? Kent provides no logical reason why criminals should be treated with dignity, and there is nothing in his theory to provide that logical conclusion. Retribution does not logically entail the dignity of punishment; the fact that Kant argues that it does may meet with our approval but cannot be derived from the initial premise. Kant has to fall back on an intuitionist stance to justify his argument, or perhaps regard it as self-evident that dignity should be bestowed. I do not disagree with the sentiment; the difficulty is that arguments based on natural law or intuition become difficult to justify.

RETRIBUTION: A PLEA FOR FURTHER
CONSIDERATION

Enough has been said, I think, to show that retribution has many
merits. I can only repeat an earlier question and ask: Why, then, is
retribution generally discarded nowadays? Why could Mabbott say
that in the theory of punishment retribution has been defended by no
philosopher of note for over fifty years, except Bradley, and that
reform and deterrence are the theories accepted in principle and
increasingly influential in practice? Why also could K. G. Armstrong
complain that retributivists have been consistently reviled? Their
theory

> has been called a polite name for revenge; it is vindictive, inhumane,
> barbarous and immoral . . . By making the punishment of wrong doing
> a moral duty, the retributive theory removes the possibility of mercy.
> The only people who today defend the retributive theory are those who,
> whether they know it or not, get pleasure and a feeling of virtue from
> seeing others suffer, or those who have a theological axe to grind.
> [Armstrong, 1961, p. 471]

Armstrong wishes to show that these criticisms are mistaken, and he
is right to do so. I do not deny that some retributivists may have been
cruel, or even simple-minded about the nature of punishment.
(Carlyle, for example, spoke of a scoundrel being a scoundrel for
ever.) Retribution can easily shift to unrestrained hatred. But
retribution has no monopoly on cruelty, and the deterrence doctrine
has produced supporters not noteworthy for their restraint, while
rehabilitation has been described as 'an exquisite form of torture'.
Perhaps the motives of some retributivists are not as pure as one
would have wanted, but they do not have a monopoly of baseness
either. I have met some ardent supporters of rehabilitation whose
motives were neither pure nor humane, and others who made me
thankful that they were not in a position to reform me. Motives after
all are not what concerns us; it is the relevant strengths of the
arguments that matter (or ought to). Motives would be important
only if it were possible to show that there was something in the
nature of a theory that encouraged cruelty or led to it directly. I also
share Armstrong's appreciation of what Hilaire Belloc called 'The
degrading slavery of being a child of one's time' and assume others
approve of such a statement.

Before leaving this section, perhaps we should sum up some of the advantages and disadvantages of a retributive theory.

First, the advantages.

(1) Retribution insists that punishment implies guilt. For that reason punishment should be imposed because of a past offence. This is not incidental to the argument but is a vital ingredient of the theory.

(2) The retributive theory demands that punishment must be equated to the crime, and therefore that a lighter offence should not be punished more severely than a serious one. It also insists that considerations of expediency or other considerations that exist independent of the crime should not detract us from the basic idea that criminals should be punished.

(3) Retribution creates strong links with justice.

(4) Retribution insists that only the guilty should be punished, and not the innocent.

Now the disadvantages.

(1) Retribution is unable to provide clear guidelines as to what equivalence should mean in practice.

(2) Retribution refuses to take adequate account of the consequences of punishment or to consider anything other than the direct relationship between punishment and the crime; no consideration is given to nature of the law or rules.

(3) Although retributivists insist on treating the offender as a moral agent, there is no proof that treatment of a person as a moral agent leads to retributive punishment. To say that punishment is an end or a good in itself can only be established by intuition, or be seen as self-evident.

DETERRENCE

The second of the grand theories of punishment is the most complex. While at one level it is reasonably clear what deterrence is supposed to mean, at another it is not at all certain if deterrence is a psychological theory based on threats, or a sociological theory based on social control, or perhaps both. Unlike retribution, it is a theory that has fostered and encouraged empirical inquiry — not with a great deal of success, I would add, for it is rarely possible to control the variables to complete a refined study.[3] The Royal Commission on

Capital Punishment (HMSO, 1953) was dominated by the deterrent argument and reviewed large amounts of evidence and empirical data provided by international experts. Those supporting capital punishment were convinced of its deterrent value; those opposed were not. The Committee concluded that they could not arrive at any firm conclusion about the deterrent effect of the death penalty, and that, while there was prima facie evidence to suggest that the death penalty had a deterrent effect on some people, its effect was not universal or uniform (para. 68). 'It is accordingly important', said the Committee, 'to view this question in a just perspective and not to base a penal policy in relation to murder on exaggerated estimates of the uniquely deterrent force of the death penalty (para. 68) — a point at variance with that of Fitzjames Stephen, who thought that 'No other punishment deters men so effectively from committing crimes as the punishment of death' (quoted in HMSO, 1953, para. 57).

Bentham is considered to be the main exponent of deterrence. Beccaria also argued from a similar utilitarian position when he said 'the aim of punishment can only be to prevent the criminal committing new crimes against his countrymen and to keep others from doing likewise' (Beccaria, 1964, p. 43). Or again, 'the political end of punishment is to intimidate others' (p. 41). Many earlier philosophers such as Grotius, Puffendorf and Locke had considered the deterrent argument, but Bentham and Beccaria give it the strength that it now commands. Bentham was its intellectual exponent, Beccaria its humanitarian.[4]

In its modern form deterrence has been linked to general utilitarian principles. 'Pleasure and pain are the only springs of human action in beings endowed with sensibility', said Beccaria. Crime then is an attempt, antisocial and ill-conceived, to promote the criminal's pleasure or relieve his pain. Deterrence operates to counteract that wish. Bentham saw it in these terms:

> Pain and pleasure are the great springs of human action. When a man perceives or supposes pain to be the consequence of an act he is acted on in such manner as tends with a certain force to withdraw him as it were from the commission of that act. If the apparent magnitude be greater than the magnitude of the pleasure expected he will be absolutely prevented from performing it. [Bentham, 1962, p. 396]

We may reject the crude psychology contained in Bentham's statement as we may also reject the assumption that offenders calculate the pains or pleasure available to them. This does not mean that men like pain, and while they dislike it they may consider the likely possibilities of having to suffer — in short, are deterred. Bentham's psychology may be crude, but it ought not to be rejected altogether. Many of our own actions operate from deterrent principles:[5] we are probably deterred by the possibility of punishment, and we may try to deter others in like manner. There is something plausible and acceptable about a deterrent argument, and in saying this we need not adopt all the psychological suppositions of utilitarianism.

From the general principles of utility Bentham was led to an examination of law. However the nature, source, ends or objects of laws need not detain us, for they are outside the main area of study, although of course Bentham's view of punishment fitted into those general utilitarian principles, namely that the end of law is to promote happiness. 'The general object which all laws have, or to have in common, is to augment the total happiness of the community, and therefore, to exclude mischief' (Bentham, 1949, p. 281). The means of excluding mischief was punishment, which though it may not promote happiness at least prevents pain.

Bentham was not sentimental about crime or criminals. He regarded unreasoning sentimentalism as obnoxious when it recoiled from the infliction of suffering as well as when it demanded it. 'All punishment', said Bentham, 'is in itself necessarily odious; if it were not dreaded it would not effect its purpose' (Moberly, 1968, p. 50). Odious it might be, but it should be used frugally, for 'all punishment is mischief: all punishment in itself is evil . . . Upon the principle of utility, if it ought at all to be admitted in as far as it promises to exclude some greater evil' (Moberly, 1968, p. 281).

It follows then, as far as Bentham is concerned, that punishment ought not to be inflicted when it is groundless (where there is no mischief for it to prevent); inefficacious (where it cannot act so as to prevent mischief); unprofitable or too expensive (where the mischief it would produce would be greater than that it prevented); and where it is needless (where the mischief may be prevented or will cease of itself without it, that is at a cheaper rate). When punishment *is* worthwhile, there are four subordinate designs or objects, said Bentham, which a legislator governed by the principle of utility ought to consider: (1) to prevent all offenders whatever; (2) if this fails, to induce a person to commit a less mischievous offence; (3) to dispose an offender to do as little mischief as is necessary to his purpose; and (4) to prevent the mischief at as cheap a rate as possible (Moberly, 1968, p. 289). Bentham followed this by providing rules or canons by which the proportion of punishments to offences is to be governed.

The limitations on the use of punishment provide one of the strongest arguments in favour of utilitarianism. No such limitations are provided by retribution — except of course the limitation placed on the prerequisite of guilt. We shall now see what other advantages and disadvantages can be found in the deterrence position.

RULES AND MORALS

Bentham considered that the immediate principal end of punishment was to control action. This action, said Bentham, is that either of the offender or of others: that of the offender by its influence, on his will, in which case it is said to operate in the way of reformation, or on his physical power, in which case it is said to operate by disablement. For others it can influence their wills, in which case it is said to operate by way of example (Moberly, 1968, p. 281). The latter is the more important.

The contrast between the two great theories is clear. The aim of punishment for the utilitarians is to control action, while the retributivists see the aim in terms of deserts. In the method of controlling actions the utilitarian argues that the purpose of punishment is for general prevention. It exists within people's minds — including that of the offender — to prevent him from neglecting or rejecting the rules (or what Barker calls 'rejecting the content of common conviction' — 1952, p. 181). Everyone is concerned and involved in each act of punishment, which operates — given the appropriate distribution of information — to remind all citizens of their obligations. Deterrence operates in the form of a permanent threat. For the individual offender it may appear to operate as if it was intended to reform, but it is not reform in the sense of changing the offender's character or refashioning a new life-style. The utilitarian would say that characters and life-styles are not the business of anyone except, of course, the offender himself. Punishment operates as reform in so far, and only in so far, as it is intended to revive in the offender the requirements to obey certain rules. It may be reformatory for some offenders in the Hegelian sense, but that is unintentional for the utilitarian.

Deterrence provides no straightforward link between rules, laws and punishment as is found in retribution. Utilitarianism is an ethical system which has had its main impact in the political sphere, and we must see the link with rules and morals as ethically based on the twin notions of pleasure and pain. When Bentham argues that the aim of punishment is to control action, he recognizes that the choice is not between moral goodness and moral evil but between two moral evils: the crime and the punishment. If a choice has to be made, said Bentham, we must choose to punish because the alternative is to connive with crime and so produce and add to the imperfections of the social order. As Dr Ewing says, the necessity to make the choice is a mark and consequence of the imperfections of society, but it is sometimes unavoidable, society being what it is (1929, p. 51). The strongest argument for utilitarianism is that punishment works by threat. Every punishment is an admission of failure, and we punish only to retain effectiveness for the future. Bentham's principle of frugality is intended to limit the use of punishment; for example, 'If any mode of punishment is more apt than another to produce any superfluous and needless pain it may be styled unfrugal; if less it may be styled frugal' (Bentham, 1948, p. 304). The most that retributivists can offer to compete with frugality is deserts; while there is no commensurate restriction with rehabilitation.

But where is the morality for the offender? William Temple once observed that there was no moral value in abstention from conduct for fear of consequences (1934, p. 26). Bentham would say that moral rewards may be present initially and may perhaps develop later. A potential offender who abstains from committing offences may eventually believe that there is some value in abstention and may even believe in the value of the rule that prohibits the intended conduct. The motive to restrain from criminal conduct may be a low one in the first instance, but presumably low motives are needed to counteract those other low motives that lead to contemplation of the crime. Moral development occurs when the offender believes in the value of the rules which in Bentham's terms exist to promote happiness.

In essence, then, the utilitarians say that punishment is to control action, and the law is the weapon to be used in control. The retributivist would see the utilitarian as falling into a basic trap — so far diligently avoided by his own theory. It concerns the oldest dispute between the two schools and one mentioned earlier. The utilitarian is accused of permitting the punishment of the innocent. So, if punishment is to be judged by its effect, then, as critics of utilitarians claim, it would be possible to manufacture evidence against an innocent man to set an example to others. The innocent may be a stranger, or perhaps a person the police believed to have committed the crime where the evidence against him was weak, or even a member of the criminal's family if the criminal had (say) died before prosecution. Alternatively, as Benn and Peters say, if the advantage of deterrence could be achieved by seeming to punish the criminal it would then be possible to *pretend* to punish him. The advantages could then be achieved without the disadvantages — especially if the criminal agreed not to divulge the pretence (Benn and Peters, 1959, p. 182). Bentham himself prompted this set of criticisms by a somewhat rash statement when he said 'It is only the idea of the punishment, the apparent punishment that really acts upon the mind . . . It is the apparent punishment that does all the service . . . it is the real punishment that does all the mischief' (1948, p. 303).

Many utilitarians have tried to defend Bentham. Benn and Peters, for example, say that punishing the innocent is a logical impossibility. Having defined punishment as being for an offence, then where there is no offence there can be no punishment. Punishing the innocent becomes an act of hostility. But Professor Hart maintains this is the wrong answer. The 'definitional stop', as he calls it, prevents us from investigating the very thing that modern scepticism most calls in question: namely, the rational and moral status of our preferences for a system of punishment under which measures painful to individuals are to be taken against them when they have committed an offence (1968, p. 6). In other words, Hart is arguing that defences that point to the definition of punishment are not capable of meeting the criticisms on a sufficiently wide front, for the criticisms are not just about punishing the innocent but about punishment in general. I can see why Professor Hart may wish to open out the discussion, but his reply is additional to the main point. Punishing the innocent *is* a logical impossibility, having defined punishment as we have done earlier, mainly in retributive terms. But again Bentham's own argument has not helped, for this dispute, if there is one, has been aided by his assertion that 'from the point of utility apparent justice is everything, real justice . . . is not worth pursuing'. Our moral horror at such proceedings, says Ewing, is not adequately explained by the principle of deterrence (Ewing, 1929, p. 54).

For the utilitarian legal rules become means to control mischief. The great strength of utilitarianism is that rules can be changed according to the demands of society. No such change is built into retribution. But who decides that rules should be changed? According to Bentham, it is for the sovereign to decide, for Bentham defined law as a 'sign declarative of a violation conceived or adopted by the sovereign in a state' (1970, pp. 1, 10). On what basis does the sovereign decide? To Bentham it must be on the basis of utility, aimed at reducing mischief. Here lies the danger of the utilitarian argument, for deterrence can easily become over-consumed with social surgery or social hygiene where the demands of a social order are such that offenders are punished according to what is regarded as socially unclean. Lacking the link between guilt and the punishment, it is easy for the utilitarian to be dominated by the mischief and see offenders as capable of manipulation. The insecurity created by an orthodoxy eager to seek out mischief should warn us of the dangers of adopting a wholesale deterrent position. We have, it is true, Bentham's twin principles of frugality and economy to fall back on, but they do not provide us with a clear sense of protection. Consider for a moment the example usually given by the utilitarians to support their case of the woman who stole bread to feed starving children. It is suggested that the woman is protected by a utilitarian philosophy, for her offence, being so exceptionally conditioned, does not threaten the general right of property and does not need to be associated with any high degree of terror in order to protect that right. The character of the act influences the sentence and takes it out of the class of offences to which it *prima facie* belongs and from which men need to be deterred by a recognized amount of severity (Bosanquet, 1965, pp. 214-15). We could ask the utilitarian how and on what basis he decides that rights are not threatened by this type of offence, and the utilitarian would be hard put to point to a simple answer. If starving children were mischievous then deterrence would surely apply, and that is where the insecurity lies. It all depends on what is deemed 'mischief'.

JUSTIFICATIONS OF PUNISHMENT

We can use the same distinction as before, considering first the general justifying aim and later the question of the distribution of punishment.

We have argued that Bentham's case for justifying punishment in general is that it is a technique of social control that is justified by preventing more mischief than it produces. Conversely, if punishment produces more mischief than it prevents then it loses its justification. As a social control technique it operates as a threat to others, but for those not deterred by the threat deterrence can prevent them from committing further offences (as it would if they were imprisoned) and by reforming them — using the term 'reform' in the sense that the offenders may eventually learn to respect the law.

The utilitarians would justify deterrence as a means whereby society can protect itself against crime. They would say that one day perhaps there will be no need for legal rules — censure may be sufficient — but until that time comes legal obligations must exist. These imply punishments. Legal rights exist also, and they require protection against violation. A utilitarian such as T. H. Green has no difficulty in justifying punishment in the following terms:

> [The right of free life] on the part of associated man implies the right on their part to prevent such actions as interfere with the possibility of free action contributory to social good. This constitutes the right of punishment, the right so far to use force upon a person as may be necessary to save others from this influence. [Green, 1910, p. 19]

The general justification for punishment, as far as Green is concerned, is to protect the body of rights. So too for Fichte, whose opposition to the Kantian version of punishment is clear: for he dismisses it as 'positively meaningless'. To Fichte punishment is merely a means by which the State can maintain public security, and the only aim of punishment is to prevent by threats transgressions of the law. The end of all penal laws, says Fichte, is that they may not be applied.

> The threatened punishment is intended to suppress all evil purposes and to promote a good disposition so that the punishment may never be applied. Hence in order to attain this end each citizen must know that the threat of law will invariably become reality if he should commit any offence. [Fichte, 1889, p. 345]

To Fichte the justification for punishment is to deter the criminal and others from crime. The execution of the penal law becomes a public act, showing that the threat will be applied. Unlike the retributivist, the utilitarian does not have to resort to a self-evident argument that punishment is good, nor does he have to avoid looking at the consequences of the punishment he introduces. The utilitarian's general justifying aim is to prevent mischief; to such an end, he can justify laws and specify what laws there should be. If the essential *prius* of punishment is that there should be laws, then the utilitarian's position is secure, provided that is he can be certain he knows what constitutes mischief, how to identify it, and how to distinguish between apparent and real.

Bentham provided elaborate rules on the proportions between punishments and offences. These were intended to be subservient to the four objects of punishment stated earlier (i.e. to prevent all offences; to prevent the worst; to keep down the mischief; to act at the least expense). The rules, as would be expected, provide general guidelines to serve the legislator and the judge. Some are intended to provide limits on the side of diminution (or limits below which a punishment ought not to be reduced), others on the side of increase (or limits above which it ought not to be increased). They operate as rules of procedure rather than of substance.

Those concerned with diminution follow the utilitarian orthodoxy. For example, the value of the punishment must not be less in any case than what is sufficient to outweigh the profit of the offence; or the punishment ought in no case to be more than what is necessary to bring it into conformity with the rules here given; or, where two offences come in competition, the punishment for the greater offence must be sufficient to induce a man to prefer the less. The second and third of these rules provides no great difficulty, for the second complies with Bentham's principle of frugality and the third is to guard against mischief at as cheap a rate as possible. But what does Bentham mean in the first rule when he says that the value of the punishment must not be less in any case than what is sufficient to outweigh that of the profit of the offence? Bentham considered this at some length, perhaps aware of its inherent difficulties.

At first sight Bentham seemed to be offering punishment based on an elementary calculation. In line with his other principles, it would seem to be wrong to punish offenders who were mentally ill or were suffering from irresistible impulses, or infants who could not be said to profit from the offence. 'Profit' implies that the offender has knowingly put himself in the wrong and can be justifiably blamed for doing so. 'Profit' also implies guilt in the retributive sense.

There are of course many other examples, some stark, others less so, where it becomes difficult to talk of profit. Consider two from the Royal Commission on Capital Punishment. The first is taken from their discussion of 'mercy killings'. 'How for example were the jury to decide whether a daughter has killed her invalid father from compassion, from a desire for material gain, from a natural wish to bring to an end a trying period of her life, or from a combination of motives?' (HMSO, 1953, para. 179). Or again from the same Commission this time a suicide pact: 'How does one distinguish between a failed suicide from one who cheated to obtain maximum advantage?' (paras. 163-76). Consider also the man who, when charged for speeding, tells the court he was hurrying home to avert a family crisis: is he to be treated differently from the person who was hoping to be the first person present at an auction?

Bosanquet argues that 'the true reason for allowing circumstances which change the character of the act to influence the sentence is that, in changing its character they may take it out of the class of offences to which it *prima facie* belongs and from which men need to be deterred by a recognized amount of severity' (Bosanquet, 1965, pp. 214-15). Or consider what we could call extenuating or mitigating circumstances: Bosanquet argues that these circumstances are not based on moral iniquity, for that is something that cannot be estimated. Rather, it is an adjustment of categories of offences based on the violation of rights. His example of the starving man who steals a turnip shows that the offender does not need to be seen as attacking the right of property. It means, says Bosanquet, that the State has to readjust its policies to remedy starvation.

Bosanquet's example is extreme, and by using it the utilitarian case is more easily justified. But there are less extreme and more common examples occurring daily in the courts, where 'profit' becomes difficult to see in such simple terms. Take the examples of the speeding offences given above. Which of the offenders is to be granted the privilege of having his offence reclassified? Both or neither? There is no simple answer, and ultimately the utilitarian fares no better than the retributivist when trying to assess moral guilt. Furthermore, when utilitarians make decisions about promoting future happiness they claim to have special knowledge of the amount of future happiness or pain to be produced. The speeding offender wishing to arrive first at the auction may produce more happiness than the one who wishes to avert a family crisis!

Within the utilitarian philosophy there lurks a measure of impersonalization. But we do not obey the law simply because of a threat: we obey it because we sometimes see it as a good in itself. Utilitarianism can easily degenerate into an impersonal philosophy. 'Man, thou are not to be hanged for stealing a horse, but that horses may not be stolen' (quoted in Moberly, 1968, p. 81). Most of us personalize our punishments, and rightly so, for they are directed at us. To see one's punishment as part of a social threat aimed at others can easily appear as cant, and to be told our punishment is not based on what we have done but so that others may not do it has little meaning when we ourselves are receiving the punishment. Yet Bentham's version of profitability places the discussion at that level. I am not saying that the utilitarians are using offenders as ends, for Bentham had always insisted that 'each to count for one and no one to count for more than one'. The point I am making here is that punishment is inflicted on a person and he may see it as hypocrisy to be told it is inflicted for reasons other than his own criminal act.

It is true that Bentham also devised rules of a more personal nature, but not such as to meet these objections. He argues that certain conditions exist where extraordinary punishments ought to apply (1970, p. 212). Six grounds are given:

(1) an extraordinary mischievousness of the offence, which makes it necessary and worthwhile to combat it;

(2) the deficiency of the punishment in part of certainty as resulting from the difficulty of detection: this difficulty, said Bentham, depends in great measure on the nature of the offence;

(3) the presumption that the offence may afford of the offender having been guilty of other offences of the like nature;

(4) the accidental advantage in point of quality of the punishment not strictly meted in point of quantity;

(5) the use of a punishment of a particular quality in the character of a moral lesson;

(6) an extraordinary want of sensibility on the part of the offenders to the force of such tutelary motives as are opposed to the offence, whether on the part of the law itself, or on the part of the other auxiliary sanctions (Bentham, 1970, p. 212).

As a general outline covering the justification for punishment, it is typical of Bentham that he should attempt to list and clarify the conditions in this way. The ground covered is remarkable in a number of respects, not least because it provides the best example of the gulf between retributive and deterrent positions. There are however apparent similarities. For example, the 'deserts' of the offence roughly correspond to the utilitarian term 'mischief'. There is also the similarity relating to the extent of punishment given; for while retribution is open to the charge of being a meaningless superstition when it attempts to fit the proportion of punishment to the crime, so the utilitarian is faced with the difficulty of identifying the conditions that constitute extra mischief. Bentham gives us no clue as to how that extra mischief could be identified. But the differences are more important than the similarities. Consider points (2) and (3). In point (2) Bentham says that, where detection is difficult, and the risk of punishment accordingly diminished, greater severity ought to compensate for the uncertainty. So a more serious but relatively easily detected crime would produce less unpleasant punishments than a minor but easily detected one. Retributionists would argue that difficulty of detection is no justification for additional punishment, for they refuse to regard the abilities and acumen of the law enforcement agencies as having a bearing on the matter. They would see this as lying outside the range of acceptable requirements and highly conducive to injustice.

In point (3) Bentham wants to punish offenders more severely if they have not been deterred by previous punishments. So offender A with previous convictions might receive heavier punishments than offender B with no previous convictions, although the current offence was the same. This is the double-track system of sentencing so common to modern penal systems (and, indeed, among parents who may punish more severely if the child insists on repeating his actions). In both examples the retributivist would regard utilitarian arguments as unjust and unfair. The retributivist would care little whether the offender had committed offences of a like nature: what matters was the offence committed now. There is no double-track system of justice in the retributive scheme of things.

RULE-UTILITARIANISM

There have been various attempts to meet the objections of utilitarian theories of punishment. Rule-utilitarianism was supposed to do this. It was said to have been introduced by Mill (although this is doubtful), but has its modern adherents in Rawls and others such as Sprigge (Rawls, 1955; see also McCloskey, 1965). Rule-utilitarianism is based on the view that an action is right if it is according to a rule that itself has a utilitarian justification. Honderich dismisses rule-utilitarianism on two grounds. First, it 'is not utilitarianism at all if one regards utilitarian moralities as those which have to do solely with satisfactions and distress, their maximization and minimization. Secondly the theories of punishment in which it can issue do not include the theory of deterrence' (Honderich, 1969, p. 85).

I do not wish to spend a great deal of time on rule-utilitarianism, for I regard Honderich's criticisms as sufficient. Yet rule-utilitarianism enjoys considerable success even though it offers an important concession to traditional utilitarianism. Sometimes it is seen to conflict with act-utilitarianism, but as Sprigge, a modern adherent, has pointed out,

> If a rule is good precisely because action in accordance with it usually advances the general good, and this is the only reason it is very odd to think that any value should be attached to action according to the rule in those exceptional cases where it hinders rather than advances the general good. [Sprigge, 1965, p. 286]

Rule-utilitarians begin at the point where they recognize that particular utilitarian punishments may be unjust, but they assert that useful systems of punishments are those that are just according to our moral consciousnesses (McCloskey, 1965, pp. 258-9). What rule-utilitarians want to do is to confer the test of utility to the rules and institutions. But surely it is the actions, not the rules, that utilitarians have sought to control, and it is for this reason alone that Honderich is right to say it is not deterrence, at least not in the sense considered here.

AN ATTEMPT TO LINK THE TWO THEORIES

Enough has been said to suggest that retribution and deterrence occupy different theoretical positions; they start from different premises and move to different aims. Some philosophers have argued that the divisions are less obvious than would at first appear. (Beccaria, for instance, argued that punishments should be deterrent *and* in proportion to the crime. This link however is not a theoretical one but an empirical one for he is joining the two theories by the word 'and'.) Anthony Quinton argues that the traditional antimony can be resolved since retribution, properly understood, is not a moral but a logical doctrine; that is it provides not a moral justification for the infliction of punishment, but an elucidation of the use of the word. Utilitarianism embraces a number of possible moral attitudes towards punishment, none of which necessarily involves the objectionable consequences adduced by retributivists — provided, that is, that the word 'punishment' is understood in the way that the essential retributivist thesis lays down. In short, says Quinton, the two theories answer different questions: retributivists, the question, when logically can we punish? utilitarianism, the question, when morally may we or ought we to punish? (Quinton, 1954, p. 134).

Quinton's widely read and important essay implies that the two major schools of philosophy are not contradictory because they have 'een directed at different questions. As such his argument is a continuation of a debate earlier formulated by Ross (1930), opened up by Rawls (1955), and extended by Flew (1954). Professor Flew argued that punishments were 'multiple justifiable', meaning by this that retributive consideration and utilitarian considerations *each* provide a sufficient justification. His argument is tenable as far as it goes, but it still leaves a number of questions unanswered; for utilitarians have often insisted that punishment is a form of coercion and a device for making others conform to one's will irrespective of their own preferences and principles (Mundle, 1954), and therefore they do not necessarily lay claim to arguments about justice or moral deserts. In the same way Quinton has been criticized, rightly in my view, for attempting a linguistic solution to a problem that involves moral decisions (Kaufman, 1959). Bradley, for example, was doing more than asking the question, When logically can we punish? He was taking for granted that one human being is involved in evil if he inflicts unjustifiable injury on another. This is a fundamental moral point, not a logical one. And Bradley himself was aware of this, for he believed that general acceptance of his argument would be said 'to mark the transition from barbarism to civilisation', in other words, he was making a moral point about the nature of society.

Essentially, attempts to reconcile the theories canot be made by reduction to logic. The debate is not analytical, but moral. Furthermore, attempts to effect a compromise produce difficulties in their own right. For example, Quinton sees the utilitarian theory as relevant to the determination in general of what kinds of actions to punish. The outcome, he says, is a set of rules; the question of whom in particular to punish has a definite and necessary answer. So, utility provides a moral justification, guilt a logical one (Quinton, 1954, p. 141). A similar distinction is made by Rawls using restricted utilitarianism. He distinguishes between justifying a practice as a system of rules to be applied and enforced, and justifying a particular action that falls under those rules. Rawls (1955) concludes that utilitarian arguments are appropriate with regard to the questions about practices; retributive arguments fit the application of particular rules to particular cases. At one level this argument, like Quinton's, is tenable as far as it goes. Retributivists have not always wanted as *an institution* legal machinery whose essential purpose is to preserve the link between moral turpitude and suffering; they have only insisted that a person cannot be punished unless he is guilty — unless, that is, he has broken the law. Utilitarians have wanted the institution of punishment to prevent mischief; therefore, says Rawls, the link is readily established. But is it? Certainly it protects the utilitarian by removing him from the unhappy position of being accused of punishing the innocent, but it still does not meet the basic requirement of retributivists that punishment should be proportionate to the offence. Utilitarians have always wanted to adjust the punishment according to Bentham's requirements and as such have been unable to see the issues in terms of equivalence or proportions. Attempts to reconcile the theories were rejected by Sir David Ross (1930, pp. 61-2) on similar grounds, and although he did not say it, he implied that reconciliation offers great potential to the utilitarians but little to others. It becomes a compromise in favour of deterrence, offering little to the retributivist except a weakening of his position.

It seems that compromises offer little hope for resolution, and perhaps it has to be accepted that the two grand theories must be forever apart. We should not necessarily mourn that, for the arguments have been sensitively stated by various philosophers who by their opposition to one theory have produced important arguments to justify another. No summary of this length can hope to bring out more than a few of the complex issues. We still have, for example, the important distinction of treating persons as ends in themselves, a point that Kant insisted upon; and no amount of utilitarianism, restricted or otherwise, can solve this dilemma. Furthermore, we still have the important distinction between the justification of punishment and the amount of punishment given to each offender.

To sum up, we can see the strengths and weaknesses of the deterrent position. First, its strengths:

(1) Deterrence is concerned with controlling action. It therefore looks to the future and not, as retribution does, to the past.

(2) It is part of a general social theory of utility and can be adjudged within the framework of that theory.

(3) Deterrence has limitations on the use of punishment largely as a result of Bentham's assertion that all punishment was mischief and also on account of his principle of frugality.

(4) Legal rules can be changed according to the demands of society if they are seen as producing more pain than pleasure. There is no possibility of social change built with the retributive argument.

Second, its weaknesses:

(1) There is no strong link with guilt. This leaves the utilitarian open to accusations of vindictive punishments.

(2) It is easy for the utilitarian to be over-consumed with mischief and so introduce harsh punishments to counteract it.

(3) Utilitarians are in some difficulty in identifying the nature of that mischief.

(4) Extraordinary punishments can be seen as unjust.

DIFFERENCES BETWEEN RETRIBUTION, DETERRENCE AND REHABILITATION

In the debate between retribution and deterrence the rehabilitation argument has gone by default. In this short note I want to bring out some essential differences between the arguments in anticipation of that which will follow in the next section.

First, retribution and rehabilitation. Those supporting rehabilitation do not accept that punishment is an acceptable method of dealing with offenders. There is thus a fundamental antipathy between the two positions at the outset. However, some rehabilitationists will be prepared to use punishment if, and only if, they regard it as a necessary aspect of treatment. Rule-breaking is not therefore the prime reason for punishment, the offender's 'needs' being the ultimate justification. Sometimes rehabilitationists will justify punishment for those who have not broken the law. Given our earlier definition of punishment, this type of rehabilitative measure is more akin to 'hostility'.

Second, there is no concept of 'deserts' in rehabilitation: 'needs' become the overriding consideration. Without deserts there can be no sense of proportionality in punishments; hence there is the possibility of those being treated receiving long sentences for relatively minor offences and short sentences for serious crimes. (Although of course, rehabilitationists oppose punishment in practical terms, they work within the penal system and have to operate within retributive controls. Their aims are to adjust and amend those controls.) Lacking a concept of desert, it follows that rehabilitationists reduce, or remove altogether, questions of moral guilt, responsibility or proportionality. On this basis alone it would be difficult to find two theories more widely apart, and understandably most of the hostility from rehabilitationists is aimed at retributivists. Those supporting retribution would resist all attempts to make the sufferer better. They would quote Bosanquet with approval:

> by a mere medical treatment of the offender including or consisting of pleasant conditions if helpful to his cure the interest of society seems to be disregarded. What is to become of the maintenance of rights if aggressors have to anticipate a pleasant or leniant cure? . . . The reformatory theory leads to the notion that the state may take hold of any man, whose life or ideas are thought capable of improvement and set to work to ameliorate them by forcible treatment. There is no true punishment except where one is an offender against a system of rights and therefore against himself. [Bosanquet, 1965, pp. 206, 207]

In contrast, the rehabilitationist may quote Ewing with approval:

> Retributive justice may be a very good thing but the saving of souls is a much better thing. [Ewing, 1929, p. 18]

The differences between deterrence and rehabilitation is more complex. Both would share the same view that punishment was mischief, and both attempt to prevent future wrongdoing and increase future happiness. The 'serpent-windings of utilitarianism' therefore applies to both. There are other similarities too: both regard the arguments about moral guilt as irrelevant; both are deeply suspicious of justice as understood by retributivists; and both have little time for proportionality of punishment and offence. However, they also differ in a number of important respects. First, utilitarians accept that the offender is responsible for his actions for the very notion of the threat presupposes responsibility. In contrast, rehabilitationists talk of the offender's having a disease or being maladjusted. Second, there is no concept of frugality in the rehabilitationist doctrine, nor any suggestion that the punishment itself should be recognized as punishment *per se.* Third, and most important, the intention behind deterrence is to act as a threat to others; in rehabilitative terms the punishment is entirely offender-centred, wherein the method of treatment is through the use of personal agencies conducting individual therapy. Rehabilitation is not a social theory directed at the social order in general, but a theory aimed at saving individual souls. It looks no further than this, not even to the effects of the offence or to the relationships between the offender and the social order, except and only in so far as the social order affects the behaviour of the offender.

THE REFORM THEORY OF PUNISHMENT

This third theory of punishment has dominated the practice of Western European societies since 1945. We speak generally of reform as if there were one major theory, but there are more, and they are not compatible. One derives mainly from Plato, the other from Hegel. Some commentators have wanted to use the term 'reform' to apply only to Hegel's arguments, and to use 'rehabilitation' or 'treatment' for that coming from Plato. Throughout I wish to use the terms 'reform' and 'rehabilitation' interchangeably, but when referring to Hegel's argument to be more specific. For convenience we can deal with Hegel first.

Hegel's theory of punishment is mainly expressed in his *Philosophy of Right* (1967, paras. 99, 100). At first sight it appears that Hegel supported retribution, and many commentators have agreed. I think this is wrong; Hegel was a reformist offering a specific type of reform in which the offender was reformed through the punishment. It is never clear how this was to occur, for pain is a sensation and reform is a moral condition, but more of this later. In contrast, the theory of rehabilitation offers a theory of reform that accompanies punishment. In rehabilitation the offender is given therapy while he is detained in prison or a hospital, or if he is on probation, detained by the compulsion of the probation order which requires that he sees his probation officer. The punishment is the coercion or the compulsion that detains or requires his attendance; the reform accompanies this. Some types of rehabilitation do not include punishment, for example where a person may see his therapist on a voluntary basis. This has misled some rehabilitationists to believe that therapy in the penal system operates similarly. If so, it becomes a dangerous misconception leading to a denial of the compulsion. For these purposes we are concerned only with the type of rehabilitation that is part of a court order, and as such with the reform that accompanies the punishment of the court.

HEGEL'S THEORY OF PUNISHMENT

Hegel believes that sin, or criminal activity, reflects and defies the moral law. He does not deny that punishments may deter, prevent or improve, but he wishes to justify punishment on the grounds that it is pain inflicted on the offender in order that the offender may, by the fact of his punishment, be forced into recognizing as valid the law that he rejected in sinning. Punishment makes the offender repent of his sin and not simply be deterred from further offending.

The object of punishment, according to Hegel, is to make the criminal repent of his crime, and by so doing to realize his moral character which has been temporarily obscured by his wrong action, but which Hegel asserts is his truest and deepest nature. Hence Hegel is led to argue that 'The criminal is honoured as reasonable, because punishment is regarded as containing his own right' (1967, para. 100). This is a curious use of the word 'right', for we usually see rights as claims that involve benefits; for example, Kant was sure there was no right to punishment, for punishment was an affront to the dignity of the person since it contained a one-sided compulsion. Hegel however was led to this view because he saw the criminal as honoured by the punishment; the punishment was a boon to him. Without it the criminal would continue to do wrong and that would be his ruin.

Now when Hegel says that punishment tends to reform criminals, and that it is pain that improves them, he says there is something in its nature that tends to produce repentence. By repentence he means the realization by the criminal with sufficient vividness that he has done wrong. Sometimes Hegel speaks as if the pain itself were a purifying agent capable of eradicating baseness; sometimes as if it leads the criminal to some wider realization — a view incidentally not shared by Beccaria, who doubted if there was a connection between pain and moral sentiments. Hegel was not concerned with the fear of pain, for this would lead him to deterrence; it was the pain itself that produced the reformative effects. Hegel may have looked on pain as evil, but he was by no means anxious to spare it. He thought the object of punishment was not to effect 'this or that good', which meant that it was not in consequence of some accidental good that punishment was to be defended, for Hegel thought punishment was capable of producing good of itself.

It is by no means clear how punishment leads to repentence, in the psychological sense that is, or why it should happen. Nor is it clear how much pain would be required to produce the necessary level of purification. Presumably Hegel would say it depends on the baseness of the criminal, but how are we to decide on that? By the nature of the crime, perhaps, or by some other evaluation? If the first, then Hegel's view is dangerously like retribution, and if the second, then it is like rehabilitation. Yet Hegel had no sympathy with either argument, least of all with rehabilitation, regarding it with distaste. As McTaggart says, Hegel hated many things, but nothing more than sentimental humanitarianism, which he regarded as endemic in rehabilitation (McTaggart, 1918, p. 134).

We can ask as McTaggart does (1918, p. 136) whether there is anything in the nature of the infliction of pain that leads the convictions of the judge to be transferred or reproduced in the mind of the offender. The answer depends on what one means by the 'nature of the infliction of pain'. I am not saying, or suggesting, that pain does not, or cannot, produce purification; for to do so would be to fail to appreciate the basis of monasticism or of many religious experiences that involve self-inflicted penances. Hegel wanted to argue that, under special conditions, like that of the person who leads a religious life, pain would perhaps purify. But these are indeed special circumstances, for under those conditions the person has already accepted the authority under which he lives, and is submissive to its moral laws. If he does wrong he will not regard his punishment as martyrdom or as an injury, but will feel it is the proper consequence of his fault. And to feel this and accept it as such is repentence. Or the person under penance may not know he has broken the law, for the law may not have been clearly formulated; yet having broken it he is punished, and the punishment may lead to regrets about his actions. We may doubt that the punishment has led directly to repentence, but at any rate a moral advance has been achieved and this is presumably what Hegel had in mind when he justified punishment in this way.

Other examples could be found where punishment might lead to repentance. McTaggart uses the instance where the authority that inflicted the punishment was before its infliction recognized faintly and vaguely as embodying the moral law, but was established thereafter when the law was broken (McTaggart, 1918, p. 141). Here as in the earlier example it all depends on the perceived validity of the law by those who break it. That is why the example of monasticism was important, for it shows the necessary connection between an offender and authority. Where that connection is weak repentance is less likely to follow. Hegel did not consider punishment in this way, for to do so would offend his views on the relationships between the individual and the state. The state was, for Hegel, comprised of an aggregate of men like himself where obedience was, within certain limits, the individual's duty (McTaggart, 1918, p. 147). He did not consider, or was reluctant to consider, that his theory of punishment placed the offender in a position similar to that of a child, regarding his parents as his teacher on morality. And yet for his theory of punishment to be appropriate, that is how the individual should view the moral law.

The Application of Hegel's Theory to the Modern Penal System

Unlike other theories of punishment, there are no apparent or immediate applications in the modern penal system. I know of no specific sets of rules or statutes that could be traced directly to Hegel's thinking, although I am certain I have met some offenders who would consider that they had been reformed through their punishment. These offenders had almost always committed offences against members of their family and recognized that their offences were morally wrong. Their punishment made them repent, or so they said. I am sure that there were others who claimed to have seen 'the error of their ways' and that their punishment attributed in some sense to their repentance. And I am also sure that there are many people who think that offenders should receive punishment in order that they repent. They would point, I think, to offences of personal violence where the offender's repentance was necessary and above all to be welcomed. I suppose it would be possible to argue, therefore, that Hegel's influence has been felt, although it has remained outside the major area of debate.

There are, however, two aspects of Hegel's thinking that have relevance for the later chapter on juvenile and juvenile justice (Chapter 4): first, Hegel's view that punishment is a person's right, and second, his assumption that reform exists when there is a recognition of the validity of the legal authority. As regards the right to punishment, when Hegel argued that the criminal had the right to be punished he saw punishment as a protection against evil ways. To decline to give punishment was, paradoxically, the major punishment, for it robbed the criminal of the possibility of maintaining the standards that he had transgressed. 'The injury [the punishment] which falls on the criminal is not merely *implicitly* just as just, it is *eo ipso* his implicit will, an embodiment of his freedom, his right; on the contrary it is also a right *established* within the criminal himself, i.e. in his objectively embodied will, in his action' (Hegel, 1967, para. 100). Yet if crime and punishment are treated as if they were unqualified evils, it may seem unreasonable to will an evil merely because another evil is there already; and to say that a criminal has the right to his punishment can appear to the criminal as hypocritical. But Hegel is not alone here, for we find similar arguments advanced by Bosanquet (1965), when he said that the criminal action was a violation of a system of rights to which the criminal is party and in which he had a vital interest. Bosanquet, however, was more concerned with maintaining the quality of life in society than with maintaining the quality of the individual's soul.

Even so, few criminals consent to punishment let alone claim it as a right. Kant's point seems persuasive when he speaks of the one-sided compulsion involved in punishment, and Ross says that it is no punishment when anyone experiences what he wills (1930, p. 63). Ross also says the law is not a promise, for a promise involves a benefit that is mutually advantageous. The law is a threat which is an intention to do harm. Yet in the modern penal system the 'right to punishment' argument has been reintroduced, not strictly in the Hegelian sense, but as a contrast to the claims of those who wish to rehabilitate offenders. The right to be punished is now seen as a means of granting protection. Those making this claim (Fox, 1974) do so by adding a retributive justification to punishment, since retribution can, and often does, produce less severe sentences than modern methods of treatment. Shorter sentences are also less costly in economic, social and human terms.

The second aspect of Hegel's thinking to be considered is the recognition of legal authority. When discussing juvenile justice, and the punishment of children generally, Hegel's argument repays closer attention. Having identified the social conditions under which punishment in the Hegelian sense was likely to be effective, the punishment of children approximates to that category. McTaggart notes that there is not the same need in education as in law for punishments to be a deterrent, for as a general rule the decisions of elders are tacitly accepted by children as being right (1918, p. 150). Modern psychology and modern penal thinking rarely acknowledge this, or if they do they tend to emphasize other factors, such as the importance of rewards in psychology, or the importance of social background as a 'cause' of delinquent behaviour in penology. It is currently unfashionable to suggest that children should be taught by being shamed of actions. Yet McTaggart is surely right when he says that a view of human nature capable of advancing by an improvement in the moral sentiments rather than according to rewards or pleasures is a more optimistic view (1918, p. 143). I am suggesting that shame about one's actions is not to be totally dismissed as archaic and outmoded. As will be shown in Chapter 4, children are punished frequently, and no less so by 'progressive' than by 'traditional' thinkers. So Hegel had a point when he said that punishment is for moral advance. The opportunities to provide such punishment may be infrequent, but they ought not to be forgotten completely.

Differences between Hegel's and Other Theories of Punishments

Hegel's theory of punishment so resembles other theories that some commentators have failed to recognize that it provides a unique contribution of its own (e.g. Ewing, 1929). Hegel himself wanted to establish a separate theory emphasizing that other theories concentrated on the subjective aspects of crime 'intermingled with trivial psychological ideas of stimuli, impulses too strong for reason, and psychological factors coercing and working on our ideas' (1967, para. 99). To Hegel the real issue was the wrong and the righting of it. Crime should be annulled, for it was crime that contained the real evil.

When Hegel talks of annulment in this way it seems as if he is leading us towards a retributive view. This I think is a mistake. Annulment to Hegel involved the equalization of the crime and the punishment in such a way as to return to a state of affairs prior to the wrong done by the crime. Now it is not easy to see how this can be achieved, for the punishment inflicted on the wrongdoer does not restore the lost fortunes of the victims. It may make the victim feel better, but little more. If it returned those fortunes, and was intended to do so, it would be forward-looking and hence utilitarian. Furthermore, Hegel's opposition to retribution is shown when he says that retribution in conception 'is an injury of the injury', by which he means that retribution is principally revenge (1967, para. 102). To Hegel revenge becomes a new transgression because it is imposed on the offender by the positive action of others who have mistakenly used their power against the offender. He also criticizes retribution for what he calls 'the absurdity of the retributive character of punishment which attempts to equal the suffering with the criminal action' (para. 101). Hegel further attacks retribution on the ground that retributivists give punishment 'the superficial character of an evil'. His own view of punishment was different. Hegel saw punishment as a positive step; a right established within the criminal himself. He saw annulment, or the equalization of crime and punishment as a value and not an external connection; what he called the inner equality of things, which in their outward existence are specifically different from one another in every way. Retribution was the external; Hegel's view of punishment concentrated on the internal, which was, he claimed, a demand for justice no longer contingent on right.

Even so, there are apparent similarities with retribution, notably that the criminal should be treated as a moral being in his own right. But these are superficial, for Hegel views the criminal as *potentially* moral, and this potentiality must be brought into existence. Retributivists make no such claims. Unlike the retributivists, Hegel wishes to inflict pain on a person for his ultimate good, and he sees punishment as an honour, not a disgrace. He also cares whether the offender can or will do good in the future. In contrast, retributivists do not wish to improve the criminal or society. It is perhaps for this reason that Hegel's theory has more application to juveniles than to adults. To Hegel, retribution is inflicted on the criminal and becomes an alien destiny, not intrinsically his own.

Hegel was firmly opposed to deterrence. He does not deny that punishment may act as a deterrent, or that deterrence may act as a way of restricting the activities of those with a proclivity to criminal actions. His major criticism is that the deterrent theory treats a man like a dog to whom a master shows a whip, and not as a free being. 'A threat presupposes that a man is not free and its aim is to coerce him by the idea of evil' (1967, Additions, para. 62). He acknowledges that the deterrent theory as proposed by Beccaria has beneficial effects, notably in the abolition of the death penalty, but these are incidental achievements which do not lead him to give deterrence unqualified support. Hegel of course cannot support capital punishment. There is no moral improvement in the death penalty, although in a later passage he seems to suggest otherwise for he says no punishment is great enough 'value' for taking a man's life (1967, para. 64).

Hegel was insistent that his theory of punishment differed from rehabilitation, which he regarded as 'sentimental humanitarianism'. In rehabilitation there is the presumption that we ought to reform our criminals while we are punishing them; Hegel says that punishment itself reforms. Unlike those supporting rehabilitation, Hegel does not apologize for inflicting punishment — it is, after all, a way of honouring the offender. Similarly, Hegel does not see the offender as a product of a background or psychological disposition, but as a person capable of exercising moral decisions. Hegel's theory is full-blooded, and not easy to reconcile with the vague and often woolly claims of many modern rehabilitationists who see the offender as partially responsible for his actions and partially a product of his environment. Taking a general overview of the argument, we could I think usefully extract from Hegel what is of value without extending or introducing a new Hegelianism into modern thinking. Hegel's criticisms of retribution, deterrence and rehabilitation are valuable for their own sake, and so is his insistence that shame can and ought to be an essential feature of punishment.

THE REHABILITATIONIST THEORY

We speak of the modern theory of rehabilitation, but the theory is modern only in so far as it has had a modern application. Its pedigree is lengthy and distinguished. Plato saw wrongdoers as morally sick, where the courts' task was to act as a physician of souls. Plato's argument is in the form of three propositions.

(1) Wickedness is a mental disease, disintegrating and ultimately fatal.

(2) The punishment of wicked acts is to be regarded as a moral medicine, unpalatable but wholesome.

(3) The State should stand to the criminal *in loco parentis.*

We find strains of the same argument in St Thomas Aquinas, who spoke of *poena medicinalis.* 'We can also look at punishment as medicinal and then not simply as a cure for past sins but as a preventative of future sins or even as an inducement to some good.' St Thomas describes this form of punishment as having the quality of medicine, where physicians administer bitter doses to the sick in order to restore health (Aquinas, 1974, Q.87, Sec. 7, p. 37). St Thomas distinguished between 'evil of fault and evil of punishment'; *poena medicinalis* arose in the former.

Whereas retribution and deterrence involve a linear method of thinking proceeding from the crime to the punishment, rehabilitation is more complex. It involves an examination of the offence, the criminal, his social system and the punishment. Rehabilitationists accept that additional problems may develop during the offender's sentence (or treatment) which are unconnected with the offence. These may require offenders to spend additional periods under coercion. So while retribution and deterrence are limited in scope and restricted to the sentence and amount of punishment, rehabilitation opens up the discussion to include the offender's social psychological world, *and* the effects of penal institutions on the offender's subsequent welfare. Criminology has followed both systems of thought, so that we can speak of formal criminology, concerned with the law, its application and the justification for punishment, and sociological/psychological criminology, which is wider and more generous in its definition of the subject matter.

The rehabilitationist theory sees crime as a manifestation of a social disease. As with all theories using a medical orthodoxy, the aim must be to cure that disease by treatment. There is no more complete definition than that described by Samuel Butler. In *Erewhon* there existed a class of man trained in soul-craft whom they called the 'straighteners', which literally translated means 'one who bends back the crooked'. The straighteners' task was to classify all known forms of mental indisposition and tell a man what is wrong with him as soon as they heard his story. Their familiarity with long names

gave assurance that they understood the case. It was hardly
necessary, said Butler, to say that the office of straightener was one
that required long and special training, for it stood to reason that he
who would cure a moral ailment must be practically acquainted with
all its bearings (Butler, 1960, p. 87).

It is not the intention here to produce definitions of rehabilitation,
for this has been done elsewhere (Bean, 1976). Plato has succinctly
stated the main feature when he says 'No punishment inflicted by
law is for the sake of harm, but to make the sufferer better, or to
make him less bad than he would have been without it.' In its modern
form the American Correctional Association describes how the
'modern philosophy of rehabilitation is put to practical application
by the development of three related and continuous phases of the
correctional process: probation, institutional training and treatment,
and parole'. The ACA show how the offender can be treated in the
community, and if this fails he can be treated in prisons and further
treated in the community when discharge becomes appropriate. The
aim is a comprehensive system of treatment covering the main areas
of the penal system.

The modern rehabilitation argument was developed by Ferri, the
founder of the so-called positivist school of criminology. Ferri wanted
to establish criminology above the level of 'mere philosophy', and
directed his attack, among other things, at the State's right to punish.
His basic idea was that the right to punishment could not be derived
from moral guilt or responsibility, because this presupposes a free
will, which on scientific grounds must be rejected as illusory. The
right to punish must be derived from the natural conditions of
existence; more precisely, from every living man's fight for survival.

> In this way the positivist school replaces the contested and indefinite
> criterion of *moral* responsibility as the reason for and basis of the right
> to punish, with the positive and precise criterion of social or judicial
> responsibility as the reason and basis of the right of honest people to
> defend society against the criminals. [quoted in Ross, 1975, pp. 64-5]

Ferri's scientific criminology was no more scientific than August
Comte's positivism from which it was inspired. It was based on a
moral theory, or rather a mixture of moral theories, some derived
from natural law, others from social contract theory and others from
what Alf Ross calls 'the assumption that the moral norm proceeds
directly from reality as an expression of immanent tendencies in the
latter' (Ross, 1975, p. 64). Ferri's methods approximated to a form of

scientific methodology, but given the nature of the subject matter and the nature of social science generally he was faced with limitations at the outset. None the less, he wanted to clarify and analyse criminological forms in order to predict criminal behaviour. To do this he rejected all suggestions of 'free will', which he regarded as metaphysical, and replaced it with a form of determinism that saw the offender as acting in a social and psychological milieu. Ferri thought this method would allow criminological laws to be developed, but he appreciated neither the complexity of the undertaking nor the difficulties of grafting a scientific method on to a study of human behaviour — and particularly on to one as delicate as that of crime.

Yet it was to Ferri that the modern treatment officials owe their debt, although the work of Freud produced the method under which most of them operated. Ferri had insisted that the study of the criminal was the major element in criminology — not crime, as was emphasized by the classical school. Immediately, problems arose as to what constitutes a criminal — whether it should be a person who had been successfully prosecuted, or one who had broken the law but not been prosecuted. The definition of the subject matter was, and still remains, contentious, and recent attempts to widen it to study 'deviant behaviour' have not extricated it from its definitional dilemmas. Ferri however produced a one-sided view of criminology, where the criminal became the central figure and the law, the moral issues surrounding law and questions of punishment were underdeveloped. Inevitably, a veiled utilitarianism was introduced where the central issues were, and still are, the success of penal institutions defined in terms of reconviction rates or some form of betterment of the offender. This was not a utilitarianism derived from Bentham but one that led criminologists to believe that some overall good could be derived by studying criminals. Moral issues were included but not extracted. Criminologists rarely asked why they believed they ought to improve the offender's welfare rather than (say) study the rights of citizens or the relationships between the offender's demands and the rights of others. It is easy to see how criminology has been colonized by neo-Marxists intent on changing the structure of society to produce the ultimate 'betterment' — the new social order, the second coming.

We shall have more to say of the dilemmas of modern criminology in a later chapter; here, I only want to show how Ferri influenced the subject matter and produced its emphasis on the offender. Modern rehabilitation was a product of Ferri's thinking and his legacy also includes the weaknesses of criminology generally which grew out of and developed alongside the growth of rehabilitation. His views flourished and became the dominant theme in the middle of the twentieth century. Only recently have we realized that the practical implementation of those demands depend on a high GNP and a similarly high commitment to government expenditure. Paradoxically, rehabilitationists have accepted these facts as of little significance, often refusing to examine the economic costs of treatment or the number of experts required to produce a successful outcome. But then, there is nothing in the reformist argument that requires treatment measures to be cost-effective. Retribution and deterrence are different; one contains a hidden economic argument related to deserts, and the other relates the amount of punishment to the amount of harm done. Rehabilitation has operated by ignoring economic requirements. It is no accident therefore that a new climate of government opinion, which has reduced government expenditure, has led directly or indirectly to the demise of rehabilitation as earlier practised.

Although we have talked generally of rehabilitation, as if it encompassed a general theory, this is much too simple. There are numerous divisions and subdivisions, some of which are antithetical to each other. The behavioural psychologist has little in common with the community worker, and the probation officer little in common with the local authority social worker — at least in the type of organization to which he belongs. Yet all retain a common thread, which is to see the offence as a justification for intervention and the offence itself as one part of, or a symptom of, the offender's background and personality disorder. Treatment consists of removing the 'need', or the symptom or disease, call it what you will. Treatment may use punishment directly or it may not. The American Correctional Association defines the position thus:

> Proponents of the theory of rehabilitation . . . do not rule out the necessity of custodial segregation, but consider custody a means to an end . . . They do not deny the desirability of using a deterrent effect if it can be done without impairing the effectiveness of rehabilitative programmes. [ACA, 1972, p. 25]

The range and possibilities become wide, and more often than not reflect the specific interests of the reformist agencies. Herein lie the strengths and weaknesses. While on the one hand flexibility is provided by the wide range of treatments, on the other, there is no 'definitional stop' to provide limits to intervention. Rehabilitation can be weak and gentle, involving nothing more than a discussion with a friendly social worker, or it can be as strong and tough as the imposition of indeterminate sentences for relatively minor offences. It can also include aversive conditioning, chimotherapy and psychosurgery. It can be humanitarian, as when it favours (say) an extension of television viewing time to prisoners, and as brutal as producing the agonies of uncertainty in the indeterminate sentence. That its proponents always claim a humanitarian component to rehabilitation should not mislead us. The range of possibilities becomes a more reliable guide to its activities.

Herein lies one of the major issues. Those supporting rehabilitation have tended to operate as if they had the monopoly of kind sentiments. Punishment is regarded as outmoded and outdated, almost as if it belonged to some atavastic age. From its inception there has been a constant stream of rhetoric from the rehabilitationists decrying the use of punishment, yet failing to acknowledge that rehabilitation *is* punishment. Often there is an attempt to bypass punishment altogether by calling it something else. Karl Menninger, for instance, emphasizes the demand for the abolition of punishment and then says, 'certainly [this] . . . does not mean the omission or curtailment of penalties; quite the contrary. Penalties should be greater and surer and quicker in coming' (Menninger, 1966). Notice: not 'punishment', but 'penalties'; the difference remains unclear. Others use a less disingenuous approach. The Kilbrandon Report, for example, wanted to take punishment out of the juvenile justice system, failing to see that this was a contradiction in terms (HMSO, 1964), while a social work lecturer could write that limitations on the powers of the court for juveniles were irrelevant since 'the whole purpose . . . is to concentrate on treatment needs and therefore what is done for a child is done in the interests of his welfare' (Boss, 1967, p. 91).

RULES AND MORALS

The essence of a rehabilitative philosophy is to deny a connection between guilt and punishment, and therefore if logically developed would contradict the retributive principle that we punish only the guilty. The link with rules and morality therefore becomes tenuous. It is not entirely absent, for presumably those who broke rules would, by the act of breaking them, be candidates for rehabilitation, and as rule-breakers they would demonstrate the disease symptoms. So too would others who had not broken rules but who might do so in the near future. Rule-breaking becomes a sufficient but not a necessary condition for therapeutic intervention.

The central difficulty is to decide what we mean when we talk of rules. Rules may be formal, as in law, or informal, as with custom. All who are candidates for rehabilitation would have broken some rules, even of an informal nature. Those attempting suicide, or experiencing marital difficulties, or even having illegitimate children could be said to violate custom — and it must be admitted that these form the bulk of the modern social workers' 'clients'. The offenders — those who have broken formal rules — become a relatively small minority. The tensions created in the penal system are often caused by the rehabilitationist insisting that those who break formal rules are not *qualitatively* different from those violating custom. Reformists suggest that all should be considered alike. Most lawyers, judges and criminologists disagree, emphasizing that legal rules imply legal punishments and in this respect are of a different order.

The theory of reform fosters and accentuates this view. Using a model devised from medicine or biology, the rehabilitationist argues that the roots of crime are to be found in the defects of the family. Hence crime is seen as no different in its origins from other forms of maladjustment. Treatment therefore becomes a family-orientated service. It matters little, say the reformists, that a person is criminal rather than suicidal, for these are mere symptoms of the same underlying disease. Reform, ideally conceived, would operate within the penal system in the same manner it operates elsewhere, namely as a service aimed at removing the disease by therapeutic methods. The reformists regard advocates of traditional legal thinking as their major opponents. Faced with such stubbornness, the reformers say, they are forced to operate in a less than ideal state, hoping and arguing that the system will change. We shall see in Chapter 5 that considerable inroads have already been made, not only in juvenile justice, which offers the most promising area for the reformist position, but also in other areas of the penal system.

When reformists ask for a family-orientated service they are unwittingly demonstrating the strengths and limitations of their position. Family-orientated practices imply a set of relationships whereby the adults, usually the parents, are the acknowledged superiors and the children accept that superiority. The sense of inferiority is based not on force but on a recognition by the children that parents mean well by them and will care for them. This is what is meant by paternalism, using the term in its less perjorative form. Punishments may operate within the family but they exist amid a wider range of other and possibly more enjoyable activities. Demands for a family-orientated service introduce the therapist, as an adult, into a social network that emphasizes the therapist's adulthood, while those who have asked for the help are placed in an inferior position. Therapy resembles punishment in this respect, in that it produces status and rankings of superiority/inferiority.

Invariably, as far as offenders are concerned, the therapist is not welcomed. There is convincing evidence that ex-offenders rarely consult the after-care services voluntarily and have little wish to change their self-image (Bean, 1976). On what basis then does the therapist operate? Under the present system, with its element of compulsion, the offender is engaged in a legal transaction under the influences of coercion (*coactus voluit* − at his wish although coerced). The therapist may play down the coercive element but it remains none the less. There may be a more relaxed atmosphere than could occur in the court, but the therapist makes the decisions, dictates the pace and has power to enforce rules. No amount of family-orientated services can remove or deny that.

But the more important limitations on family-orientated services lie in the field of prevention. In medicine the history of prevention has made valuable inroads into the levels of health in society, and on this basis it would seem entirely reasonable that the reformist should adopt similar practices − given the models from which he operates. Prevention of delinquency has therefore become an important platform. Now there are many ways in which this can be done. Generally speaking, we tend to warn people about the dangers of (say) leaving luggage unattended, and allow the potential victim to make his own choice. But in reformist programmes there is less choice. Sometimes these programmes operate in a mild form and sometimes not so. Professor Eysenck advocates the mild form when he says 'once this particular aspect of the child's nature was well known we could . . . pick out those who by virtue of their poor conditionability are predestined to become criminals and delinquents, and recommend to their parents a kind of upbringing that would minimize that possibility' (quoted in Honderich, 1969, p. 99). Others have been less reluctant to *recommend* to parents but have advocated direct intervention and control. This is vindictive punishment at its worst and most dangerous, ignoring the rights of those who have been selected as potential criminals. As such it runs counter to Dicey's dictum that men are to be interfered with or punished not because they may or will break the law, but only because they have committed some definite assignable legal offence (1962, p. 245). A similar point was made by Bosanquet, who foresaw some of the political implications when he said that rehabilitation leads to the notion that the State may take hold of any man whose life and ideas are thought capable of improvement and set to work to ameliorate them by forcible treatment (1965, p. 207).

Within the framework of rehabilitation it seems there are rules, but these are of a different order to those related to retribution or deterrence. In rehabilitation rules are flexible and are related to the requirements of the 'needs' of the offender. They are certainly not the rules of retribution, for there is no guilt; there are only symptoms and diseases. And there is no specific link with legal rules generally except and in so far as legal rules provide the compulsion under which rehabilitative regimes operate. We can no more talk of rehabilitation being a theory of jurisprudence than we could talk of medicine being one. All that can be done is to identify the framework within which rehabilitation operates and show the normative requirements and implications related to that setting.

The same is true of the link with morality. Rehabilitation sometimes operates as if it makes no claims to be part of an ethical system, and as such it appears as a practical problem-solving device using the model of medicine to promote its ideals. The language of Freud may be used, or rather an extension of Freudian principles, and where it is there is no social or moral theory linking the offender to the social order. Rehabilitation has little to say about the way human beings are sufficiently equal in their capacity to hurt one another, or that it is in their interests to give respect to the interests of others. Crime cannot easily be condemned as antisocial or immoral. Rehabilitation has nothing to say on these wider moral principles when it is encapsulated into a framework of 'needs', 'diseases' and 'problems' of the individual offender.

And yet it has within it a set of assumptions that have a certain moral appeal. First, it has provided its own restless morality where its supporters claim they represent the criminal against an obdurate and often inflexible penal system. Rehabilitation has often led the way in a search for new policies and for improvements to the criminal's position. On the other hand, sometimes claims have been excessive. Many reformist programmes are, within the strictest sense of the term, more likely to be humanistic services. That they have been claimed as rehabilitative perhaps in the long run does not matter, for without a rehabilitative framework it is unlikely that those policies would have been suggested let alone implemented.

Second, rehabilitation has sharpened the focus, and highlighted the difficulties surrounding the position of children in the juvenile justice system. That children are young, vulnerable and capable of being influenced is a matter of some significance; that they may have committed offences that are qualitatively different in terms of intent is important also. So too is their future welfare. Regrettably, supporters of deterrence and retribution have ignored this, for their theories start from the premise that punishment is either deserved or deters, and as such applies only to those who are morally responsible for their actions. Children are clearly not responsible — at least, under a certain age. So it is worthwhile to note that rehabilitation has for many decades been the only possible alternative for the juvenile justice system. It has reached its prominence by default rather than design — but it at least offered a coherent alternative.

Third, rehabilitation has emphasized the personalities and social lives of offenders. It may have done so to the exclusion of victims, and to the exclusion of the rights of others, but on moral grounds it is to be welcomed, for it has often shown the levels of desperation in which many offenders find themselves. These are positive achievements and should not be lightly dismissed.

THE JUSTIFICATION OF PUNISHMENT

It is not easy to discuss the justification of punishment in rehabilitative terms, for more often than not there is a refusal to believe that punishment is being operated. Where it is, it is justified invariably in terms of the offender's own good. This does not mean that traditional theories of punishment are excluded, for deterrence has been incorporated into the theory to promote the 'betterment' of the offender. The American Correctional Association defines it thus:

The proposition taken by proponents of the theory of rehabilitation may be summed up as follows. They do not rule out the necessity of custodial segregation but consider custody a means to an end in the vast majority of cases and an end in a very few cases. They do not deny the desirability of achieving a deterrent effect if it can be done without impairing the effectiveness of rehabilitative programmes. [quoted in Bean, 1976, pp. 7-8]

So while deterrence may be used, it becomes an adjunct to the main reformist programme, for rehabilitationists do not consider it has value of its own accord. They then become prone to Dr Ewing's criticisms that it is wrong, on moral grounds, to sacrifice the majority of potential non-offenders for the good of the few who offend. Reformists would argue that their preventative programmes meet Dr Ewing's point, but whether they do so is of course another matter. Prevention by its very nature must have a limited appeal, for it would be impossible to screen all potential offenders. Deterrence has this much; it is capable of permeating through all the recesses of a given society, whether we like it or not.

Preventative programmes of course are allied to social defence. And by social defence I mean more than the protection of society but an administrative approach to rid society of its problems. However, social defence is rarely discussed by rehabilitationists as an active justification for punishment. It exists wherever there is the assumption that something has to be done now to avoid problems later. The Kilbrandon Report makes this plain. 'What we mean by persistent truancy is often the first sign of serious maladjustment of psychological disorder. If unattended, like all disease prognosis it may have repercussions in after life more serious than delinquency itself' (HMSO, 1964). (Presumably the Committee meant 'later life' rather than 'after life', for rehabilitation must have some limits!) The justification for intervention is based on requirements derived from medicine: if unattended the symptoms will increase and the prognosis will worsen.

The general justification of punishment becomes bound up with a number of themes, but is dominated by one: the requirement of treatment. The model of medicine produces the thrust of the argument. Treatment is provided because the offender needs it, and where he does not recognize his need he would resemble others whose sickness prevents that realization — the mentally ill. (The Freudians have always believed that the therapist could understand the patient better than the patient himself, and treatment, heavily indebted as it is to Freudian theory, has had no difficulty in transposing that belief to the world of the offender.) The general justification of punishment goes no further than this. Social defence fits into that theme.

The distribution of punishment is similarly based. The extent of treatment must be related to the extent of need, and given the difficulties of establishing need it is not possible to decide in advance the amount of treatment required. For this reason rehabilitationists favour an open-ended system of sentences where decisions are made according to the progress made in the treatment programme. Hence there have been demands to replace the fixed sentence of the court with semi- and indeterminate sentences, and to replace the courts with sentencing panels, as well as to produce a flexible sentencing system where custodial and non-custodial sentences are used as alternatives to treatments.

Comparisons with retribution are instructive. Whereas retributivists insist that punishment is for deserts, rehabilitationists make no such claim. (We can for the moment ignore the occasional wilful refusal to see rehabilitation as punishment and accept that it is, and can note also that in rehabilitation the punishment is for the disease of which the crime may be one symptom.) Whereas retributivists claim that punishment is 'for something', by which they mean for a specific offence, rehabilitationists offer their punishment for more diffuse reasons, such as needs or social and human problems. The differences between rehabilitation and retribution are most marked when retributivists talk of 'deserts'. There is no similar concept in the rehabilitative framework. In contrast, retributivists speak of deserts that are 'just', marking a relationship between the offences and the punishment. 'Just' or 'commensurate' deserts prescribes the maximum punishment appropriate for the offence. Theoretically the maximum punishment under rehabilitation is infinity. These differences perhaps explain why rehabilitationists decry retribution as inhuman or vindictive, and wish to rid the modern penal system of its influence, while they in turn are accused of opportunism.[6]

To sum up, we can see the strengths and weaknesses of the rehabilitation position. First its strengths:

(1) Rehabilitation places emphasis on the personal lives of the offenders.
(2) It treats people as individuals.

(3) Rehabilitation has often produced new thinking in an otherwise inflexible penal system.

Second, its weaknesses:

(1) The assumption that crime is related to disease is unwarranted; so is the additional assumption that social experts can diagnose that condition.

(2) Treatment is open-ended, related neither to the offence nor to anything except an ill-defined term like 'need'.

(3) The offender, not being seen as fully responsible for his actions, is capable of manipulation.

ADDITIONAL AREAS OF INTEREST

The debate so far has tended to follow somewhat traditional lines and concentrate on legal punishments. Perhaps this is because philosophers have found the subject matter more interesting, or perhaps it is because legal punishments provide form and shape to the arguments. Occasionally someone provides a glimpse of alternative forms — for example Mabbott when he cites his experiences as warden and punished students who broke rules — but these are rare. For my purpose it has suited me to go along with this debate, for the aim of the book is criminological as well as philosophical and the extent of the debate has fitted neatly into those arguments. And yet I cannot but hope that others concerned with punishment will not adopt such a narrow framework. Punishment, after all, is for an offence that need not be a legal offence, and although legal punishments are the most severe, they are not the most common.

Consider the case of a parent and children. A parent does not legislate but gives orders. (Baier, 1955, p. 26); he does not specify in advance the maximum and minimum penalties, and he rarely takes much trouble to find out whether the child is really guilty; nor does he formally find him guilty or pronounce sentence. Sometimes the child may not even know there was a rule to be applied, yet he is punished for having broken it. This is often part of the nature of parenthood, for the aim is to demonstrate to the child that there is a rule and thenceforth those who break it will be punished in this manner. We think there is nothing odd in this, and it is possible for the child to be punished retributely in these circumstances. Yet we cannot really say the child deserves punishment in the sense in which deserts are usually implied. Nor can we assume that he knows the rules (or would have known these had been taught), for the purpose of this type of punishment is to teach the rules to him. To say the child is guilty of an offence then is only partly true (McCloskey, 1962, p. 313). We could say that children were a special case and retribution does not apply to them, but it obviously does, for parents punish retributively. We can agree with McCloskey, who sees an over preoccupation with legal punishments in the debate generally, and less concern with other forms (1962, p. 307). Legal retribution is institutionalized in what Baier calls the 'game', which is preceded by 'giving orders or laying down laws, affixing penalties to them, ascertaining whether anyone has disobeyed the commands or laws, sentencing persons found guilty . . . These activities must be performed and must precede the infliction of hardship if we are to speak of punishment at all' (Baier, 1955, p. 26). No such 'game' occurs with children.

Consider also the case of the large numbers of adults who break social rules as part of their day-to-day activities, or break the rules of institutions. Are these punishments to be justified in the same ways as legal punishments? Presumably yes, but they approximate to the punishments of children in so far as there is an absence of a trial or 'game', although they may resemble legal punishments in other respects. Yet while it may be reasonable to assume this is so, the point is that we really do not know. There may be qualitative differences of a kind not discovered, and who knows, perhaps careful study may throw further light on the debate about legal punishment. Again, many people are 'sacked' from their jobs and are punished, but how different is this in principle to those who are made redundant? Members of professions who are 'struck off' are punished too, but is this a different type of punishment, and if so in what way? Again, we do not know. Perhaps one day these defects will be remedied.

NOTES

1. We find an equally crude argument linking retribution to child development and showing why retribution should be discarded (Whiteley,

1948, in reply to Nowell-Smith). The early phase of development is what Whitely calls 'spontaneous resentment'. As we grow older we replace this with a sentiment of sympathy for the wrongdoer, or by a wish to discover the best method of preventing crime. In these early stages the child believes that punishment has everything to do with the results of action and little to do with the state of mind of the agent. Apparently, we never grow out of this completely, and retribution is a left-over from this childish thinking (Whiteley, 1948, p. 231). Whiteley also believes that societies follow similar stages of development, and he suggests that it is not unreasonable to suppose that less sophisticated societies which believe in crude retribution have not grown out of it as far as we have. I apologize to Mr Whiteley for retaining some of those childish thoughts, but dare I suggest explanations for the other theories on similarly crude lines; deterrence being a left-over from a fear of the dark and rehabilitation from 'Mummy kisses everything better'.

2. In making this distinction, Hart acknowledges his debt to Locke who, when writing his chapter 'Of Property', distinguishes between the labour of a man's body and the work of his hands. Locke's distinction corresponds to Hart's 'General Justifying Aims and Distribution' (Hart, 1968, p. 4).

3. Many of the theoretical issues discussed below are relatively simple compared with those involving what is customarily called the Deterrence Doctrine, i.e. an empirical description of the manner in which someone is deterred, as opposed to the *a priori* theory itself (Beyleveld, 1979a, b). Deryck Beyleveld has distinguished nine separate ways in which the deterrence doctrine can be tested, ranging from what he calls general deterrence, i.e. the effect a sanction has on a particular offender who has not had the sanctions inflicted on him before, to particularized deterrence, when a sanction for a particular type of offence deters that offence only, to vicarious deterrence, which occurs when there is deterrence of an offender by a sanction accompanied by replacement of the offence for another offence (e.g., a potential offender may consider armed robbery to be too risky and switches to burglary. Beyleveld, 1979 (a), p. 213). For those wishing to pursue the empirical discussion further see Zimring, and Hawkins, (1973); and Gibbs (1968, 1975).

4. Sir Walter Moberly describes them in terms of Beccaria being the Luther of the new reformation, and Bentham its Calvin, its chief systematic logician; while Radzinowicz said 'Beccaria had indicated certain principles with the light touch of an essayist, Bentham grasped them with astonishing firmness, gave them sharpest definition and developed into numberless consequences' (Moberley, 1968, p. 43).

5. As a method of social control, deterrence is widely used in the courts and in schools or in families. It is also used to justify the stockpiling of nuclear and strategic armaments, although in these instances the term 'deterrent' is used in its secondary sense. One talks none the less of nuclear armaments being of 'deterrent value' and in a sense, of course, supporters of this argument suggest that there is a deterrent effect, but do not suggest that the effect is other than particularized, i.e. does not necessarily stop the possibility of wars by strategic arms.

6. Finally, we should consider one of the major criticisms of rehabilitation which has come from the influential American Friends Service Committees report (1971) *Struggle for Justice*. The American Friends document is important if only because the Friends have publicly stated that they no longer support reform. They argued that there was 'compelling evidence that the individualized treatment model, the ideal towards which reformers have been urging us for at least a century, is theoretically faulty, systematically discriminatory in application and inconsistent with some of our basic concepts of justice' (1971, p. 12).

Why theoretically faulty? The Committee saw rehabilitation as a theory based on the assertion that crime has its roots in the defects of individual upbringing and where the defects are symptoms of an underlying disease. The Committee believed that the medical model was inappropriate and misplaced. It is not possible to talk of 'social diseases', for there is no defective structure or functioning in the social organism as there is in the human organism. Crime is related to values, not to anatomical defects, be they social or otherwise.

The Committee believed that rehabilitation is systematically discriminatory because those coming from worse backgrounds are deemed to require longer periods of treatment than those from more acceptable backgrounds. Furthermore, decisions are based on impressionistic pieces of evidence, rarely validated, which have the overall effect of giving greater punishment to those who are said to need the most treatment. The extent of treatment provided is regarded as independent of the offence, for the offence is regarded as one symptom of disease.

Rehabilitation is seen as inconsistent with justice because the offence is regarded as a symptom. This means that some offenders will serve long sentences, others shorter ones, although the offence may be the same. It is also inconsistent with justice because it encourages the indeterminate and semi-indeterminate sentence where decisions to release the offender are usually taken in secret based on impressionistic views of the offender's response to the treatment. Or in Beccaria's terms, 'who can defend himself from slanders which are secure inside tyranny's strongest armour, secrecy' (1964, p. 27).

These are recent criticisms. They relate not only to the general justifying aim of rehabilitation but also to its distribution. Earlier (in 1928) Bosanquet had complained of the danger of rewarding the deviant 'by a mere medical treatment of the offender, including or consisting of pleasant conditions' (1965, p. 206). What he did not foresee was the possibility of *longer* sentences. Had he done so he would have highlighted the dual thrust of the criticisms which appear paradoxical but are contained within the rehabilitative framework; that of sentences that are too short, that fail to protect other's rights, and those that are too long, which fail to protect the offender's rights.

3

Punishment and Justice

To the offender, punishment is the key in a system of justice in which he has become a central if unwilling figure. Sir Walter Moberly once observed that the moral quality of punishment lies in its intrinsic justice rather than in its possible effect in causing or averting pain (1968, p. 69). Yet if justice is a central requirement how can the debate on punishment lead us to establish what we mean when we say that justice was done and a just decision was made? Or perhaps we should go back further and ask if it matters? We could, as the utilitarians often suggest, regard crime as a public nuisance or a public danger, or, as the rehabilitationists suggest, regard the criminals as candidates for therapy. Or we could, as Kant urges us to do, retain the strongest moral condemnation for any punishment if it were to be regarded as unjust. Clearly then our arguments about punishment will affect our arguments about justice. In this chapter I wish to establish how and in what way theories of punishment can be linked to justice generally, and to just decisions in particular. And by justice I mean specifically penal justice rather than distributive justice common to the taxation system or welfare provisions.

JUSTICE DEFINED

There has been no shortage of definitions of justice in the philosophical literature. Aristotle defined it in terms of proportions (*Ethica Nicomachea,* 1925, Book V, p. 1131a): 'Hence one term becomes too great the other too small as indeed happens in practice; for the man who acts unjustly has too much and the man who is unjustly treated too little of what is good.' Aristotle thought that justice occurred when a man acted wisely; injustice occurred when, from choice, the act violated the proportion or equality. For Aristotle, justice meant treating equals equally and unequals unequally, where equality is defined according to criteria deemed to be relevant. Others, such as Spinoza, have suggested that justice consists in the habitual rendering to every man his lawful due; injustice consists in depriving a man under the pretence of legality of what the laws rightly interpreted would allow him (Spinoza, 1951 (a), p. 208). Spinoza goes on to say that those who administer the law are bound to show no respect of persons but to account all men equal, and to defend every man's right equally, neither envying the rich nor despising the poor.

The major features in justice can be extracted from these definitions: the sense of balance, the quality of proportions, impartiality, and the giving a person what is rightful due. The same themes were picked up and developed by John Stuart Mill, who, in his discussion on the common attribute of justice, saw injustice as occurring when a person was deprived of his liberty, his property or any other thing that belonged to him otherwise than in accordance with law; whereas justice was related to deserts and was inconsistent with partiality i.e. with showing favour or preference to one person over another in matters to which favour and preference do not properly apply (Mill, 1964, pp. 298-301). Allied to impartiality was equality.

We can follow Aristotle further to indicate the special features of penal justice. Aristotle distinguished between what he called the 'government to law' and 'the government of men'; the former he defined as government by passionless reason.[1] By this he meant a method of government where decisions are made according to rules that are themselves justified by public debate, where the rules are made known to the public because they are drawn up in advance, and where decision-makers are expected to decide, on the basis of those rules, what is generally understood. In contrast, the government of men more resembles the Khadi justice of the Moslem market-place where decisions are less in terms of established principles, more on the basis of intuition, and always apart from public scrutiny. Khadi justice has fewer built-in safeguards and lacks an established right of appeal.

Of course, the contrast in the forms of justice presented here creates the impression that justice by the government of men is qualitatively inferior to that of the law. The slight is not intended; the contrast has been presented deliberately and in this extreme form to show the essential features of justice by laws; i.e., justice by law is likely to be more circumspect, it is related to defined rules which by their very nature provide built-in safeguards to those who violate them, and it often guarantees the right of appeal. Obviously there are many instances where 'the government of men' provides justice according to equally strict canons, but it is justice of a different order with different aims and methods.

Now justice is a prescriptive and protean term. Curiously enough, it was not one of the 'triumvirate of virtues' fostered by the French Revolution (liberty, equality and fraternity being preferred), but it has at all times been regarded as an ultimate value capable of existing only in refined consciences. Aristotle praised it, as have all legal jurists and philosophers since. We demand that our legal system be just, and also that justice should be manifest; for, as lawyers never tire of saying, it is not enough that justice be done: justice should be seen to be done. Philosophers such as Kant have wanted to link justice to other virtues such as freedom, although Bentham regarded it as a metaphysical concept having little meaning.

Punishment is part of justice. John Stuart Mill has, I think, captured the essential link, for he regards it as a moral one. So we do not call anything wrong unless we imply that a person ought to be punished in some way or other for doing it, if not by law then by the opinion of his fellow creatures (Mill, 1964, p. 304). This is the nature of a moral wrong. Justice involves a correlative right, and implies not only something that is right to do, and wrong not to do, but something that some individual person can claim from others as his moral right. Where a moral wrong has occurred punishment follows, and those being punished can claim the moral right of justice.

Mill went further and claimed that there was a sentiment of justice which involved two essential ingredients: the desire to punish a person who has done harm, and the knowledge or belief that there is some definite individual or individuals to whom harm has been done (1964, p. 306). Others such as Adam Smith have argued that the punishment of the wicked is deeply rooted in human instincts, or what he calls the moral sentiments, so that in every religion, and in every superstition that the world has ever held, there has been a place provided for the punishment of the wicked as well as one for the reward of the just (Smith, 1808, p. 216). When the wicked are punished they are properly dealt with according to ideas of justice. 'When justice is violated', said Adam Smith 'it is injury: it does real and positive hurt to some particular person, from motives which are naturally disposed of. It is therefore the proper object of resentment, and of punishment,' (1808, p. 185). Here Smith was talking of the violation of justice leading to punishment; later he shows how the punishment produces the justice, which he regards as a means of promoting wellbeing in the Commonwealth (1808, p. 190).

Perhaps the debate about sentiment is less important now with the development and growth of modern psychology; although Adam Smith has this: he speaks of *moral* sentiments and links those to normative requirements. Yet it is the moral link established by Mill that is for our purposes the most important. Mill was clear on this point: punishment occurs when a wrong occurs, and a wrong is a moral term. Justice exists to determine the nature of that punishment within a moral framework. And this is so whether the wrong is legal or otherwise, and whether the punishment is legal or otherwise.

RETRIBUTION AND JUSTICE

We have defined punishment as being imposed on an offender for an offence. Here I wish to expand on this and examine the view that if punishment is unjust it is also unjustified. This is a recurring theme in moral philosophy and one to which retributivists and utilitarians have devoted considerable attention. Indeed, the key objection to utilitarianism has been that it cannot exclude the possibility of justified injustice; in contrast, retributivists are able to assert that they can. Later I wish to examine these questions within the context of just decisions being imposed on offenders, or more specifically to ask under what circumstances could offenders be seen to be the recipients of just decisions.

The great strength of the retributivist's position is his insistence that retribution stands for legal justice. If we accept Aristotle's definition that justice is concerned with proportions, balance and the equal treatment of equals, then retributivists are assured that the link is well made. So Kant talks of 'the justice of punishment; and the right of retaliation (*jus talionis*) which properly understood is the only principle which in regulating a public court . . . can definitely assign both the quality and quantity of a just penalty' (Kant, 1897, pp. 195-7). Elsewhere he goes further: 'All other standards are wavering and uncertain; and on account of other considerations involved in them they contain no principle conformable to the sense of pure and strict justice' (1965, p. 101).

What did Kant mean when he spoke of 'pure and strict justice'? I think he meant, first, that justice must be in the forefront of all decisions about punishment, and second that justice was an ultimate value, unwavering, and not affected by other considerations, notably that of the needs of the offenders, or demands of society. I do not think he saw it as an absolute value, although he said that judges must sentence only according to requirements of a 'pure and strict justice', which to Kant meant the principle of *jus talionis*.

For the present let us concentrate on Kant's demand for justice. Consider how his principle would affect many of the procedural requirements of the modern courts. First, it is doubtful if on Kantian terms the probation report, the psychiatric report or the school report would be acceptable with their hearsay evidence, nor would the common practice whereby the report writers rarely attend court to permit cross-examination. It is also doubtful if the use of remands in custody for such reports would be acceptable. Similarly, decisions in the Court of Appeal probably could not be made without the defendant being present as is the practice at the moment; and Kant probably would not have approved of a system whereby legal representation was variable in quality and content (Baldwin, and McConville, 1977). At these purely formal and procedural levels Kant requires us to keep a watchful eye on changes that may act against justice 'strict and pure', and as such impose a standard that protects offenders and public alike. Modern judicial systems have not always been as careful in this as they might. More often a mixture of expediency and what Kant calls 'the serpent-windings of utilitarianism' has begun to dominate. And by 'serpent-windings' I do not mean only those that pertain to the doctrine of utility but also those pertaining to others that invoke claims for social justice to be made consistent with legal justice. In a later chapter this point will be developed further.

Kant demands that standards of justice remain consistently high, although this is a rule of procedure rather than substance for he does not tell us how to achieve or recognize a correct standard. What then would be a just decision in terms of the offender? Earlier it was noted that Kant dismissed Hegel's argument that the offender had a right to be punished, arguing instead that punishment was imposed not negotiated. This I think is the essence of the retributive position; it is authoritarian, authoritative and unyielding in its attitude to those who have broken the law. A just decision in retributive terms is imposed, and must be if the offender is to receive justice. Kant would see the argument in the following terms.

First, he would regard it as a public and social duty for any society to operate with his same high standards. In an oft-quoted passage Kant shows that justice is a means of exonerating the deed as far as other members of society are concerned.

> Even if a civil society resolved to dissolve itself with the consent of all its members — as might be supposed in the case of a people inhabiting an island resolving to separate and scatter themselves throughout the whole world — the last murderer lying in prison ought to be executed before the resolution was carried out. This ought to be done in order that everyone may realise the desert of his deeds, and that blood guiltness may not remain upon the people; for otherwise they will be regarded as participators in the murder as a public violation of justice. [Kant, 1965, p. 102]

What are we to make of this? Obviously Kant believed that whoever commits a crime must be punished in accordance with his desert, but the last section of the last sentence is tantalizing. Why should the people be 'otherwise regarded as participants in the murder as a public violation of justice'? Did Kant mean that the crime had to be annulled, or did he, in Hegel's terms, see a just punishment as being the negation of crime, as not being arbitrary but grounded in the nature of the moral order? I think he did. The parallels with Hegel are not always clear, but in this instance both Kant and Hegel use similar language. Hegel talks of 'the criminal's act returning on himself' or 'the other half of crime that judges itself'; Kant argues that 'his own evil deed draws the punishment upon himself'.

But there is more to it than this. The passage quoted above gives an entrée into the justification of punishment that is central to retributivism. It will therefore repay closer attention, for it is the criminal's rights that are at issue and the relationship between the criminal and society. To examine the relationship with justice it is necessary to retrace some of the earlier steps.

It will be remembered that Kant saw punishment as an end in itself and believed that human beings should be treated as ends in themselves. There is obviously a logical difficulty in treating people as ends in themselves, since it gives no means of reaching decisions where two men's interests clash. If each is an end in himself, how are we to arrive at a principle for determining which shall give way? Bertrand Russell says that such a principle must have to do with the community rather than with the individuals. In the broadest sense of the word it must have to do with the principle of justice (Russell, 1946, p. 205). But Kant did not want to see justice in that way. His was a more formalistic system. To appreciate it we need to see it in terms of his basic justifications of punishment and to repeat an earlier quote:

> Now the notion of punishment as such cannot be united with that of becoming a partaker of happiness; for although he who inflicts the punishment may at the same time have the benevolent purpose of directing the punishment to this end, yet it must be justified in itself as punishment, that is as more harm, so that if it stopped there, and the person could get no glimpse of kindness hidden behind the harshness, he must yet admit that justice was done him, and that his reward was perfectly suitable to his conduct. In every punishment as such thee must first be justice and thus constitute the essence of the notion. Benevolence may indeed be united with it but the man who has deserved punishment has not the least to reckon upon this. [Kant, 1949, p. 149]

When Kant says the criminal must admit 'that justice was done him' he accepts that benevolence may be part of the punishment, but this has nothing to do with the infliction of punishment. Punishment is inflicted because the criminal has deserved it. We cannot, therefore, tell the criminal that he is being punished for his own good or to make him a better person, for that is to treat him as a means to an end. Nor can we debate with the criminal the value of punishment, for that leads to the 'serpent windings of utilitarianism', and if good consequences or future happiness are to be considered, then justice vanishes. Once good consequences intrude, the criminal loses the essential protection granted by retribution.

But punishment *is* inflicted, and while criminals may say they deserve it they may doubt the essential justification. As a rational being the criminal can question the ends of punishment; but we have no right, says Kant, to demand that he sacrifice himself for any public wellbeing. There is no duty upon the criminal, or anybody else, to be benevolent. In questioning the ends of punishment the criminal would then, in the Kantian system of thought, be confronted with the categorical imperative. The argument would go like this. As a free agent the criminal has exercised his choice to make punishment necessary because he has drawn the punishment upon himself. He has hindered freedom, and punishment as 'a hindering of the hindrance of freedom'. By hindering freedom the criminal has set himself in direct opposition to others and has perversely operated the categorical imperative which is to act as if that behaviour can be universalized. If the criminal has committed crime he has suggested explicitly that crime could be universalized, and if it were it would destroy the social order. Therefore, to punish the criminal is to show that we are proceeding on the same lines as he, but our aim is to prevent the hindering of freedom. If the criminal steals, we must symbolically steal from him; this is how 'he draws the punishment upon himself'. The punishment is a way of showing the logical consequences of criminal behaviour and the dangers of that behaviour if universalized. The criminal has willed it and we show what he has willed.

The link with justice consists also in showing the criminal what he has willed. There is no attenuation here; the criminal is confronted with his misdeeds and with the implications of his actions. The deeds of the criminal are accepted, but turned against him, and he is presented with the results of those deeds. That is why, said Kant, he must always be punished, even if society were to dissolve itself: to do less is to avoid showing the criminal what he was willed.

Justice in Kantian terms is inevitably imposed upon the criminal. The criminal has no way of avoiding this. Were he to question the system and say he has not drawn punishment upon himself, but that others have drawn it on him by their actions, he would find this rejected as firmly as would be suggestions that the punishment might do the criminal no good — or might in fact do him harm. We can see how far modern thinking is from the Kantian view of justice. For example, it is a common complaint that prison does the offender no good and may make him worse. Consideration of those arguments would, Kant would say, lead again to those 'serpent-windings', but even if it didn't it is of little consequence, for the debate is not about future benevolence: it is about justice. And justice is about returning to the criminal what he has willed. It is about showing that hindering the freedom of others produces punishment, for if the criminal act were made universal it would destroy freedom. Justice is about showing the criminal that the compulsion we use on him proceeds according to the same rule by which he acts.

I have given some time to the Kantian argument if only to show that retribution requires that punishment is imposed on the offender and that a just decision does not involve considerations other than those pertaining to the offence. Of course not all retributivists support Kant, nor do they have the elaborate theoretical structure on which to base their arguments. They would I think still accept the general principles that have been extracted, particularly the authoritarian nature of the punishment.

And yet within the Kantian position as it relates to justice and punishment there are two defects, which are elegantly pointed out by Bertrand Russell. The first concerns Kant's principle that we ought so to act as to treat every man as an end in himself. This, Russell argues, is an abstract form of the doctrine of the rights of man and is open to the same objections. The obvious difficulty arises in political philosophy, where principles are required by which the interests of some can be sacrificed to those of others. If there is to be an ethic of government, the end of government must be a major principle, and the only single end compatible with justice is the good of the community. The second difficulty relates to the categorical imperative which, according to Kant, is deduced from the concept of law.

If I think of a categorical imperative I know at once what it contains. For as the imperative contains besides the law only the necessity of the maxim to be in accordance with this law, but the law contains no condition by which it is limited, nothing remains over but the generality of a law in general to which the maxim of the action is to be conformable and which conforming alone presents the imperative as necessary. Therefore the categorical imperative is a single one and in fact this:

Act only according to a maxim by which at the same time will it that it shall become a general law

or

Act as if the maxim of your actions were to become through your will a general natural law. [Kant, 1965, p. 26]

Kant gives as an illustration of the working of the categorical imperative that it is wrong to borrow money, because if we all tried to do so there would be no money left to borrow. It follows easily that murder, theft, violence, etc., are condemned by the categorical imperative. However, Russell argues that there are some acts that Kant would certainly think wrong but that cannot be shown to be wrong by his principles, for example, suicide. A person seriously contemplating suicide may believe that the world is an abominable place in which to live and might genuinely believe that everybody should commit suicide. Russell says that Kant's maxim gives a necessary but not a sufficient criticism of virtue. A sufficient criterion would lead us to abandon Kant's purely formal point of view and take some account of the effects of action, a position firmly rejected by Kant as being utilitarian (Russell, 1946, pp. 737-8).

But on the positive side, if justice in retributive terms is imposed on the criminal, it none the less has a strong democratic flavour. Whereas Plato and Aristotle believed that justice should consist of a relationship between the person's social position and his behaviour (those in higher positions are entitled to share a greater amount of privileges), the retributivists, at least since Kant, make no such claim. Punishment is just when it is based on the proportionality for the crime; it matters not about the offender's background, his social position or his subsequent career on release from prison. For example, if a doctor of medicine commits a crime which deserves imprisonment, then so be it. In Bradley's terms, it is 'external to the matter' if on release he has been struck off the Medical Register. The criterion for punishment is the crime, and this gives it the democratic flavour (unlike rehabilitation, which has an aristocratic tendency, for under rehabilitation the most favoured and those having fewer needs will require the least treatment, whereas those most favoured will often be those of highest social position). So under retribution justice and punishment become universal in their application.[2]

Yet some critics, notably Ewing, go as far as to say that all retributive punishments are unjust (Ewing, 1927, p. 40). Ewing argues as such because of the impossibility of assessing moral guilt and finding proportionate sentences. Injustice, says Ewing, is worse than no punishment at all. 'Ought the State to aim at retributive justice if the overwhelming probability is that each time it tries to inflict it will do serious retributive injustices?' (1927, p. 40). He adds that injustice is greatly increased if criminality is, in the majority of cases, associated with special weakness of will and intellect which is likely to diminish the responsibility of the criminal. His point is worth making, but not of overwhelming importance. Certainly it illustrates one weakness in retributive justice, but no system yet devised is able to provide a greater measure of security for the population at large.

Ewing, however, is making a more substantial point when he says we are no surer that justice requires the punishment of a brutal murderer than we are that it requires the infliction of a severer punishment than a petty assault committed under dire provocation (1927, p. 41). Kant, of course, would not agree; in the *Critique of Pure Reason* he showed that, although our knowledge may not be able to transcend experience, it is none the less in part *a priori* and not inferred indirect from experience (see also Russell, 1946, pp. 732-4). We can, therefore, know that *a priori* there is a relationship between punishment and justice — but to accept this point is to accept the whole of Kant's methodology. He also maintained that the proposition was synthetic (i.e. not analytic but known through experience), and accordingly argued that our experience tells us that punishment and justice are linked. Kant was doing more than appealing to the view that 'everybody knows' that a link exists, although Bradley was content to leave his argument at that level: Kant was demonstrating a wider philosophical system, far beyond the boundaries of the debate on punishment.

But if we accept that punishment is imposed what type of punishments ought to be imposed on a given offender? Or is it that retribution allows us to discuss legal justice in the abstract without coming to grips with what that means except in terms of the just decision? What sentences ought a judge to give if he is faced with an offender whom he wishes to sentence retributively? Unfortunately, retribution is silent on this matter. Yet it is of some importance if the argument is to have serious practical applications. Bradley, if anything, made the situation worse and has rightly been taken to task for it. He says that we may have regard for whatever considerations we please — our own conscience, the good of society or the benefit of the offender — but, having once the right to punish, we may modify the punishment according to the useful and the pleasant. He later says these are 'external to the matter', but by modifying punishment he enters the utilitarian arena and confuses an essentially strong initial position. Dr Ewing rightly suggests that Bradley has inadvertently exposed himself to the weak spot in the retributive argument. Bradley, however, later recoups something of his position by stating that punishment is justice and that justice implies the giving what is due (Bradley, 1927, p. 29). In so doing he returns the argument to a retributive base.

But Bradley, like Kant, cannot or does not tell us anything about the sentences to be passed. We may agree with Bradley that there is a scale that 'the vulgar' (as Bradley calls them) have to decide upon based on the proportion between offence and punishment; but again, this remains a criterion of procedure rather than substance. In practice, judges in modern penal systems wishing to abide by retributive considerations would appeal to the 'tariff'. This is a rough and ready guideline which approximates to some degree of proportion. It is a subjective scale related to an acceptable view of a proportionate sentence and based also on what judges generally believe is acceptable to the claims of the offender and the community. It may be unsatisfactory and less formal than Kant would have wanted, but it remains the only standard so far devised. And it remains so for this very reason: that no scale can be devised that is satisfactory.

For on what basis would such a scale be made? Not on the basis of the good of society, for that is utilitarian; and not on the basis of the offender's welfare, for that is rehabilitation: only, then, on the basis of the offence. But the offence is not such as to provide much assistance except in the extremes where murder could be compared with petty pilfering or minor cases of assault. Bosanquet was right: equivalence of offence and punishment is a 'meaningless superstition', and this criticism of retribution may be hackneyed but is no less important for that. When we examine the principles of justice in retributive terms the argument is strong; when we hone it down to consider a just decision it becomes considerably weakened.

If we cannot make a just decision, is retribution unjustified? I think not. For although there can be no just decision in the specific sense of that term, there can be just decisions in the general sense noted above. Kant's requirement that punishment is for deserts provides a basis, which is further strengthened by the retributive position related to the punishment of the offence, and by the democratic overtones implied there. The candour with which retributivists accept that their decisions are imposed gives credence to their point and helps them lay claim to a position that should be accepted and recognized as being honest if nothing else. It may not be a position free from defects, but it has certain elementary advantages. Furthermore, it may not be simple but it is not one overburdened with complexity. We now turn to examine the more difficult question of justice within a utilitarian framework.

JUSTICE AND UTILITY

Bentham had little time for justice. He said:

> sometimes in order the better to conceal the cheat they set up a phantom of their own which they call justice; whose dictates are to modify (which being explained means to oppose) the dictates of benevolence. But justice in the sense in which it has a meaning, is an imaginary personage, feigned for the convenience of discourse, whose dictates are the dictates of utility, applied to certain particular cases. Justice then is nothing more than an imaginary instrument, employed to forward on certain occasions and by certain means the purposes of benevolence. The dictates of justice are nothing more than a part of the dictates of benevolence which on certain occasions are applied to certain subjects; to wit, to certain actions. [Bentham, 1948, pp. 240-1]

There is no ambiguity about this statement. Bentham also cared little for jurisprudence, calling it a fictitious entity: 'nor can any meaning be found for the word but by placing it in company with some word that shall be significative of a real entity' (Bentham, 1948, p. 423). By that he meant that jurisprudence can have but one of two objects: to ascertain what the law is (and Bentham was sure he had already done this), or to ascertain what the law ought to be. Both questions could be answered by reference to the principle of utility, defined by Bentham as 'that principle which approves or disapproves of every action whatever, according to the tendency which it appears to have to augment or diminish the happiness of the party whose interest is in question: or what is the same thing in other words to promote or to oppose that happiness' (1948, p. 26).

The principle of utility could be applied, said Bentham, to every action whatsoever, whether it be the action of a private individual or every measure of government. Terms such as the 'law of reason', 'right reason', 'natural equity', 'good order' or 'natural justice' are, therefore, redundant. The three last terms, said Bentham, are more tolerable than others because they do not claim to be anything more than phrases. On most occasions said Bentham, it will be better to say 'utility': utility is clearer, referring more explicitly to pain and pleasure (1948, p. 141). Nor did he concern himself with the origins of our notions of right or wrong. 'I do not know [the origins]; I do not care'; or, again, 'Whether a moral sentiment can be originally conceived from any other source than a view of utility is one question; whether . . . it can be justified on any other ground by a person reflecting within himself is another' (1948, p. 142). Crime or mischief, as Bentham called it, promotes unhappiness; therefore, it is to be punished in order to reduce unhappiness and promote happiness. This is not to say that justice could not be achieved, although Bentham himself did not consider it in quite that way. Bentham saw justice as consisting of a consideration of the total amount of happiness involved, without favour to one individual or class as against another. Russell puts it this way: when two men's interests clash the right course is that which produces the greatest total of happiness, regardless of which of the two enjoys it or how it is shared among them. If more is given to the better man than to the worse, that is because in the long run the general happiness is increased by rewarding virtue and punishing vice, not because of an ultimate ethical doctrine that the good deserve more than the bad (Russell, 1946, p. 205). To Bentham, justice meant equality, where equality was related to the general levels of happiness in the community.

Bentham's concern for justice was more a concern for legal procedure, always aimed, of course, at promoting the concept of utility. His classification and sub-classification of laws are his particular hallmark. Yet it is not to this aspect that we shall be concerned; our particular interest is in the ways in which utilitarians have considered justice, or attempted to promote it.

The fact that utilitarians rarely considered justice is a point often made by their opponents. As was shown earlier, retributivists have consistently argued that deterrence does not rule out the punishment of the innocent; nor does it rule out the possibility of lengthy sentences for relatively minor offences if the demands of the general deterrent effect require it. But deterrence is more complicated than this; for we can distinguish different forms of deterrence, some aimed at a deterrent effect for each particular sentence, others at a general deterrent effect aimed at reducing the level of crime generally, others being less of a general effect and more a specific one, aimed at directing the offender to a less serious crime, such as shoplifting instead of robbery (Beyleveld, 1979b).

Consider first the general deterrent effect for each sentence. Andenaes argues that, if a judge wishes to attach weight to the general preventative effect of a particular sentence, he should consider the publicity that the decision will receive and the possible reaction to that decision: if a case has attracted great publicity, a severe sentence could be expected to have a deterrent effect (Andenaes,

1970, p. 656). Adenaes recognizes the possible injustices that could exist in operating this type of general deterrent effect for each sentence, but he suggests that this approach could be adopted, although he says it ought to be used with caution. He none the less quotes approvingly the deterrent sentences passed on offenders in the Notting Hill race riots in 1958, which it was claimed led to a reduction in racial tension. (I am not concerned with the empirical validation of these sentences, although it was claimed that they reduced racial offences immediately.) But consider those who committed similar offences some time after the tension of the riots had died down: presumably they would receive light sentences, for the publicity would be reduced and there would be no need to operate a deterrent effect so severely. Consider also those who had committed that offence at an early stage of the riots (assuming they lasted for two or three weeks), and in the intervening period between the commission of the offence and their sentences a new burst of offences arose. Under a deterrence doctrine the offender who was to be sentenced first would likely receive a more severe sentence than he would if there had been no spate of similar offences later. It is difficult in these circumstances not to view deterrent sentencing as objectionable from the ethical standpoint because it imposes unequal punishments on offenders who may be equally blameworthy. But of course the out-and-out utilitarian would say these criticisms merely reflect a retributive viewpoint, showing how retributivists have influenced sentencing by their views on proportionality. The requirements, say these utilitarians, must be that of utility. Yet Andenaes has clearly adopted a retributive position (as incidentally did Beccaria) for later he says that the general deterrent effect for each punishment is ethically defensible, both in legislation and sentencing, if the punishment is in reasonable proportion to the gravity of the offence and does not violate the principle of equality before the law (Andenaes, 1970, p. 663). This is retribution wrapped up in a deterrent argument.

In order to operate the general deterrent effect for specific punishments publicity is a key variable. Most utilitarians would agree that publicity is a central aspect of a system of justice. The aim of publicity would be to act as part of the threat to be used on others so as to increase, or rather not decrease, the extent of happiness. Yet as Mabbott rightly says, we sentence a person to three years in prison, not three years plus three column inches in the press (Mabbott,

1939). If the threat works without the punishment then so much the better; if not, then publicity comes to the aid of the deterrent. But what if the publicity is not forthcoming for some inexplicable reason? Should punishments increase until they are sufficiently severe to attract the publicity? Presumably yes, and if this is so then the retributive charge of utilitarian injustice is well formulated. We are returned, therefore, to the older difficulty of deterrence using an offender as a means to some further end.

For the deterrent effect related to crime generally, the problem of justice takes on a wider set of issues. Dr Ewing says of the retributive theory that the object of the retributivist is that the punishment should be just. Every excess over the just amount must be in the same ethical position as punishment of the innocent, leading, says Ewing, to an injustice that seems much worse than non-punishment of the guilty (Ewing, 1929, p. 39). So, presumably, by the same argument, too light a penalty is injustice also. If we assume for a moment that this argument is accepted, it does not as Ewing thinks become an argument for accepting the utilitarian position. For Mundle, I think, makes an irrefutable point when he says that, if we reject the retributive theory on the ground that God alone knows the extent of our moral guilt, we ought equally to reject a utilitarian theory on the ground that God alone knows what constitutes and conduces to our long-run welfare (Mundle, 1954, p. 223). Mundle goes on to say that people responsible for imposing punishment can often be more confident in estimating what penalty is deserved than they could be in solving the formidable problem of the 'net welfare productivity' of alternative penalties (1954, p. 223). Yet this is what the utilitarian must do. He must decide according to the requirement of future happiness, and this involves the judicial system in a form of prediction. But how does it do this? How could one have predicted the future happiness of a society when confronted with a conscientious objector or an active feminist at the turn of the century? These were crimes that have influenced future morality, and who would have been brave enough to have predicted the direction that would take? Deterrence becomes no less obscure than retribution, but retribution is at least able to avoid predictions about the future.

The utilitarians have often been criticized for ignoring justice; and rightly so. G.E.M. Anscombe is adamant that the claims of justice ought never to be compromised: 'if someone really thinks in advance that it is open to question whether such an action as procuring the judicial execution of the innocent should be quite excluded from consideration. I do not want to argue with him; he shows a corrupt mind' (quoted in Kleinig, 1973, p. 84).

Justice to G. E. M. Anscombe is self evidently good and absolute. Others are not so sure. McCloskey, in a way somewhat surprising for a retributivist, argues that sometimes it is morally obligatory to override the dictates of justice where the good it achieves is so great that it outweighs the evil of the injustice involved (1967, pp. 91-2). McCloskey justifies his position by pointing again to the multi-faceted nature of retribution which makes it capable of assessing other goods and evils. Utilitarianism is by contrast restricted to utility. However, McCloskey's method for assessing competing claims is made on the basis of intuition rather than a calculation of utilities (Kleinig, 1973, p. 84). And in spite of McCloskey's disclaimer to do otherwise there is a hidden form of utilitarianism contained in his argument. It goes further, for by claiming to assess other goods and evils it now seems as if some retributivists are willing to compromise on justice and in so doing hand one of the greatest strengths of retribution over to the utilitarians. Justice, it appears, is not as absolute as Kant would have us believe.

This does not of course let the utilitarian off. A further criticism is that utilitarians confuse aggregates with distribution (Kleinig, 1973, p. 79), for the two may conflict. Bentham, it will be remembered, was concerned with promoting happiness whether to individuals, to a number of individuals or to government, and so presumably was concerned with the happiness of a number of individuals. He was primarily concerned with maximizing happiness to the point where the justice of each case can be overridden. We can use the following example given by Kleinig.

(1) Suppose we have nine units of advantage. In one course of action A will have 6 units, B will have 1 unit, C will have 1 unit and D will have 1 unit.

(2) Suppose we have eight units of advantage. In another course of action A will have 2, B will have 2, C will have 2 and D will have 2 units.

Kleinig says it is proper here to consider the choice between courses 1 and 2 as between utility and justice where course 1 promotes the greatest utility. However Kleinig is being unfair to the utilitarians, for Bentham himself had argued that each was to count for one and no one to count for more than one. In spite of the extra unit of advantage in course 1 Bentham would I think have favoured course 2 on the grounds that course 1 violates his principle of 'each to count for one' and because the unhappiness produced in the distribution of units in course 1 would be likely to neutralize the additional advantage. Yet on the other hand Russell interprets utilitarianism as a doctrine that does not concern itself with how advantages are shared, and is concerned only with the maximization. We then have two opposing views about utility, and it is a criticism of Bentham and the utilitarians generally that they are less than clear on this point.

If we accept Kleinig and Russell's version, a just decision on Utilitarian grounds becomes a decision related to the maximization of utilities. This being so, it becomes a matter of some importance to decide whether a just decision could exist within a utilitarian framework. Utilitarians have always regarded this criticism as a serious objection to their views and have devoted strenuous efforts to show that, rightly understood, utilitarians can operate justly. Rule-utilitarianism has been part of that search, but as was shown earlier, rule-utilitarianism does little to remove those objections.[3] Nor can it be said that Bentham's dictum, 'each to count for one and no one to count for more than one', solves the utilitarians' problems completely: it helps them without offering a complete solution, for there is nothing in the classical utilitarian position to question the justness of a law that maximized advantages at the expense of equality of treatment. In this way, individual decisions become subsumed under the general demands of utility. Herein is its central weakness.

REHABILITATION AND JUSTICE

The essence of rehabilitative justice is that emphasis is placed on social justice rather than on legal justice. Where justice is to exist it has less to do with making the punishment proportionate to the crime, more to do with assisting the redress of social wrongs that are considered to be major contributors to the offence. The rehabilitationist argument would go something like this. Crime is a symptom of a disease that is social or psychological in origin, where the aetiology lies in the social system. The disease is present because of the injustices in that social system, and those having that disease have invariably been the subjects of that injustice. The disease may manifest itself in criminal behaviour, but need not do so. Criminal behaviour is likely to be one symptom out of a wide range of symptoms which could include suicide, divorce, child battering, etc. Long-term aims are to eradicate social injustice generally; short-term aims are to eradicate social injustice for that particular offender. Again; the method of eradication may be social or psychological, depending on the nature of the condition. The function of the court, therefore, is to provide facilities in order that treatment can be effective.

I hope that this provides a fair summary of rehabilitation, although Francis Allen has suggested that the rehabilitative ideal is a complex set of ideas which perhaps defies exact definition (Allen, 1964, p. 26). However, if the above account is accepted, then it appears that the sentence of the court becomes a means to an end, and justice is defined according to that end. Rehabilitationists would, therefore, regard the debate about legal justice as irrelevant, unless and only in so far as the sentence of the court ensured that rehabilitative justice would be possible. It would be unjust for an offender to be sent to prison if a probation order would be more likely to help his condition, and unjust to discharge an offender if a custodial sentence would be more appropriate. Justice consists in the neutralization or cure of the disease and in the allocation of resources to meet the offender's requirements. Lawyers, entrenched in a tradition of legal punishment, are not likely to view rehabilitation with sympathy. This is why H. L. Hart, for example, argues that reform can have a place within a system of punishment only as an exploitation of the opportunities presented by the conviction or compulsory detention of offenders (1968, p. 26). To the thoroughgoing rehabilitationist, Hart misses the point. It is not the intention to have rehabilitation within a system of punishments; the intention is to work within the system in order to produce social justice at a later stage. Nowhere is this more obvious than in the juvenile court, where the juvenile justice system becomes a means to the pursuit of social justice for the child. Legal justice becomes a stage in that wider process.

Nor does Hart appear to understand the rehabilitative position if he insists on discussing principles of justice in terms of different kinds of offences being related to different levels of severity of sentence (Hart, 1968, p. 25). He may be right to believe that, where the legal gradation of crimes expressed in terms of the relative severity of penalties diverge sharply from the rough scale, then there is a risk either of confusing common morality or of flouting it or bringing the law into contempt (1968, p. 25). And the throughgoing rehabilitationist may recognize this too: but argue that Professor Hart is dealing with matters that have little relevance to rehabilitation, and, more to the point, that Hart is concentrating on a different scale of justice. Hart insists on comparing offences; rehabilitation consists of comparing different kinds of offenders, of which the offence is merely one aspect of that offender's personality. Rehabilitation would not be at odds therefore with the Aristotelean requirement to treat equals equally. Offenders with the same needs should be treated in the same way, and offenders with different needs would have to be treated differently. Doctors after all have a standardized method of treating broken legs, and it matters not to them how the legs came to be broken. Rehabilitationists would argue that the difference between their position and that of Hart's is the criterion of relevance. Hart's is limited to the offence; theirs is less circumscribed and is not reducible to legal categories. Certainly, they would say, equals should be treated equally and unequals unequally; but the respect in which they are considered unequal must be relevant to the difference in treatment that is proposed. The rehabilitationist would say to Hart, 'You have chosen the offence as the attribute; we have chosen the total personality.'

I do not wish to be involved in the debate as to whether it is ever possible to assess the 'total personality', or to debate what 'total personality' may mean, for this has been done elsewhere (Bean, 1974). For the purposes of this discussion let us accept that assessment is possible, and concentrate on matters of justice. If the rehabilitative argument is framed in this way, then it is consistent with certain requirements of justice even if it is of a different order. There are defects, but we can come to these later. Rehabilitation becomes a different method of justice, not subject to the same constraints as retribution or deterrence. It is, of course, of some consequence whether the type of justice advocated by rehabilitationists is ever attainable, but they could make the perfectly reasonable reply that the more traditional forms of justice are not without defects. Faced also with the criticism that a rehabilitative system of justice relies in part on the willingness of the offenders to accept it, the rehabilitationists could equally assert that those on the receiving end of the retribution and deterrence systems have rarely been enthusiastic about it. And so we could continue to swap charges and counter-charges almost indefinitely without ever coming to the main area of discussion.

It is not necessary however to be a supporter of rehabilitation to accept their complaint against traditional forms of justice. The defects are too widely known. But the weaknesses of the rehabilitationists' own case are sufficiently numerous to require a separate examination. First, there are those weaknesses related to the claims of other parties. These seem to be ignored to the exclusive claim of the offender; the victim, the police and the community at large have no claims in the rehabilitation perspective. The offender is the key party — or so it appears — but this is deceptive, for the offender has no more claims than anyone else. His diagnosis is made for him and the treatment plan is decided for him. The parallels with medicine are clear: the doctor diagnoses and the patient accepts the prescribed treatment. But the differences are also clear: under a rehabilitative regime the patient may be a less willing party to the treatment. Second, in spite of the humanistic rhetoric underpinning rehabilitation it is possible that an offender may serve longer in prison than under a retributive doctrine. This is why Professor Hart is only partially right when he says that rehabilitation forgoes the prospect of influencing those who had not broken the law (by presumably lacking a deterrent effect) and 'thus subordinating the prevention of first offences to the prevention of recidivism' (Hart, 1968, p. 27); for he is confusing the rhetoric of rehabilitation with the practical possibilities. The long sentences under a rehabilitation regime may unintentionally act as a deterrent — even though this was not the original aim of the reformist position. Supporters of rehabilitation have always been able to create the impression that they are, in Professor Flew's phrase, 'adopting a molly coddler's charter' when they are often doing something else.

Third, there is the question about the *nature* of justice under rehabilitation. The refusal to acknowledge claims other than those of the therapist renders it justice by expert. It becomes impossible to appeal against the expert's decision except to a more advanced expert. Of itself, justice by experts can disguise the nature of the punishment inflicted, and the language of therapy can easily become another form of disguise which one may regard as disingenuous or dishonest depending on one's point of view. But disguise it certainly is.

Inevitably, then, the question of justice appears meaningless, for justice is not the ultimate aim in rehabilitation. The closest approximation to justice for rehabilitationists is annulment, and the term is used here not in the Hegelian sense, nor in the sense of undoing the past, but in the sense of annulling the evil effects of the past. Rehabilitation aims at making the sufferer better by removing the effects that produced the crime, which is itself one symptom in a social disease or maladjustment. Ewing describes this as 'analogous not to locking the stable-door after the horse has bolted, but to trying to recover the horse' (1929, p. 102). Rehabilitation offers distributive rather than retributive justice, but uses the retributive to secure the distributive effect. The aim is not to look backward to the crime, but to look forward to the future effects.

As a social theory, rehabilitation is tied to definitions of social need. There is no necessary connection between guilt and punishment and, as stated earlier, if logically developed rehabilitation would contradict the principle that we punish only the guilty. Inevitably this raises the general question of the State's right to punish and the possibility of a totalitarian tyranny under which the State claims the right to rehabilitate anyone considered in need of it. Under a fully developed rehabilitative regime we would no longer ask if the offender committed the offence or whether he deserved his incarceration, but what is the nature of his condition, and how is treatment progressing? Justice would be granted only if treatment was provided, and denied if not. The rights of the offender would become the rights to receive treatment, and the duty of the State would be to provide conditions conducive to social health — and, where this was not possible, to supply the experts in sufficient quality and quantity to provide treatment.

There is no logical objection to this form of justice, but there may be strong political ones. The insecurity created would certainly produce a political climate where fear of the State dominated all else. It would also depart from the liberal doctrine derived from Aristotle between the 'government of man' and the 'government of law', for all would be the government of men. The minimum area of personal freedom claimed by Mill as a necessary prerequisite for a tolerant society would be violated. Mill saw legal constraint as a generating idea in the notion of justice (1964, p. 303), and rehabilitation has no built-in legal restraint. Mill also saw injustice existing when a person was deprived of his personal liberty, his property or any other thing that belonged to him by law (1964, p. 298). This principle would be violated also. It could be objected that I am offering an extreme set of examples, and that rehabilitation as it exists at present is a relatively harmless operation, concerned with helping a small number of criminals who deserve help rather than providing retributive or deterrent punishments. As will be shown in the next chapter, the rehabilitative ideal is already well advanced in modern penal systems, and I do not think it is an exaggeration to say that some of the dangers can already be seen.

Justice under rehabilitation is more complex than under retribution or deterrence. Rehabilitation, like other theories of punishment, reflects a type of social order; for rehabilitation thrives under a collectivist ethos. It diminishes under classical liberalism, where individuals are seen as responsible for their actions but are condemned when they violate others' rights. The liberals' objection to rehabilitative justice is not simply that it is collectivist, but that it is paternalistic, or in Plato's terms places the offender *in statu pupillari.* It follows the Platonic tradition in that vice is contrary to every man's essential nature, and so in the wrongdoer's own interests wickedness should be subdued or channelled into new and virtuous pursuits. The modern doctrine has been influenced by social science, but we should still see it for what it is: a way of treating offenders as naughty children, rather than public enemies, open rebels or wilful law-breakers. As a form of justice it creates an unusual relationship between adults where one is seen to possess the truths and wisdoms of the teacher, the other to learn the error of his ways (or in modern jargon to acquire sufficient insight into his motivations to combat them in future social situations). It is a form of justice that attempts to break away from traditional methods. Yet as it currently operates it remains within the traditional system, although the strains towards separation are always present. At best rehabilitation shows a concern for the individual offender; at worst it could produce its own form of inflexible tyranny. We may agree with Carlyle that saving souls is important but believe that this is the task of the Church, not the judicial system.

A JUST DECISION

We now need to consider the nature of a just decision. Whereas justice relates to proportions in the sense that Aristotle defined it, a just decision is more specific, relating to the application of rules, and presupposing the existence of rules. Differences in treatment must in a loose sense be proportionate and justified by reference to relevant differences of attributes or conditions that are recognized by the rules. Distinctions are legitimate if the rules are amended universally and preclude exceptions. Amendments require elaboration of new criteria which are then to be applied universally (Benn and Peters, 1959, p. 128). Just decisions operate within existing frameworks; justice is the means whereby the framework is established.

Public justice, like private justice, involves decisions that must themselves be just. Public justice or legal justice does more than reflect the personal whims of the judiciary, for those who pass sentence are representatives, as it were, of society generally, and their decisions are open to public scrutiny. They must have integrity and must not make decisions according to personal gain or to likes and dislikes. They are not required to make the law, nor are they required to agree with it; their task is to punish according to rules not of their own choosing. Of course, judges make law in the sense that they interpret law and their interpretations reflect their personal views. This is acceptable and to some extent encouraged, for we would find it objectionable if decisions were taken out of the human context and made according to some pre-ordained computer programme (described by Max Weber as 'vending machine justice'). Individual interpretations are accepted, if they remain in the bounds of what is generally acceptable and are known to be made with integrity. Dishonest, corrupt or prejudiced judges attack the very essense of a social order.

THE CLAIMS ON A JUST DECISION

We can concentrate for the moment on legal or public justice and compare it to private justice using the example of a parent and a child. In private justice a parent may punish a child within the confines of his household, but a judge does so publicly. A parent may forgive, but a judge cannot, for only the victim is able to offer forgiveness. A parent has no higher parental authority to which the child may appeal, nor a set of rules that must be considered before punishment is given. A parent has no organization, group or community interests to serve — or if he has, then they are marginal to his main interest, which is to bring up his child. Nor does a parent have to satisfy anyone other than himself and his child that justice has been done. The difference between public and private justice is the difference between a private and public conscience. I would therefore agree with James Doyle when he says that a just response to legal wrongs is primarily a matter of providing legal recognition, adjudication and satisfaction of the variety of claims invoked by criminal violation (1969, p. 168). Without acknowledgement of those claims justice cannot be preserved. If as Doyle says one were to ask why this should be so, then the answer would be in the form of another question: on what basis can men hope or be reasonably expected to live together? (Doyle, 1969, p. 168). Doyle is implying that human beings are sufficiently dependent on each other to need to support institutions designed to give them reasons for respecting others; and that, without the satisfactions gained from those institutions, respect would quickly vanish. Legal punishment does more than demonstrate the enforcement of rules: it provides and reflects an avenue for the public affirmation of what is considered to be right.

I have used the word 'satisfactions' here in its widest sense. Some satisfaction may involve agreement about moral principles — some of which we may not like, but they exist none the less. Judicial sentencing may, for example, satisfy desires for revenge, hatred or sadist impulses on behalf of some members of the community. It may also thwart those desires by not going far enough, but as long as it goes some way to meeting them it may be important. (Durkheim talked of 'healing the collective conscience' and in so doing pointed to an important function of punishment.) But there are other satisfactions that require consideration.

First, consider those whose task it is to enforce the law. Mr Barry Pain, Chief Constable of Kent, in evidence to the Royal Commission on Criminal Procedure suggested that, unless the police are given the satisfaction of seeing the law punitively implied by the court, they may opt out of some areas of law enforcement altogether (reported in the *Justice of the Peace,* vol. 143, October 1979). This is not to say that the police salaciously support punishment; merely that the extent of legal punishment adds credibility to their own position by demonstrating that they — the police — are bringing serious offenders to justice. They might, of course, have vested interests in seeing some offenders given lengthy sentences, but this is not I think how Mr Pain ought to be interpreted. He was implying that a lengthy sentence or serious punishment is seen by the police as proportional to the effort required to detect certain types of offenders. There is little satisfaction to be gained where a great deal of effort results in a minor sentence. In this sense the balance becomes unequal.

The claim is almost Hegelian in the manner in which it is made. The annulment of the crime becomes related to the correct balance between the effort involved in detection and the severity of the punishment given. In this example, the police are making what they think are reasonable and just claims to have their expertise and effort acknowledged. They believe that their work and dignity as professionals are under scrutiny. We, as outsiders, may not see it that way and may say that the police *ought* not to be concerned with the outcome of the trial and sentence, i.e. that their role and function should end at the point where the jury are asked to make their decision. But as long as judges commend them for their work, as long as the public claim to affect the deployment of the police force (even if it is only by pressure of opinion), and as long as politicians pronounce on the rights of citizens, the police will believe that their work and the outcome of the case are linked.

The victim also claims that the punishment will reflect his rights as a citizen. Bishop Butler once observed that it was the resentment and indignation against the injury that brings the offender to justice (Butler, 1729, p. 101). He was, I think, showing us that some of the motivations for reporting offences were not always noble. Others may be more so, for example those based on the belief that legal punishment protects rights, and may perhaps help to restore them in some way. Sometimes restoration would go further and involve the return of the victim's property; sometimes it would involve compensation for injury. Where children and the mentally ill are concerned legal punishment may be the only way for the offender to receive official assistance, especially if the child was neglected or deprived, or if mentally ill then a danger to himself. The possibilities are endless, but we should not forget that the victim, where there is one, often begins the proceedings that ultimately lead to the punishment. Parenthetically we could add that criminological studies of the victim tend to disregard his motives and claims. This is a serious omission; for we ought not to ignore Butler's observation, and it links to Durkheim's point that theories of punishment that do not require suffering to be inflicted on the offender are seen as subversive to the social order because they do not heal the collective sentiments.

To the offender we may also reasonably ascribe a just claim to be dealt with as a person of some worth and dignity. Doyle regards this as the basis for further claims such as the right to protection from arbitrary restraint and detention and to the satisfaction of all the requirements of impartial public hearing, trial and sentencing (Doyle, 1969, p. 164). We can add the offender's claim to be seen as someone who is responsible for his acts unless proven otherwise, and as capable of deciding who shall legally act for him. He may in some circumstances have a claim to be seen as capable of advising and conducting his own defence. He most certainly has a claim not to be intimidated in his plea, nor to be seen as a cartoon figure whose only function is to demonstrate the power and authority of the State (as in so-called show trials). In the event of his plea of not guilty being accepted, there is the claim to have his reputation restored in the community.

As far as the punishment itself is concerned, the offender has a claim to a right of appeal to a higher authority, and the right to petition a higher authority to remedy grievances. He also has a claim to be punished in ways that do not lead to physical mutilation, or to irreversible forms of treatment, at least without his valid consent. While he is being punished, the offender has other claims. These unfortunately are less clear than those that can be made during the court appearance. The offender's general claim to be dealt with as a person of worth and dignity covers, and indeed ought to cover, all areas relating to his punishment. Or, as Doyle says, the ideal of just punishment would be the complete satisfaction of all legally acknowledged claims without prejudice to any of them (1969, p. 166).

We should not forget the claim of others involved in the trial and sentence. That judges make claims to make moral pronouncements may not always be to our liking, nor need we necessarily approve of what is said. Even so, claims are made and reflect the image of judges as upholders of public morality. Claims of lawyers, jurymen and other personnel are valid and need to be respected too. The trial, the sentence and the business of the courts may operate within fixed roles, but the claims emanating from these roles must be considered. Where any activities operate against the general interests of justice, as in (say) plea bargaining, they violate the claims of others. Plea bargaining operates to the benefit of administrators and violates the claims of the offender, the victim and the police.

Finally, there are the claims of the community itself. Numerous competing moral demands make the community heterogereous, and for that reason difficult to assess as having a single moral claim. But claims exist none the less. The community claims to be protected from mischief, and the law itself reflects the promise that mischief will be dealt with in the appropriate manner. The community's claims differ from the victim's, being less personalized, but no less personal. It is not simply a measure of public censure or the reprobation of legal wrongs, for those claims more properly belong to the courts. The claim of the community is to see legal punishment as an affirmation that the State is protecting the public from wrongdoings. In a way I think Hegel summed up the position when he said that the important feature of punishment as far as the community is concerned is that crime is to be annulled — by removing 'real evil' wherever it lies (Hegel, 1967, pp. 69-70). (In saying this I wish to avoid the more obvious utilitarian argument proposed by T. H. Green; not because the argument is defective but because it pre-supposes a justification of punishment which for the moment I wish to avoid.) In Hegelian terms the process of annulment operates by transferring back to the community, through the act of punishment, the wrong that the offender committed. That is what Hegel seems to be saying when he talks of infringing 'the right as right'. The removal of real evil is part of the promise of the State. Inevitably, that promise cannot always be fulfilled, but while it remains a promise the State must continue to show that it will do its best not to break it.

So, legal punishment differs from private punishment in a number of respects, most of which relate to the claims of outside groups. The police, for example, have no direct claim in matters of private punishment except as members of the community who may see it as morally excessive — or perhaps not excessive enough! In private punishment there are no claims from bodies such as the courts, lawyers or jurymen. However, in public and private punishment the person punished remains self-evidently a person to be treated as someone of worth and dignity, whether he be child or adult.

The judge passing sentence is obliged to recognize these external claims, but so too is the offender. Criminological theories have also neglected this point, often depicting the offender as being attenuated from the social institutions, or in Bosanquet's term as being a person without a shadow. More specifically, psychological theories have tried to explore the offender's psychological situation at the time he committed the offence, or perhaps to relate his offence to early childhood development. Freudian theory is an extreme example of this type, where the offender's psyche is seen as the product of faulty development. With Freud's theory, as with others less extreme, there is no recognition that the claims of others may be as valid as that of the offender's. Sociological theories fare no better. Sub-cultural theory depicts the offender as trapped in an unfair class system; anomie theory shows the offender as being the victim of a confidence trick involving a discrepancy between culture goals and legitimate means; while labelling theory sees him as a product of irrational social control mechanisms. Sub-cultural theory mocks or ignores the claim of others while anomie theory has no place for such claims, and labelling theory sees those claims as irrelevant, irrational or both. In contrast, penal theory starts from the point at which the offender is sentenced and so avoids consideration of the claims mentioned above. The sociology of law is the only criminological theory capable of making the necessary links, and these are often made with hesitancy.

To summarize, a just response to legal wrongs consists of providing recognition, adjudication and satisfaction to the variety of claims invoked by criminal violation. These claims come from the police, the victim, the offenders and the community. Private punishments involve fewer claims. In contrast, an unjust response occurs when certain claims operate to the detriment of others. Plea bargaining has already been mentioned as an example of an unjust response, but so too would be the manufacture of evidence or the intimidation of witnesses, for in both the claims of certain groups dominate to the exclusion and detriment of others. For example, plea bargaining may satisfy the claim of the court and court staff, but will neutralize that of the victim, offender and community. The manufacture of evidence enhances the claims of the police to the detriment of the offender, while the intimidation of witnesses enhances that of the offender to the detriment of all others. Legal justice, therefore, becomes a delicate balance of competing claims where the balance demonstrates the quality of justice.

EXTENUATING CIRCUMSTANCES

By extenuating circumstances I mean those that advance a case for a reduction in the offenders sentence, but are not related to the complicity in the crime, or to the intentions of the offender concerning his crime. All penal systems offer opportunities for the offenders to ask for extenuating circumstances to be considered, since without them punishment becomes inflexible, and perhaps inhuman. We say that some decisions are unjust if they do not take account of the special circumstances of the case, and unjust if the judge is not allowed to permit his sympathies to intrude. I wish to look at three forms of extenuating circumstances — forgiveness, mercy and the social backgrounds of the offender — and to do so in terms of the three theories of punishment — retribution, deterrence and reform. Forgiveness and mercy are more traditional forms of extenuating circumstances; the social background of the offender is a modern equivalent drawing heavily on psycho-social theories of development.

Forgiveness

Let us deal first with forgiveness, in relation to retribution. Rashdall has argued that:

> it is one of the great embarrassments of the retributive theory that it is unable to give any consistent account of the duty of forgiveness and its relation to the duty of punishment. It is seldom that one finds anybody so logical as to maintain that it is always a duty to punish and never right to forgive . . . If the duty of punishment is to rest upon an *a priori* deliverance of the moral consciousness which pronounces that . . . sin be punished, it is difficult to see how forgiveness can ever be lawful. [Rashdall, 1910, p. 199]

Rashdall is involved in an elementary confusion. First, as far as judicial punishment is concerned forgiveness does not arise. Only the victim can forgive, and legal punishment is imposed by the State who is not a victim. It could be argued that the State forgives when it offers a 'royal pardon', but this is quite different again. A pardon is the remission of a punishment. It is not lessened but obliterated from the offender's record. A pardon can be for an administrative defect in the trial, for an injustice that occurred at the trial, or for some other reason, such as providing evidence leading to the conviction of others. The State is not forgiving but wiping out the punishment by a further administrative act.

But what of those circumstances in which the victim and punisher are one and the same, or the victim hands over the offender to be punished by someone else? I have wanted to argue that punishment is more than legal punishment and that retributive punishment can exist other than in the courts. If the schoolteacher punishes a child for retributive reasons how can he forgive him? The answer is that forgiveness and punishment are not opposites, as Rashdall suggests, but adjacent or complimentary. John Kleinig gives the example where it is quite appropriate for a person to ask after he has been punished, 'will you forgive me?' (1973, p. 92). The opposite of punishment is not forgiveness, for the opposite of forgiveness is resentment and ill-will. To forgive is to refuse to nurse resentment, or to try to refuse to nurse resentment; it means that one no longer says to the person 'you have done me an injury which I shall always remember and hold it against you'.

Rashdall falls into this confusion because I suspect he believes there is a connection between forgiveness and the remission of punishment. A person may say 'I forgive you, you will not be punished', but strictly speaking he means 'I forgive you *and* you will not be punished', or 'I forgive you *and* you will be punished'. The statements are analytically separate. So when Rashdall says that it is 'difficult to see how forgiveness can ever be lawful', he is right in the sense that the State cannot forgive, but wrong in the sense in which he singles out retribution, for retribution is no more able to offer forgiveness than any other theory of punishment. By this I mean that forgiveness and punishment do not operate as counteracting influences.

By the same argument, deterrence and rehabilitation are unable to offer forgiveness. It may be true that forgiveness is more likely to take place if the offender has been rehabilitated (or even received his just deserts), for the offender is able to show that he has placed himself in a position where he is asking for forgiveness; but again, forgiveness is not a means of remitting punishment, but a way of removing resentment. Forgiveness is a moral sentiment where ill-will is no longer retained. It may occur before or after punishment but does not affect it. The three theories of punishment are therefore independent of forgiveness.

Occasionally we do speak as if there were a connection. The offender may be remorseful, and we say 'in these circumstances you are forgiven' and we remit the punishment. I would suggest however that this is a way of using forgiveness in a manner that more closely resembles mercy, although as will be shown later remorse is only one of the conditions of mercy — others must also apply. Even so, it is possible that remorse itself is sufficient to ask that the punishment be remitted, and forgiveness does appear to be connected in some way; if the offender is remorseful we may be more inclined to forgive and on the face of it appear more inclined to remit the punishment. But again, remorse and forgiveness can be independent of punishment; there may be remorse and forgiveness prior to the punishment or after the punishment, and forgiveness can take place at either stage. So, where it occurs before the punishment and the punishment is remitted, the remission is akin to mercy and the forgiveness operates alongside it; where it occurs after punishment it is forgiveness on its own.

Mercy

Mercy is much more complex. To show mercy is not to condone, for to condone an offence is to act as if it didn't matter — in other words, as if it were not an offence (Smart, 1969, p. 217). To condone an offence is to look the other way when it happens and try to ignore it and say that no action is to be taken. Nor is mercy a form of pardon. A pardon is an acknowledgement that an offence has occurred and an official administrative decision involving the remission of a punishment. Mercy, according to Alwynne Smart, exists when a judge acknowledges that an offence has been committed, decides that a particular punishment would be appropriate or just, and then decides to exact a punishment of lesser severity than the appropriate or just one (Smart, 1969, p. 218).

Under what conditions would it be appropriate to talk of mercy? First, the opposite of mercy is not injustice but cruelty. Judges who are not merciful are said to be hard, unbending and cruel, and above all lacking in compassion. Unmerciful judges take no account of human frailty, distress or possible destitution. Merciful judges, on the other hand, temper punishments with mercy by avoiding suffering regarded as excessive. Mercy is not in opposition to justice, nor is it an alternative to justice: it is a way of softening justice.

Second, mercy is a good in itself, and is not justified in all cases. In some it would be immoral. Alwynne Smart gives the example of a vicious habitual rapist who showed no sign of repentance or remorse. To be merciful — to adjust a possible sentence of imprisonment for a probation order — would be to expose others to the possibility of future crimes. 'One ought not to be merciful at the cost of others — to do so would be to defeat what is thought to be the main point of exercising mercy, namely to avoid suffering (Smart, 1969, p. 218). There must be certain appropriate conditions under which mercy can be provided, and because the rapist in this example was habitual this fact above all others ruled out mercy in his case.

Third, mercy is not to be confused with the remorse of the offender. The offender who is remorseful and/or likely to be reformed may present good grounds for having his sentence adjusted in some way, perhaps on account of the circumstances of the offence, but of itself remorse is not sufficient to expect the judge to be merciful. The offender who is repentant might be a candidate for mercy, but only when certain other conditions apply.

Finally, mercy is not to be confused with so-called 'mercy-killings', or with degrees of complicity. The Royal Commission on Capital Punishment noted that recommendations for mercy were usually successful in the following circumstances:

> Unpremeditated murders committed in some sudden excess of frenzy, where the murderer has previously had no evil animus towards his victim, expecially if he is weak-minded or emotionally unstable to an abnormal degree; murders committed under provocation which though insufficient to reduce the crime to manslaughter may be a strongly mitigating circumstance, murders committed without intent to kill, especially where they take place in the course of a quarrel; murders committed in a state of drunkenness falling short of a legal defence especially if the murderer is a man of hitherto good character; and murders committed by two or more people with differing degrees of responsibilty. [HMSO, 1953, para. 39]

These examples are not of mercy but of crimes where the prescribed penalty does not fit the case in question. Law, by its very nature, cannot take account of every possible contingency, nor can it anticipate the likely circumstances under which crimes could be committed. The circumstances listed above are examples of grades of murder regarded as less serious than others such as those premeditated or committed with the intention to steal. I agree with Alwynne Smart, who says that this type of case requires not mercy but a form of legal judgment, and the judge (or Home Secretary) who rigorously applies the law and declines to exercise his judgement is unjust (Smart, 1969, p. 217). Were it possible to have grades of murder covering all known contingencies — as opposed to the relatively crude distinctions existing between (say) murder and manslaughter, then those given by the Royal Commission would be less than the first grade, and some less than the second or third.

Mercy, and merciful decisions, are not then about gradations of crimes or about indiscriminate beneficence to those under threat or need (Kleinig, 1973, p. 89). Mercy is more limited in scope. It is to give less than the deserved punishment to an offender; in Armstrong's definition, 'to be merciful is to let someone off all or part of a penalty which he is recognized as having deserved' (1961, p. 487). Mercy is not about redressing a potential wrong or adjusting the punishment to fit a less serious crime. Genuine mercy is about considering claims made upon the judge by others, usually the offender's family but sometimes the offender himself. Two examples will illustrate the point, both used by Smart.

The first is of a man who has a wife and a number of young children to support. He has no previous convictions but was recently made redundant. Before leaving his job he stole £500 from the cashier. He promised to return the money when he could. The second is of a man who ten years ago deserted from the army. He has now given himself up. In that ten-year period he had not pursued a criminal career but was in every sense a respectable citizen. Both cases would qualify for mercy; the first on the grounds that to punish the man by a period of imprisonment would place an intolerable burden on his family, especially as he had shown every indication that he would keep his word about repayment and was not an habitual offender. Mercy becomes a means of extending assistance to those who are not offenders but whose lives would be seriously disrupted by the offenders punishment — but as long, and only as long, as certain other conditions about the offender are satisfied, such as remorse, previous character, etc. In the second example, the passage of time has reduced the seriousness of the crime; this plus the offender's behaviour over the ten years, and his remorse, would permit the judge to be merciful. So it is not the offender but the claims of others that is the important factor. In the first example it is that of the family; in the second that of the victim — the army — who after ten years was no longer prepared to take the offence as serious.

Notice that mercy does not include the destitute, the poor or the fatherless. With these there may be good reasons for adjusting the punishment because the prescribed penalty does not fit the case in question. The widow may qualify for mercy if she had young children, but only if this was accompanied by the additional features of previous honesty, remorse, etc. Without these she may have her punishment reduced because of the nature of the offence. It is not possible to determine which of those would produce the lesser punishment. It depends how merciful the judge is and on the gradation of the crime.

Some retributivists — at least those who regard other moral considerations as of equal value — are able to consider mercy within their theories. Not so the rehabilitationists, and less so the utilitarians. We can use the two earlier examples to demonstrate the point. Consider first the offender who stole the £500. A retributivist might say that the offender deserved a certain punishment, say two years in prison, but that moral considerations permit an act of mercy. Presumably most retributivists would not wish to involve pointless suffering although deserved suffering is another matter. And the offender has certainly deserved some punishment. However, the moral considerations of the offender's family must count for something, since only the harshest judge would wish to ignore these completely. These examples show that, where the retributivist ethic is multi-faceted, it is capable of allowing the retributivist to weigh one group of moral considerations against the other.

With the army deserter a different argument would apply. Alwynne Smart talks in terms of a different person 'who over a period of time has shown by his character and biography that he is not the same person who deserted from the army' (1969, p. 226). Being different, the retributivist can justly say that this new person hardly deserves the penalty that should have been given to the man ten years earlier. In both these examples the retributivist is able to demonstrate that his is not the inflexible system sometimes supposed.

The utilitarian is on less certain grounds. Utilitarian justice is concerned with producing the most happiness, and in one sense this is conducive to being merciful. The man who stole the £500 may have his sentence reduced because he may qualify under one of Bentham's criteria, namely where punishment is useless or the offender's character is such that he may not require a sentence that is necessary to deter him from future crimes, especially where the unhappiness created by the punishment would possibly be greater than was required to deter others. Similarly, the army deserter may qualify in a like manner. The utilitarian may appear to be acting kindly because he was avoiding pointless suffering and in both cases not wishing to add to the unhappiness already caused. But this is not mercy: it is another example of Bentham's principle of frugality at work. The punishments are reduced in both examples because severe punishment would create more unhappiness than was necessary.

Both examples show the strength and weaknesses of utilitarianism. On the one hand, its strength is that utilitarians do not have to invoke a separate moral position to account for a reduction in sentences. The principles of frugality, and the categories given by Bentham covering unnecessary punishments, are sufficient. Yet on the other hand utilitarians are tied to the principle of happiness. This makes all other moral considerations superfluous. They cannot account for mercy for it becomes another moral consideration, which cannot be fitted into the existing framework. Furthermore, utilitarians could reasonably ask why such considerations are necessary. A utilitarian could say that his own philosophy was capable of subsuming concepts like mercy which are, after all only another way of looking at utility.

The rehabilitationist faces more difficult problems. In the two previous examples rehabilitation can neither offer mercy nor forgiveness. Mercy does not arise. To be merciful is to impose less than the deserved penalty, and since rehabilitation has no interest in deserts, mercy does not apply. In the example of the man who stole £500 the reformist could point to specific defects in his character that require attention. Whether these defects are due to the pressures placed on him as a result of losing his job, or whether the theft was a symptom of some deeper malaise must be a matter for future investigation. But these would be the important matters for consideration. The appropriate sentence would depend on the outcome of these investigations. Family matters may be relevant to the sentence but not necessarily in the direction of a leniency. Perhaps the family are making excessive demands, perhaps even placing unwarranted pressure on the offender. This being so, it would be reasonable to argue that a period of imprisonment might relieve those demands. Conversely, treatment could be family-based, i.e. involve all the family. The outcome would be a matter for the diagnostic experts.

The army deserter offers more hope under a reformist position and would confidently expect leniency. His offence occurred ten years ago and his settled and respected life would suggest that the symptoms have disappeared. But again, the prognosis would depend on detailed investigation. Assuming that it was good, the sentence would be light. But the sentence is not based on mercy any more than a patient being treated for a fractured leg could be said to be receiving mercy. Treatment is appropriate to the disease, not to moral considerations.

The Offender's Background

We can now turn to examine what is meant by a just decision in terms of the background of the offender. Occasionally the details of an offender's background are presented as if they were a form of mitigating circumstance. I do not mean by this that backgrounds are presented in order that the offender be forgiven, nor on the grounds of mercy, although they perhaps become closest to this; often they are presented in order that the court should be sympathetic to the offender and show leniency. The aim would perhaps be to encourage the court to see the offender's background as a way of absolving him from the full responsibility of his crime — or, if not, then to change the grade of the crime in some way. The aims are not always clear. To try to sift through them we ought to first consider what is meant by just decisions in rehabilitative terms to see how this would operate.

Generally speaking, it seems as if the offender's background is used to explain the offender's involvement in the crime. Presumably this explanation would be couched in ways that would imply that a different sentence should be passed if the offender came from a different or more unpleasant background. If this is so, then the argument can belong to one of three categories: it can be an argument based on the grounds that the person's background was such that he could no longer help doing what he did (in other words, it is determinism); or it can be because of infancy, mental illness or irresistible duress, in which case the offender is exonerated in morals and in law; or, finally, his background can be such that it is felt his offence should be taken out of the class of offences to which it belongs and placed in a different category (because it is a different type of offence).

It is unlikely to be the first or the second of these cases, for in the first neither moral blame nor punishment can be attached to someone who has not been responsible for what he has done, and in the second the offender would also be said to lack responsibility. The third example is likely to be more appropriate. But how can an offender's background change the offence into a different category? It is reasonable to argue that different sentences should be passed according to the complicity of the crime, according to the severity of the crime and perhaps even according to the offender's motives, intentions or temptations. But these have little to do with background except in the most general way. To say that a person came from a deprived home tells us nothing about his degree of involvement in a crime or of his intentions. It may tell us something about the amount of temptation he felt, but even then the connection is a loose one. More likely, the way the argument is usually presented, it is implied that the offender's background places him as a 'prisoner' of his past; that his background in some way made him unable to act in a way other than he did.

The influence of Freud, and certain types of social science, can be detected here. In Benn and Peter's terms Freud spoke of causes as if they were mechanical pushes and pulls — forces in the depths of the unconscious which impelled a man to behave in a certain way (Benn and Peters, 1959, p. 207). People in Freudian terms are seen as prisoners of their pasts, controlled by unconscious forces which push them into activities that are neither to their liking nor according to their conscious wishes. Marx presented a similar picture of 'men caught up in an unwinding historical pattern' (Benn and Peters, 1959, p. 207). Both theories are plausible, for we do occasionally behave in ways that we say are out of character, and clearly our parents have influenced our attitudes and ways of behaving. Our social background has influenced the way in which we view the world, and a person who was diligently taught that stealing is wrong is likely to have more qualms about committing such offences than someone who was as a child encouraged to steal.

But there is a world of difference between an influence and an uncontrollable force. Influences can be evaluated, examined, reduced and even removed, but uncontrollable forces require that we act only in that manner. Yet the theories of Freud have suggested that we behave in ways similar to that of the uncontrollable force, or, if not uncontrollable, at least in ways that are compelling. Benn and Peters are right when they say that Freud's arguments have suggested an indefinite extension of the concept of acting under compulsion (1959, p. 207). For if men are seen as being pushed and pulled in certain directions it is easy to see them as being compelled.

Tied into this argument is that of an explanation. If a person behaves in a certain way, and came from a poor background, there is a tendency, again fostered by Freud, to 'explain' the behaviour in terms of the background. And by explanation I mean nothing more than making a connecting link between the two variables. The production of a cause is then seen as offering a means of exonerating the behaviour. 'To know all is to exonerate all' seems to be what is being said. So the person with the bad background has his offence 'explained' by that background, and explanation is associated with exoneration, or, if not, then with a reduction in deserts.

We may well challenge the nature of the explanation offered in criminological terms (for example, the supposed criminological link between poor backgrounds and criminality). We may also challenge the nature of the explanation in terms of the assumptions underlying it (for example, the tendency in social work to seek out an evil, i.e. the crime, and attempt to link it to another evil, i.e. the background); and we may also challenge it on the grounds that its aim is to produce a sympathetic response from the judge rather than to explain the criminality. All such challenges are worth making. But the most important point is that the production of causes or explanations of this nature are irrelevant to the question of whether the offender acted in the way he did and could have acted in no other. Explanations are not descriptions of compulsions or, descriptions of events whose causes are not known, or of events which are unavoidable. That they are often presented as if they were is a reflection of the influences of those such as Freud who alerted us to ideas about 'inner drives', 'forces' and 'impulses'.

This type of explanation rarely goes the whole way towards embracing a full-blown deterministic position. The description of the person as 'having freedom within a cage' is a more accurate one. It is a form of semi-determinism, if that is not a contradiction in terms. Often it exists within a rehabilitative framework but it need not, although when it does it is usually a way of presenting a sentimental account of the offender's background in order that the judge can be persuaded to take the offence out of one class and place it in a lower one.

Now I am not suggesting that the offender's background is unimportant. A just decision requires consideration of this — or at least of some specific portions of it. For the retributionist it is of value in estimating deserts related to complicity, and for the utilitarian it is of value in determining mischief. Bentham spoke of the offender's previous criminal habits, whether they had been detected or not, and the intentionality of the offender (1948, p. 294). These are background factors to be considered, but unlike those mentioned above they have a direct bearing on the offence and the way it was committed. They do not suggest compulsion, nor do they suggest an explanation: their value is to assess the level of future mischief.

It is interesting that the debate in criminological circles rarely involves a discussion on forgiveness or mercy, but that is because of the dominating influence of rehabilitation. Perhaps forgiveness and mercy are altogether too theological or metaphysical for modern social science. In contrast, the background of the offender is well discussed, criminologically that is, for criminology has often been parasitic on rehabilitation, offering the data to support a rehabilitative argument. But without forgiveness or mercy the decisions of judges become routine or technical or perhaps hard-faced — and justice and a just decision less apparent in consequence.

We also hear much criticism of the inflexible judiciary, or the absence of understanding of the offender — and rightly so, in my opinion — but if the judiciary is to be capable of a moral advance it will not come from areas where morals are not discussed, or from a belief that the offence and the harm done is of less significance than the background assessment of the offender. It can only come from an awareness of the nature of a just decision of which forgiveness and mercy are integral elements. To forgive an offender may not affect his sentence but it does permit him to take his place in society once his punishment is completed; and to have mercy on an offender allows considerations to be given of the influence of the punishment on others. Both encourage human sympathies. So too, of course, does an examination of the offender's background, but under modern rehabilitative programmes this becomes too easily incorporated into treatment techniques where the sympathy is overridden by other requirements. For my part I would wish to encourage greater discussion about forgiveness and mercy, and a more active debate about just decisions.

NOTES

1. As in many other aspects of the debate, my attention was drawn to this by

Benn and Peter's admirable book, *Social Principles and the Democratic State* (1959).

2. Yet while retribution can be democratic, the older criticisms of its barbarity constantly reappear, almost as if it were an atavistic theory left over from less enlightened times. Consider Sidgwick's criticism.

> History shows us a time in which it was thought not only as natural but as clearly right and incumbent on a man to require injuries as to repay benefits: but as moral reflection developed in Europe this notion was repudiated . . . In its universal form the old conviction still lingers in the popular view of criminal justice. It is still widely held that justice requires pain to be inflicted on a man who has done wrong, even if no benefit result . . . Personally I am far from holding this view that I have a strong instinctive aversion from it, and I hesitate to attribute it to common sense since I think it is passing away from the moral consciousness of educated persons in most advanced countries. [Sidgwick, p. 281, 1901]

Sidgwick's hope is premature. Retribution has still found a place in legal justice, and if anything is making something of a comeback. The early link with the Church and the biblical requirement of *lex talionis* helped produce the barbarity of sentencing, but to consider it in terms of the sociology of the theory is not to condemn the theory as such. It is true that Kant supported the death penalty, while Beccaria opposed it, but John Stuart Mill also supported it, and for the most dangerous of reasons: that 'of humanity to the criminal . . . as the least mode in which it is possible adequately to deter him from the crime' (in Feinberg, and Gross, 1975, p. 121). Whereas Kant said a murderer deserves capital punishment, Mill arrived at the same conclusion but by the deterrence route. Mill thought it more humane to execute a murderer than to condemn him to hard labour for life. In an uncharacteristic way, Mill's view is paternalistic, but my point is that deterrence has successfully escaped the accusation of being 'barbaric'. The theory itself does not automatically lead to barbarity.

3. Rule-utilitarianism stemmed from a somewhat oblique passage by J. S. Mill:

> As we do not call anything justice which is not a virtue we usually say that justice must give way to some other moral principle, but that what is just in ordinary cases, is by reason of that other principle not just in a particular case. By this useful accommodation of language the character of indefeasibility attributed to justice is kept up, and we are saved from the necessity of maintaining that there can be laudable injustice. [Mill, 1964, p. 59]

4

Special Provisions for Juveniles

In general terms, children* have fewer rights than adults and are often held less accountable. Parents and schoolteachers have duties to provide the child with care and support, and parents have a duty not to neglect the child, expose him to moral danger or allow him to be beyond control. Children normally cannot undertake contractual obligations and are not normally entitled to their own earnings; nor can they manage their own property. Moreover, children younger than certain statutory limits are not allowed to vote, hold public office, work in various occupations, drive a car, buy alcohol or be sold certain kinds of reading material, quite apart from what they or their parents may wish (Coons, and Mnookin, 1978, p. 391).

In England and Wales a parent or person standing *in loco parentis* has the right to punish a child under his charge. This right is expressly guarded by Section 1(7) of the Children and Young Persons Act 1933 and is still operative (in 1980). 'Nothing in this section shall be construed as affecting the right of any parent, teacher, or other persons having the lawful control or charge of a child or young person to administer punishment to him.' In law such punishment will not be unlawful if it is inflicted with 'moderation and with a proper instrument'. Whether or not the punishment is reasonable must depend on all the facts of the case, and in particular on the age and strength of the child and the nature and degree of punishment. If it goes beyond what is reasonable it is unlawful and would therefore render the parents criminally liable for assault or, if the child dies, manslaughter; if the parents' act or omission was *intended* to cause death of the child, then the parents would be guilty of murder if it could be shown that serious harm or death was highly probable. Only a person *in loco parentis* has the right to inflict moderate and

---

* The term 'child' will be used interchangeably with 'juvenile', and unless specified refers to any person under the age of 17.

reasonable punishment. The court has held it to be unlawful for an elder brother to administer corporal punishment where both sons are living with their father and consequently the elder brother could not be considered to be *in loco parentis* of the younger (Goodman, 1972, p. 14; Bromley, 1976, pp. 336, 340).

A schoolmaster being *in loco parentis* has the same legal right to inflict punishment as a parent; there are also the same liabilities should the punishment prove excessive. The schoolmaster's rights are coterminous with the authority given to him, and cease as soon as that ceases. Difficulties arise in law about the rights of schoolmasters to punish children for behaviour that takes place outside the school, or even to punish for not learning lessons that were not authorized by the education code. These marginal areas do not affect the main legal position *vis-à-vis* schoolteachers' rights to punish children generally, although they help define the legal boundaries.

Chidren in the care of the local authority are governed by different regulations, although the local authorities' rights are not dissimilar to those of parents. However, regulations define the method of punishment and who should be able to apply it. Generally speaking, the rights are invested in the person in charge of the institution and the amount of punishment to be inflicted is controlled[1] (Goodman, 1972, pp. 469, 981). Corporal punishment is still permitted.

Children appearing before the juvenile court on criminal offences are subject to certain legal provisions relating to general defences to crime (i.e. as opposed to the specific defences, which apply to particular crimes). Legal discussions surrounding criminal prosecution for juveniles, therefore, takes place alongside other defences such as insanity. Modern lawyers have inherited from Bentham and the neo-classicists the basic premise that, where a person caused an *actus reus* with the appropriate *mens rea*, he will generally be held liable. There are certain defences available that reduce or remove liability, and persons under the age of 18 qualify in some degree for those defences (Smith, and Hogan, 1978, p. 156).

In England and Wales juveniles who are likely to be prosecuted for criminal offences are classified into one of three categories according to age. The first concerns those under the age of 10. Professors Smith and Hogan say that under common law a child is exempt from criminal responsibility until the day before his seventh birthday. Under the 1969 Children and Young Persons Act (to be called the 1969 Act from now on) responsibility begins at the age of 10, which for these purposes can be called the prosecutable age. This rule is commonly stated as a conclusive presumption that the child is *doli incapax*. Even though there may be the clearest evidence that the child caused an *actus reus* with *mens rea* he cannot be convicted once it appears that he had not, at the time he committed the act, attained the age of 10. This is no mere procedural bar, for as Smith and Hogan show, no crime can be committed by an infant and any one who instigated the child to do the act therefore becomes a principal, not a secondary, party. So, for example, the court has ruled that where a husband and wife were charged with receiving from their son aged 7 a child's tricycle knowing it to have been stolen, they must be acquitted on the ground that, since the child could not steal, the tricycle could not have been stolen (Smith and Hogan, 1978, p. 156).

The second category of children, those between 10 and 14, are in a twilight zone in which they are exempt from criminal responsibility unless it is proved, not only that they caused an *actus reus* with *mens rea*, but also that they did so with a 'mischievous discretion', in other words that they could discern between good and evil at the time the offence was committed. It is not necessary for the juvenile in this category to know that the act was against the law: the child must simply know that the act was morally wrong.

The third category of juveniles — those over the age of 14 — have no special consideration for criminal offences but do for care proceedings. For criminal offences the child is presumed to be entirely responsible for his actions (Smith and Hogan, 1978, p. 157-8).

In addition to these specific requirements relating to criminal proceedings, additional requirements have been introduced by recent legislation (mainly under the 1969 Act) for care proceedings. Juveniles under the age of 10 may be subject to care proceedings and dealt with in a juvenile court sitting as a civil court, on the grounds *inter alia* that the child is exposed to moral danger, or beyond the control of his parents or guardian, and is also in need of care and control that he is unlikely to receive unless the court makes an order in respect of him. The commission by a child under 10 of what would in the case of an adult be a criminal act would be evidence of moral danger or lack of parental control (Cross, 1975). In the case cited above, where the husband and wife were charged with receiving a child's tricycle from their son aged 7, it is possible that the child could have been brought to court under care proceedings had the family circumstances been considered appropriate.

Juveniles over the age of 10 may be subject to care proceedings to the same extent as those under the age of 10 except that, where an offence has been committed when they have reached the prosecutable age, they may be prosecuted according to the age requirements listed above. Under the 1969 Act it was intended that no juvenile would be prosecuted unless he was also in need of care (that is, with the exception of certain offences such as homicide), but this section has never been fully implemented (see Cross, 1975, pp. 68-72).

Finally, there are legal requirements relating to the child's attendance at school. The original Act was the Education Act 1944 (S40(3)), but is now substituted by the 1969 Children and Young Persons's Act. Under the original Act it was stated that,

> where a child has failed to attend regularly at school at which he is a registered pupil . . . the court may direct that the child be brought before a juvenile court, and the juvenile court may if it is satisfied that it is necessary to do so for the purpose of securing the regular attendance of the child at school make any order which such a court has power to make under Section 62 of the Children and Young Persons Act, 1933, in the case of children and young persons in need of care or protection who are brought before it under that Section.

This Act has the effect of bracketing children who do not attend school and who are under the minimum school-leaving age with those who are otherwise endangered. Subsequent regulations have not affected this main point.

This summary is a brief and somewhat simplified account of complex legislation. However, three major principles appear to dominate. First, parents or others *in loco parentis* have legal rights to punish children. As there are no corresponding rights to punish adults, children therefore constitute a special group in society. Second, for criminal proceedings there are defences in law based on age graduations where more and more responsibility is attributed to the child as he grows older. Finally, children can be subject to care proceedings which for those below the prosecutable age may include an offence as evidence that the child may require care. Above the prosecutable age other factors are needed to show that care is requried.

Surrounding and underpinning these principles listed above is the legal requirement that the court should place emphasis on the child's welfare. The court is obliged to consider the welfare of the child in all cases, criminal or civil. Section 44(1) of the 1933 Children and

Young Persons' Act states that 'every court, in dealing with a child or young person who is brought before it, either as an offender or otherwise, shall have regard to the welfare of the child or young person, and shall in a proper case take steps for removing him from undesirable surroundings and for securing that proper provisions are made for his education and training'. This section is still operative (in 1980). The key phrase is 'shall have regard to the welfare of the child or young person'.

This section was intended to remove doubts that had existed in earlier legislation by affirming the basic principle under which juvenile justice must operate. It did not do so. First, there is a definitional problem about the term 'welfare'. The term is wide and capable of flexibility. For example, while the dominant matter for the courts' consideration must be the welfare of the child, this is not to be measured by money or physical comfort. Accordingly, the word 'welfare' must be taken in its widest sense. The moral and religious welfare of the child must be considered as well as its physical wellbeing, as too must be the ties of affection (quoted in Goodman, 1972, pp. 50-1). Second, where should the emphasis be placed? Does 'welfare' mean that welfare considerations should be *paramount,* or that they should only be *considered*? In short, the legal requirements are ambiguous. However, in practice it seems that courts sometimes regard welfare considerations as being paramount but sometimes as adjacent. The decision depends on the specific circumstances of each case, and on the personal views of the magistrates.

In England and Wales, unlike many parts of North America, a form of retributive justice is retained. Nothing can override the principle that the court must first try the case and determine whether what is alleged is proved. This applies to criminal and care proceedings alike. If a case fails for want of proof the court cannot act, even though the child's welfare is precarious (Goodman, 1972, p. 50).

A PHILOSOPHICAL OVERVIEW OF
JUVENILE PUNISHMENT

There has been no place for juveniles in the grand philosophical theories of punishment. Bradley, for example, regarded pedagogic punishment as qualitatively different from that of adults. He did not think that juveniles could be regarded as being fully responsible for their actions and as such could not be said to deserve suffering in the same way as adults. He thought the aim of punishment was different. For Bradley the principle aim of juvenile punishment was improvement (1927, p. 31). The amount of punishment to be given was a practical question based on the decision of parents and tutors. Interestingly enough, Bradley also used the terms 'discipline' and 'corrections' to apply to juvenile punishment; the latter is now widely used in North America and contains many of the assumptions incorporated in Bradley's thinking.

Punishment for juveniles has been neglected by utilitarians too, and for similar reasons, for both theories rely on the offender being responsible for his actions. Bradley talks of wrongdoing as desert, while for the utilitarians, T. H. Green sums up the position when he says of punishment generally that 'the idea of punishment implies on the side of the person punished at once a capacity for determination by the conception of a common or public good . . . and an actual violation of a right or omission to fulfil an obligation' (Green, 1910, para. 185). To the utilitarians juveniles are unable to have an understanding of the nature of rights as founded on relations to such public good; neither do juveniles have awareness of the violation or omission of rights that may have been prevented. This is most clearly stated by Bentham, who thought that punishment could produce little effect in influencing juvenile conduct, for children were too young to face consequences and appreciate future events (1948, p. 284). Bentham was not however persuaded to grant juveniles complete immunity, for he recognized that there were instances where children were capable of perceiving the effects of their actions. The difficulty was to decide whether a given case satisfied a given rule.

Philosophers have tended to agree on the aim and justifications for punishment for juveniles, that is when they have considered the matter at all. We find agreement among those where we would not normally expect harmony. Hegel thought the punishment of juveniles was not directed at justice as such but was to be more subjective and moral in character. It was to stop children from exercising a freedom still in the toils of nature 'and to lift the universal into their consciousness and will' (Hegel, 1967, p. 117). We find similar views expressed by Plamenatz, without of course the attended metaphysic. Plamenatz thought that we should not punish our children in order to reform them, for they are as yet innocent, and we do only to some extent in order to deter them. According to Plamenatz, our immediate purpose is to train them to feel as they ought. Juveniles may be blameless, but they are capable of hurting others and themselves, and if we do not punish them we will find later that, when they are old enough, the appeal to reason will be in vain (Plamenatz, 1968, p. 175). Presumably this is why Bradley said pedagogic punishment varied in occasion and amount; why Hegel thought punishment for juveniles was not to be aimed at justice; and why Plamenatz could say that punishment for children was an appeal to feelings that in later life act as a censor for moral behaviour.

The general agreement between philosophers of widely divergent positions may appear unexpected but is none the less relatively easy to explain. Once the initial premises on which the grand theories of retribution and deterrence are based are found to be no longer applicable, the theories lose their impact and collapse into well formulated reformist sentiments. If deserts cannot be allocated to children, then retribution is not applicable; and if there is no prospect of foreseeing consequences, the utilitarian argument is similarly placed. Only the reformist argument becomes meaningful, for reform emphasizes improvement and reduces arguments about responsibility. Modern versions of juvenile justice have eagerly embraced the reformist position, finding on the one hand active support of reformist doctrines from its own theory, and on the other tacit agreement from philosophers who under other circumstances would be expected to deal harshly with reformist aims. Philosophical opposition to the reformist position occurs immediately the child becomes an adult; while he remains a child the retributionists and utilitarians are rarely critical and if anything retain a passive silence.

The general theme underpinning philosophical arguments is that pedagogic punishment is for improvement. This, it seems to me, is based on a number of assumptions. First, there is the assumption that children are amenable to discipline — or, rather, that their characters are still pliable. We find examples of this from Plamenatz, who talks of the child's inability to reason and its dependence on adults for approval and disapproval. Plamenatz sees the child as self-centred and capricious but also imitative. He concludes that blame and punishment may be effective, indeed indispensable, where it is a question of forming character not already formed (Plamenatz, 1968, p. 176). We find further examples in Kant and Rousseau, both of whom gave some consideration to the education, and therefore punishment, of children (Kant 1960; Rousseau, 1969). Kant placed great emphasis on discipline and was prepared to use physical punishment to supplement the insufficiency of moral punishment, although he believed the former was a poor substitute for the formulation of moral character. He was stern enough to believe that disobedience was always to be followed by punishment in some form (pp. 88-9). Rousseau employed different methods to bring up 'Emile'. The very words 'obey' and 'command' were to be excluded from the child's vocabulary; still more so those of 'duty' and 'obligation' (p. 53). Rousseau was not, however, persuaded to be overpermissive, or to accede to all the child's demands, for 'the child who has only to ask and have thinks himself the master of the universe; he considers all men as his slaves; and when you are at least compelled to refuse he takes your refusal as an act of rebellion, for he thinks he has only to command'. Unfortunately, Rousseau does not tell us how to control a child who will not accept refusals from adults.

Second, there is the assumption related to society's future and the need to safeguard it. We can call this the 'reserve capital argument'; it occurs in almost all discussions of punishment, education and welfare. Traces of this argument can be found in Hegel's writings, where he views the duty of society as an act of stewardship or trustee. Extravagance in children destroys the security of society, of the families and of the child itself. Society, said Hegel must substitute for extravagance the pursuit and ends of that society against the individuals concerned (Hegel, 1967, para. 240). Kant placed great emphasis on the value of education as a means of realizing a better world. He, like the Abbott of St Pierre, hoped for a 'senate of all the nations', for only by such a method could mankind advance. 'If this proposal were carried out,' said Kant, 'it would be a great step forward, for the time now occupied by each nation in providing for its own security could then be employed for the advancement of mankind'[2] Kant, 1930, p. 252). This remarkably advanced view was dependent on the fruits of education, conceived by Kant as having two strands. One was negative, which he called discipline, and aimed at restraining whatever was unnatural; the other was positive, which he called doctrine or training. Discipline had to precede doctrine. Discipline was correction, and man must be disciplined because he is by nature raw and wild (Kant, 1930, pp. 248, 249). Doctrine was applied at a later stage when the child was ready to receive it. Children were Kant's reserve capital, and the improvement of mankind the destined final end.

Third, children are assumed to require protection. Pedagogic punishment protects by providing stability for the child, for it provides boundaries to the child's wilful nature. It protects him by helping to establish his place in the universe. Discipline — the imposition of order by authority — is often regarded as self-evidently good, a view not shared by all modern writers on education, who regard discipline as an interference with personal liberty and as such always in need of justification (Dixon, 1967, p. 163).

These three assumptions dominate the debate. As will be shown later, they also dominate the modern debate on juvenile justice. Furthermore, in spite of the limited attention given by some philosophers to questions about the punishment of juveniles, their arguments remain relatively bland compared with the complexity of their writings on other matters. Kant's views on education and punishment consist mainly of moral exhortations to which parents should adhere. For example, we find Kant asserting that everything in education depends on establishing correct principles and leading children to accept them (1960, p. 108); or that every transgression of a command in a child is a want of obedience which ought to bring forth punishment; or that commands that are disobeyed through inattention ought also to bring forth punishment. There is no debate about the justification for punishment or about the complexities of bringing up children generally. The modern psychologist has overtaken the philosopher in the interest and quality of the debate, although as one psychologist admits the subject matter is still bedevilled by potent and misleading legends (Herbert, 1978).

A GENERAL OVERVIEW OF THE
PUNISHMENT OF CHILDREN

We have touched briefly on the way in which most philosophers have discussed the punishment of children, and have shown how the grand theories have had little to say on the matter because of the difficulty of establishing the child as 'responsible'. But there are more difficulties, some of which are empirical, others theoretical. Consider first an obvious empirical limitation. Most parents do not punish their children solely for improvement: they punish because children occasionally exasperate them, and they punish too for retributive and deterrent reasons. Thus parents know that some children may not always appreciate the consequences of their actions but feel that they are able to do so occasionally. Most of us notice that children can be generous at times and not so at others. Children are not just the plastic and pliable creatures depicted in some popular accounts.

Children also have a sense of fairness. 'It's not fair' is a frequent complaint, both of other children and of their parents. That sense of fairness can be acutely felt, and in some children appears to be highly developed. Fairness as far as children are concerned involves commensurability and comparability; that they should be treated as others of similar age and condition and treated as others who have done similar acts. Mr Quintin Hogg during the parliamentary debate on the 1969 Act cited evidence of injustice which he said 'stood out like pebbles in [his] memory making a permanent mark on [his] personality. I speak of the times I was punished for something I did not do, when I was accused of something of which I was innocent or was treated, as I thought, as another child more favoured than myself would not have been treated' (*Hansard,* vol. 779, p. 1200).

Unless that sense of fairness is acknowledged, improvement can be a tyranny. A sense of fairness, with its strong retributive undertones, provides limitations on punishments. We may think the child needs punishing, but without recognizing that the child sees punishment as fair we may, in Mr Hogg's tremulous phrase, produce pebbles that leave a permanent mark. In Mr Hogg's view (stated during the same debate), 'it is my belief that we can talk about [improvement] with all the sincerity, companionship and love that we know . . . but we forget at our peril that the child has a sense of justice which though unsophisticated and immature like all its undeveloped faculties is none the less as acute and real as the sense of justice of the Lord Chancellor himself' (*Hansard,* vol. 779, p. 1200). And indeed it may be, and no amount of appeal to improvement will alter that.

The other empirical limitation involves an adult judgement about what children can or cannot do. It makes no sense to ask a young child to be responsible for taking control of a classroom during the teacher's absence and then punishing the child for failing to live up to adult expectations. Neither does it make sense to punish children for failing to live up to the sophistications required by adult consciences and to expect them to sympathize with the sufferings of others.

Children are children, a point sometimes forgotten by those who argue that the rights of children ought to coincide with the rights of adults. Approximate they might; coincide is something else.

There is also the form of punishment to be considered. In general terms, the punishments of children are mostly mild; in schools they amount largely to detentions, reports and loss of privileges, which are of a transient nature. In the home similar punishments are used, mainly comprising loss of privileges. These types of punishment, because they are mild, direct attention away from the punishment itself to the effect they have on the person punished. Severe punishments produce estrangements (Peters, 1966, p. 279); mild punishments are more likely to take place within an existing relationship between punisher and punished. Deterrent punishments of a mild form become qualitatively different from a severe form, for the aim is to deter and perhaps educate at the same time. A child for example who is behaving badly may be punished on deterrent grounds, but done so in a manner that is also comforting and reassuring. A child given a severe deterrent punishment loses the personal contact. The distinguishing feature is the severity of the punishment, not the agency imposing it.

Punishment in schools has the added dimension of being aimed at maintaining social order. The influential Plowden Committee saw punishment in deterrent terms (HMSO, 1967). They asserted that few teachers would consider punishment to be good for children, and few would regard it as a cure for deep-seated ills such as persistent cruelty, laziness or even poor work. The Committee said that punishment should be defended solely as a means of inducing social order, adding that it needs to be understood by the child, or to be seen to be just — thereby giving a nodding acceptance to retribution. Corporal punishment constituted a separate category of punishment, said the Committee, and as a general rule the Committee was opposed to it — a view, incidentally, not shared by the teaching profession generally in England and Wales, who claim that corporal punishment has the ultimate deterrent to maintain order.[3]

These empirical limitations place the study of punishment for juveniles within a more complex — or, rather, a more untidy — arena than the punishment of adults. But the theoretical issues are no less important. The major one concerns the child's level of responsibility. To say that a person, in this case a child, cannot avoid or help doing what he does amounts to saying he is not responsible for his actions.

Of course at the extremes we could confidently assert that a young baby was not responsible for his actions, and a 16- or 17-year-old probably was, given, that is, that he was of a certain level of physical and psychological development. (If he was not we would probably be provided with justificatory pleas if he was subnormal, or excuses if he was immature. Justificatory pleas remove the blame from the offender; excuses reduce the blame.) Between those two extremes of age and development there would be varying levels of responsibility. The law reflects this and, as shown earlier, provides a rough and ready method of acknowledging the child's development. It is not perfect, and no legal system could be faced with the immense difficulties relating to levels of childhood development or to the fluctuations within and between each child. To call it 'rough and ready' is not intended as a cheap criticism.

But responsibility is more complex than this. It is often confused with 'cause' inasmuch as it is believed that, if we know what 'caused' a child to act in a certain way (for example his home background), the child (or adult for that matter) is not regarded as responsible. The point has been noted earlier when we discussed the influence of writers such as Freud and Marx who spoke of forces as if they were mechanical pushes and pulls — unconscious forces which impelled men to behave in a certain way, making them prisoners of their past or catching them up helplessly in an unwinding historical pattern. These 'causes' are irrelevant to the basic question of whether a child or person was responsible for what he did: they do not compel; they merely provide plausible explanations of why a child acted in the way he did.

We need to look more closely at what 'responsibility' means. Bradley has provided the classic exposition of what we mean when we ascribe responsibility to a person (1927, ch. 1.). There are three major conditions.

(1) Self-sameness. By this Bradley means that throughout the act the person must be one identical person, i.e. one to whom the deed belonged, and it must have been *his*, which means it was issued from his will.

(2) Intelligence. The doer must know the particular circumstances of the case. If he was ignorant, and if it was not his duty to know, then the deed was not his act. A certain amount of intelligence or 'sense' is thus a condition of responsibility.

(3) Responsibility. This implies acting as a moral agent. No one is

accountable who is not capable of knowing the moral quality of his acts. He must be familiar with the general rules of what is required, and in this sense must know good from bad.

Responsibility, then, in Bradley's terms means that the man must act himself, be now the same man who acted, have been himself at the time of the act, and have had sense enough to know what he was doing and to know good from bad[4] (Bradley, 1927, p. 9). When these or any of these are absent the classical defences of compulsion, non-culpable ignorance of fact and defect of reason can be applied (Benn, and Peters, 1959, p. 206). Yet, as Professor Hart has shown, 'responsibility' is more a negative than a positive quality. We decide that a person is responsible when we have satisfied ourselves that those features listed above are *absent*; that he was *not* compelled, *not* ignorant of fact and *not* defective of reason. If these features were not absent the act was avoidable (Hart, 1951).

In the first of Bradley's conditions, the self-sameness, no special place would be granted to children, for they as well as adults could be subject to compulsion. It may be easier to compel children than adults to do certain acts, but that is only a marginal consideration. The second condition, that of intelligence, is more appropriate, and by intelligence Bradley meant not innate IQ but 'sense' or 'knowledge of' the surroundings. Children and especially young children could not always be said to have intelligence of the act. Similarly, Bradley's third condition, that of being a moral agent, applies to children. Bradley himself said: 'Wherever we can presume upon a capacity for apprehending moral distinctions in such cases, for example, as those of young children . . . there is and there can be no responsibility, because there exists no moral will (1927, p. 7). Bradley would be joined by many other philosophers and psychologists who would see the child as having a limited capacity for apprehending moral distinctions.

We talk of 'responsibility' as if it were present or not present, and we can easily confuse it with actions that are voluntary. But as Aristotle maintained, children share in voluntary actions but not in choice, and acts done on the spur of the moment we describe as voluntary but not as chosen (1925, Bk 3, ch. 2). Now the problem is to assess degrees of responsibility and degrees of choice. The argument presented so far has no higher value than that of producing principles about responsibility. It does not tell us how to recognize examples when responsibility is expanding, enlarging or developing.

It is an argument of procedure rather than substance. It does not prescribe specifically one method of recognizing responsibility, although if we try to understand responsibility our arguments must be within this framework. We are left then with the private judgement of parents and schoolteachers based on the child's development within that framework, and a grudging acceptance of the crude legal divisions in juvenile justice. For punishment is for something, that is for something that has been done. We cannot say we will punish a child if the child does not know what is wrong. When Mill said punishment is responsibility he made the correct link. There is no magical age at which full responsibility arrives, nor any magic to produce that responsibility. We cannot say we will punish a child if the child does not know what is wrong; we may coerce him, expecting him to learn what is right and wrong from the coercion, but that is a different matter altogether. It is not punishment, either.

These limitations, empirical and theoretical, perhaps account for the lack of interest shown by the retributive and deterrent philosophers in the punishment of children. If punishment is deserved, then the actions of the offenders must be the actions of a responsible person. It makes no sense to say otherwise. Similarly, if the principle object of punishment is deterrence, it can be effective only in the case of deliberate acts, for on utilitarian grounds it would be pointless mischief to do otherwise. With little to offer from retributive and utilitarian theories, we have been left with a wholesale adoption of the reformist, or improvement, philosophy. As will be shown, this produces its own testimony to failure, at an empirical and theoretical level. As R. S. Peters says, 'the treatment position depends on sacrificing liberty and fairness to an over riding regard for the interests of the weaker brethren. It is paternalism dressed up in a lab-coat' (1966, p. 287).

THE AIMS OF JUDICIAL PUNISHMENT
FOR JUVENILES

Official aims of juvenile punishment vary over time although some threads remain permanent. The modern conception of juvenile justice began in Britain under the 1908 Act which made juvenile courts mandatory, although they had already been established earlier in some cities in England and Wales. In the United States juvenile

courts were first introduced under the 1898 Act of Illinois, although
there is some dispute as to whether Illinois can claim the honour[5]
(Parsloe, 1978, p. 53). A separate, or rather special, form of
jurisdiction was developed to attempt to break with the harsh
penalties of earlier years, and because of a growing recognition that
the aims of juvenile justice were different from that of adults. Yet
from the outset the juvenile court has contained within it a series
of unresolved conflicts which appear as anomalies to those whose
business it is to operate the system. While it has retained the
obvious humanitarian undertones, it remains an institution of
remarkable complexity. It performs a variety of functions, assumes a
variety of roles and expresses a wide range of values and aspirations
(Bean, 1975, p. 58). It also encompasses wide variations in its social
organization. Edwin Lemert (1971) says it is no mean task to
comprehend the protean local adaptions of the juvenile court and yet
capture some of the features that make it distinctive as an institution
in its own right. To talk then of 'the juvenile court' as if it was a
homogeneous institution means that we do so only at the risk of over-
generalizing.

Yet I think we must speak in general terms if we are to understand
the principles of the legislation. The first point therefore is less of a
principle, more an acknowledgement of the differences in the social
situation of punishment inflicted by parents or schoolteachers and
by a court. A number of obvious differences exist; the former involves
the parents, who are victim (usually) and are also the prosecutor, the
judge, the jury and the executive. In the courts the functions are
separate and apportioned accordingly. Some writers have insisted
that these differences are important and cite the example of corporal
punishment, comparing the pain inflicted by (say) a teacher for an
act that is immediate with pain inflicted by a disinterested court
official for an act occurring in the relatively distant past. The
differences are said to affect the child's perception of the punishment
and the possible outcome — and probably do.

The differences in the social situation of punishment by the courts
and by the parents would be as follows. First, the rules governing
punishment differ between parents and the courts. In the courts
stricter canons apply as to notions of guilt, while witnesses,
prosecutors and defendants speak according to ordered requirements,
and rights of appeal exist that are equally ordered and can suspend
punishment until appeals are heard. Second, judicial punishment is

the result of an outcome of negotiation that has taken place between police and defendant, and where the decision to prosecute is usually unrelated to the personnel sitting in the court. Furthermore, if the defendant is guilty the courts *have* to punish, even if they grant an absolute discharge, for that is a record of judicial action which is a punishment in itself, although not necessarily a legal punishment in the strict sense of the term. Third, usually but not always, parents punish for less serious offences; or perhaps it is more accurate to say that courts have a monopoly of punishment for the most serious offences. Fourth, courts have an obligation to protect others as well as to consider the needs and welfare of the child. In contrast, there is a weaker obligation given to parents to protect other members of society. Fifth, parents usually punish for immediate offences, whereas courts have inevitably to deal with a time lag between offence and court hearing. Finally, the relationships differ within which punishment is inflicted. Parental punishment is not reduced to mechanical implementation. As stated earlier, in parental punishment affection usually precedes the punishment and is re-established afterwards. With courts personal affection does not exist prior to, during or after punishment has been inflicted.

These differences may not affect the justifications of punishment, but they affect the aims. The aims of the court are more socially orientated, those of parents more individually orientated; the schools fall somewhere in between. It is conceivable that the intensity of punishment given by parents is equal to that given by the court, but the court would have aims more directed towards the social order.

Of course there will be an overlap. The 'reserve capital' argument has already been considered as one aim of punishment for children generally. It operates in the courts as well as in the home, but as with all other judicial arguments the emphasis on the future of society in more pronounced. That is the major difference. The Earl of Lytton made the point in the parliamentary debate in 1908. He said, 'the whole of the part of the Bill (Part V on juvenile offenders and juvenile courts) is concerned not only in a spirit of tenderness and affection for the child's life, but also with real interest in the future welfare of the State. Its provisions hold out to us hopes for a marked diminution of crime in the future' (*Hansard,* 20 October 1908, col. 227). We find the same argument reiterated some sixty years later during the parliamentary debates on the 1969 Act. The then Home Secretary Mr Callaghan said the aim was 'to prevent the deprived and delinquent children of today becoming the deprived, inadequate, unstable and criminal citizens of tomorrow' (*Hansard,* vol. 779, p. 1176).

In both quotes the model of the reserve capital is clear. The young people of today will be the citizens of tomorrow. As with all investment there has to be a return, which in this case is the future quality of society. The juvenile court is a form of capital outlay almost in the manner of Bentham's cost accountancy system. The quality of society can be measured in terms of low crime rates, which make the reserve capital argument more pertinent. Many adult offenders have been juvenile offenders (about 70 per cent), and the argument goes that if the juvenile supply is cut off then adult crime becomes reduced. (There is some force in this argument, although nowadays there is a growing tendency for there to be more late-comers to crime, that is, offenders prosecuted for the first time over the age of 21.) In practical terms, the reserve capital argument has led to a wider range of penal provisions for juveniles than for adults aimed at reducing adult recidivsm. On this basis the juvenile court has become a key variable in the overall crime rate.

Emphasis on the reserve capital ties the child to the requirements of the State. But the State has other aims, one of which is the protection of children from their parents. The Earl of Lytton implied this when he spoke of 'real interest in the future welfare of the State'. Traditionally, protection has existed under the ancient concept of *parens patriae* — literally, the State as father of the people. This concept is directed towards protecting members of vulnerable groups unable to care for themselves or who may be exploited or neglected. Under *parens patriae* the State has an obligation to intervene and offer protection. Few of us would I think wish to remove that obligation, and the many tragedies of recent years show how important protection has become.[6] Mary Carpenter described these children as coming from the 'perishing classes'; they were ignorant, destitute and a risk to themselves. She thought they required a 'helping hand to raise them'.

The third aim has also been mentioned earlier: that of justice for the child. The juvenile court has always required that a case be proven before action is taken. There have always been requirements of legal procedure, albeit weakened over the years, and some rights of appeal. In North America many of these requirements are absent, making the juvenile court more akin to a statutory social service than a judicial enterprise. In suggesting that one aim of the court is to pursue justice for the child, I am not suggesting that this aim produces one particular form of justice, merely saying that principles of common law intrude and demand that offenders be punished according to statutory requirements.

The fourth aim shows itself in the Earl of Lytton's comments when he spoke of a spirit of affection and tenderness for young children. The humanistic and sometimes sentimental side of juvenile justice has been present since its inception. We think it morally wrong to subject children to unpleasant conditions, irrespective of whether we are concerned about the future of society or the way they will develop in later life. As members of vulnerable groups we regard them as being poor at helping themselves to the basic necessities for their own welfare. As Patricia Morgan says, socially, morally, intellectually and physically the child is dependent on the adult's position and choices (Morgan, 1980). We have also linked the child's development to the demands of maternal values, so much so that legislation in England and Wales requires that one magistrate sitting in the juvenile court must be a woman. In so doing we have implied that children have certain 'needs' that can be met only by reference to the role and function of women.

THE METHODS OF JUVENILE JUSTICE

In an area as wide and embracing as juvenile justice the aims and methods of justice tend to be merged. Sometimes methods appear as aims ('We need to keep children out of the courts') and vice versa. By a 'method' I mean the implementation of some of those aims delineated above, but I recognize that this is not a wholly satisfactory distinction.

The favoured method of most modern juvenile justice systems is based on a balance between the requirements of justice and the requirements of children as members of a vulnerable group. Legally, that balance was produced by the 1933 Act, which required consideration of the defendant's welfare. In effect this led to a juxtaposition of demands rather than a theoretical link. The juxtaposition was tenuous and potentially fraught with conflict; it was also a compromise between demands that had traditionally produced ambiguities and diversity of sentencing practices. The

Ingleby Committee reporting in 1960 summarized the position thus:

> The combined effect has been to produce a jurisdiction that rests at least in appearance on principles that are hardly consistent. The court remains a criminal court in the sense that it is a magistrates court, that it is principally concerned with trying offences, that its procedure is a modified form of criminal procedure, and that with a few special provisions it is governed by the law of evidence in criminal cases. Yet the requirements to have regard to the welfare of the child and the various ways in which the court may deal with an offender suggest a jurisdiction that is not criminal. It is not easy to see how these principles can be reconciled; criminal responsibility is focused on an allegation about some particular act isolated from the character and needs of the defendant, whereas welfare depends on a complex of personal family and social considerations. [HMSO, 1960, para. 60]

In spite of the apparent defects, the Committee were not disposed to recommend changes. They considered the strength of the existing system to lie in its pragmatism; it was reasonably acceptable to the community because it satisfied the general commitment to welfare, and it provided a defined base for state intervention. Even so, state intervention was relatively wide, constructed as it had to be according to welfare considerations. The method prior to 1969 was a compromise then between two conflicting principles. It was acceptable to the Ingleby Committee because it restricted excesses. In practice, a balance was attained by recognizing the inherent ambiguities linked to a refusal to be dominated by competing philosophies. The juvenile court did not operate as if it was wholly committed to welfare; or, to use an example from the Ingleby Committee report, it did not operate as if it were a medical practitioner who, if he felt that the child needed some particular medical treatment, provided that treatment for the patient's best interests. Treatment was tempered by retributive controls. Similarly, welfare requirements demanded that the court paid attention to the child's biography.

The instability of such a system was obvious. Juvenile courts often appeared to act as if disparities in sentencing did not matter. Child A could be sentenced for retributive reasons to one type of sentence; child B convicted of the same offence could, and often was, sentenced to a different type of sentence for the same offence but for welfare reasons. As a compromise it satisfied few and was open to the scorn of many. Some critics pointed to the high reconviction rates, and others insisted that penal institutions such as the approved schools were seen to be marking time. As a compromise it was an easy target for attack, and few felt able to defend a system that had apparently so little to offer.

Yet in spite of, or perhaps because of, those ambiguities, the system still operated reasonably well as far as the requirements of justice were concerned. In retrospect it was probably an advance on the present system. The Ingleby Committee, therefore, was right to have reservations about changes. The Committee recognized that it is always possible to produce a more logical system, but feared that its implementation could paradoxically produce more ambiguities than before. Few who criticized the juvenile court system prior to 1969 saw a return to more retributive methods as a feasible alternative. And so treatment offered the only possibility of advance.

As a method of juvenile justice, retributive controls contain the obvious advantages noted in earlier chapters. Retribution (and deterrence also) requires an assumption of desert based on some degree of blameworthiness, even though that assumption is suspect owing to the age and likely sense of responsibility of the child. Even so, retributive controls determine the extent of intervention in children's lives and act as an accepted feature of court procedure. Children, it appears, accept and believe that retribution is the only justification for punishment. So apparently do their parents. In one of the few empirical studies to determine the child's and parents' view, Miles Hapgood found a finely attuned appreciation of retribution. He was able to demonstrate that sentencing decisions were more likely to be viewed as fair when taken according to tariff considerations than when based on principles of individualized justice (Hapgood, 1979, p. 508). Parents were no more disposed to the treatment model. They too believed that there should be a relationship between the offence and the sentence.

Of course, asking children what they thought of their sentences could easily appear to be vulgar popularism. In questions concerning punishment it may be inappropriate to canvass the views of the recipients. Punishment is imposed rather than bargained about. Yet for too long we have made assumptions about children that may be incorrect and have assumed that children are incapable of perceiving differences that we take as given. The Ingleby Committee was aware of this when it considered the difficulties that children face in distinguishing between treatment and punishment — a problem basic to their compromise. The Committee thought that the confusion often led to a belief on the part of the child that he had been unfairly treated. Such feelings, said the Committee, result from the nature of the situation and were probably inevitable. Their solution: the feelings should be expelled by explanations as far as it is possible to do so. But explanations for these matters seem hardly sufficient. How does one tell a child, or an adult too for that matter, that the length of time to be served in a penal institution results from a conflict between principles of punishment and welfare?

If Hapgood's results are generalizable, and they are sufficiently plausible to suggest that this might be so, there is still the thorny problem of the child's welfare based on assumptions that the child is a member of a vulnerable group. It is not easy to escape from this, and I do not think we should try. Here I only wish to acknowledge the point and argue that previous attempts to juxtapose the retributive/welfare philosophies were found wanting, and all proposed solutions pointed to a more logical system which emphasized the child's vulnerability. These solutions involved a move towards treatment and welfare with a correspondingly minimum of retributive controls.

The shift towards treatment was inevitable given the spirit of the times and the accepted failings of the previous system. By the late 1960s juvenile justice in Britain was to be dominated by a philosophy that accentuated the perceived needs of the child. The argument was not new. As far back as 1928 it was asserted during a House of Commons debate that 'the modern version was not that punishment should fit the crime, but that treatment should be fitted to the mentality of the offender. That is the new doctrine, and a very much more desirable one than the old rigid rule that a certain crime merited a certain definite punishment' (quoted in Bean, 1975). This point has been reaffirmed over four decades; that punishment is sterile but treatment is new, imaginative and humane.

Finally, there is the argument that for want of a better name we can call decriminalization, or the means by which offenders are administratively removed from legal jurisdiction. With children the argument assumes an importance over and above that for adults. Many commentators on juvenile justice have insisted that a great deal of juvenile crime is not crime in the usual sense of that term, but is more akin to 'naughtiness'. All children, particularly boys, are said to be naughty and to behave in ways likely to break the law. 'Naughtiness' lacks the heavier moral connotations of criminality, and it is thereby assumed to be a transient phase in a child's development. Frequently one hears comments to the effect that all children are involved in naughtiness at some time, implying that it is unfair that some children are selected for criminalization. The argument is not without its merits but does not show how to distinguish between crimes that are 'naughty' and crimes that are 'crimes'.

A related argument concerns the stigma attached to criminal proceedings. Accepting that some children are 'naughty', it has been suggested that it is unfair for children to carry around with them the previous convictions recorded in a juvenile court for offences that reflect childhood behaviour.[7] Similarly, it is argued that for those offences that could be called 'crimes' a child should not be expected to have a criminal record for behaviour that may be transient or reflect a particular stage of development. This argument has been accepted in principle for some four decades, for under Section 53 of the 1933 Act children are said to have not 'previous convictions' but 'findings of guilt', which are not to be evaluated in the same light. The legal solution is an acknowledgement of the deterrent argument but presented in a weak form. It meets the criticisms neither of the 'decriminalizers' nor of those supporting deterrence. It could I think be usefully abandoned, or if not then amended in such a way that all juvenile court appearances cease to be resurrected once the child reaches adult status.

Another strand of the same type of argument is based on the view that the court appearance itself deepens criminality in some way, or does some form of irreparable damage. It is not clear how nor why. The argument goes as follows.

> I want to ensure not only that young children are not charged with having committed a crime — which is important — but that as far as possible we shall keep young children out of courts altogether. This is the important thing. It is not just the nature of the charge made in court; it is the appearance in court which can do so much damage to a young child. [quoted in Bottoms, 1974, p. 326]

If 'damage' means that the child retains a live impression of the court appearance, it is difficult to see why this should be regarded as objectionable. On utilitarian grounds this would presumably be a major instrument in deterrence. If the argument is that 'damage' is created by criminalizing minor indiscretions (or for what one modern sociologist has called 'Micky Mouse' offences), then this is something else again. If so why use the term 'damage?' However, a more sinister implication lurks behind this and all other decriminalizing arguments, for if children with less serious offences are not to be prosecuted does not this increase the stigma for those who are? Decriminalization could quickly lead to the juvenile court becoming an institution of last resort, resembling a warehouse dealing with incorrigibles.

The value of the decriminalization argument is that it offered a view of juvenile offences as a reflection of normal processes of development. It has been picked up subsequently by those supporting treatment and has been turned into an argument in a way never intended originally. Supporters of treatment have always viewed the juvenile court with suspicion and eagerly latched on to arguments that supported their case. Those who wanted to keep children out of the court did not necessarily believe in treatment but found their position taken over by the treatment lobby.

TREATMENT IN JUVENILE JUSTICE

A modern version of the treatment philosophy, at least as far as it applies to the juvenile court, has been provided by the British Association of Social Workers (BASW). The arguments are worth stating in full.

> It is doubtful whether any child makes a conscious effort to be a criminal. An accumulation of social and psychological factors and circumstances predisposes him to criminality. If punishment could help rehabilitate him its use may be justified. It does not seem to do so. It is, therefore, surely inappropriate to punish young offenders for behaviour for which they are hardly responsible.

Or again:

> The government should make a firm public commitment to the principle that young offenders need help and not punishment and that the 1969 Children and Young Persons Act affords a splendid means of assisting and treating the delinquent whose problems are mainly of an emotional or inter-familial nature. [Minutes of Evidence to Expenditure Committee, paras. 5.58 and 6.52, pp. 220 and 222]

It is not necessary to make a detailed criticism of these statements although certain inconsistencies can be recognized. For example, there are many assertions about the aetiological nature of juvenile criminality and about the supposed lack of intent by juvenile offenders that are questionable. The BASW evidence closely resembles Plato's arguments: that no one willingly does wrong; that vice is the expression of a disease of the soul; and that treatment should rest with the Guardians.

The 1969 Act was not an isolated piece of legislation but one reflecting a wider debate about the role and position of social work in modern society generally. In Scotland the Kilbrandon Report had earlier recommended the transformation of juvenile justice to a panel system; in England and Wales the Seebohm Report in 1971 had led to the Local Authority Social Services Act 1970 and to the formation of social services departments. Hitherto social work had been directed towards specific problem areas, administered, staffed and financed by specific organizations. The Social Services Act provided a new organization which operated as an umbrella and included all forms of social need within. Juvenile justice was readily included and became part of a comprehensive family-orientated social work service. Indeed, the terms of reference of the various committees were such as to make their reports complementary, and given the ethos at the time it would have been inconsistent to do otherwise. The Probation and After-Care Service, traditionally responsible for juvenile offenders, was obliged to abdicate its position within the juvenile court, for it was said to be too tainted with criminality and not sufficiently linked to a family service.

Treatment, social work and juvenile justice became one and the same thing. The court *qua* court was retained but with limited powers. The care order was to be the sole custodial sentence — for offenders and endangered children alike — but the provisions to phase out the use of borstal and detention centres for children under the age of 17 have not been implemented (in 1980). The care order is a semi-indeterminate sentence which can last until the child is 18, and in exceptional circumstances until 19 (Section 21 (1)). Care orders are orders made by the court but operated by local authorities whose duties are 'to receive a child into their care and notwithstanding any claim by his parent or guardian to keep him in their care while the order or warrant is in force' (Section 24). While in care the local authority 'shall have the same powers and duties with respect to a person in their care by virtue of a care order . . . and may restrict his liberty to such extent as the authority consider appropriate' (Section 24 (2)). Care orders follow the principles stated by BASW, i.e. the demand for a family-based service to meet the problem of delinquency which 'are mainly of an emotional or inter-familial nature'.

The major non-custodial sentence is the supervision order

(Section 11), with powers granted to the court to include requirements (Section 12) such as

> (a) directions requiring the supervised person to live for a single period specified in the directions at a place so specified;
> (b) directions given from time to time requiring him to do all or any of the following things:
>
> (i) to live at a place or places specified in the directions for a period or periods so specified
> (ii) to present himself to a person or persons specified in the directions at a place or places and on a day or days so specified
> (iii) to participate in activities specified with directions on a day or days so specified
>
> but it shall be for the supervisor to decide whether and to what extent he exercises any power to give directions . . . [Section 12(2)]

There are no sanctions for children who break the conditions of their supervision order.

The care order provides treatment in institutions; the supervision order provides treatment in the community. Both are designed and framed to be operated by local authority social workers. The principles underpinning the supervision order are the same as for care orders, and follow the assumptions of those supporting a family-based service. The courts have powers to make the orders, but it is up to the local authority Social Services Department to decide how and under what circumstances the system operates. The care order and supervision order have been selected for closer examination because they are the major forces of sentencing available to the juvenile court. They operate for offenders and endangered children alike. Of course the 1969 Act is more complicated than this, but for these purposes the necessary points can be made using the care order and supervision orders as illustrative.

First, and with the benefit of hindsight, it seems hardly credible that any government should believe that this form of treatment, or indeed any other form of treatment, could do anything about the overall problem of juvenile crime and the increasing crime rate. The expressed aim of the 1969 Act was to reduce juvenile offending, but since reform concentrates on the offender, its effects must inevitably be limited. Furthermore, there is no empirical evidence to support treatment, whether for juveniles or adults, although a small number of studies have produced results against the general trend. The poor results are now well known and have been stated countless times. It was therefore naive to believe that treatment programmes would be effective in reducing delinquency.

Second, the assumptions behind the family-based service are that delinquency is a product of maladjustment within the family. It may well be so in some cases, but this is hardly sufficient to produce a general theory of crime prevention. Even if it were so, the specific features of family life that predispose to delinquency are not discussed in the Act, nor does the Act make or imply a theoretical connection between the offence and the morality of the crime. Yet it will not do to assume that the child will learn a moral code from his peers or through some treatment programme, however family-based, unless there is a commitment to morality within that programme. I know of no discussion about such a commitment, and would not expect there to be, for it is against the spirit of treatment to include moral training. Yet children do not pick up morality as they go along, or pluck it out of a vacuum: they need to be taught it as they need to be taught other social skills. A child may well be more disposed to moral ideas if he is not maladjusted and not hostile to adults, but this is only part of the process. Modern methods of treatment emphasize the value of psychological insights. They need not do so, for there is nothing to say that a visit from a psychotherapist or social worker is the only method of reform of juvenile offenders. Conceivably, educational training or trade training, or perhaps even poetry reading, would do just as well. That we concentrate on one version rather than the other is a matter of social custom mixed with a deeply held belief that therapy is the most effective. In Britain the treatment of offenders is controlled by social workers trained in therapeutic techniques. Other aspects, such as educational or moral training, are either adjuncts to the main theme or are not included.

Third, terms like 'care order' or 'supervision order', mask the nature of the enterprise. They become deceitful if there is a corresponding refusal to acknowledge that treatment involves punishment. The deceit has been most succinctly illuminated by Francis Allen when he says that the business of the juvenile court, like that of all other courts, consists of dispensing punishment. He suggests that a candid recognition of this fact avoids confusion and ambiguity. For, as he says, whatever one's motives, however elevated one's objectives, if the measures taken result in a compulsory loss of the child's liberty or the separation of the child from his family, or even in the supervision of a child's activities by a social worker, the impact on the affected individual is essentially a punitive one. Good intentions and a flexible vocabulary, says Allen, do not alter that reality (Allen, 1964, p. 18).

Indeed they do not. Punishment involves the infliction of suffering brought about when certain ills have been done, and whenever that suffering is imposed on a person against his will it cannot be covered up or denied by the use of terms that suggest otherwise. Therein lies the deceit. It makes no difference to say that a supervision order involves benefits for the child, or that a period in a community home under a care order is beneficial, when the supervision order or care order has been imposed initially against a person's will. It is the imposition of an order that involves the suffering. The gains, anticipated or otherwise, are incidental.

The most obvious example of this elementary confusion exists in Scotland under the Children's Hearing System, which was set up by the Social Work (Scotland) Act 1968 along the lines suggested by the Kilbrandon Report (HMSO, 1964). The Kilbrandon Committee rejected the 'crime—punishment concept' arguing for a 'new alternative' which in the words of the Act requires a sentencing panel to consider the course to be decided in the best interests of the child. The methods to be used are 'the continuing application, by persuasive action, of skilled advice and guidance, with the aim of evoking in turn from the parties concerned a constructive response, based on an increased awareness and understanding of their underlying problems and responsibilities' (HMSO, 1964, para. 88). But what happens when no such awareness arises? The panel must, of course, impose its will, and we are then back to simple punishment again. The will of the panel must prevail, for the aim of any panel system is to reduce juvenile delinquency. This was the basic question addressed by the Kilbrandon Committee, and the panel hearings are methods to achieve this aim (Campbell, 1977). Neither will it do to say that the present sentence is not punishment because it is concerned with the best interests of the child. Take the example given by Campbell, who poses the situation of a child conducting a flourishing blackmail business. Here we may take the child into 'care' or some similar institution 'in his best interests'. Yet as Campbell points out, in this and in most other cases it is principally *society's* interests, not the child's, that are at stake and his interests are simply identified with those of society. Those supporting treatment would perhaps argue that the child should be placed in care in order that he is to be helped to stop blackmailing because society will inflict punishment on him as an adult if he does not change his way now. But this means the hearings are currently inflicting compulsory treatment to avoid punishment later, and by doing so show that children are part of a wider system of punishments (Campbell, 1977, p. 82).

So an elementary confusion prevails. The BASW proposals exemplify this when they say 'the government should make a firm public commitment to the principle that young offenders need help not punishment'. The BASW proposals start from the premise that the children's institutions are therapeutic, and under those circumstances it is inappropriate to see the child as requiring protection. (For the same reason, it would be as absurd to see the child being punished by medical staff because he was physically ill.) If of course one believes that the impact on the child is essentially punitive, then different considerations apply. And, it must be admitted that some children may see the institutions in the way described by the treatment officials. Not all see them as punitive; some may welcome the protection they afford. This does not weaken the main point; it merely shows that some children prefer the punitive environment of the care order to the lack of safety provided in their home.

The confusion is exacerbated by the method of 'flexibility' in sentencing. Under the 1969 Act it is possible that a child under a care order could be detained for nearly nine years, which had he been an adult and sentenced according to retributive principles, would have been far less. In the Scottish system a booklet, *Childrens' Hearings: Questions and Answers,* states that 'a child who has committed a very slight offence . . . may have to reside away from home because he displays problems which his own home cannot help him with' (quoted in Campbell, 1977, p. 79). A psychiatrist, Dr J. Gunn, notes that the 'period of imprisonment which would be awarded on punitive grounds alone using the tariff system can frequently be less than a period of secure management thought necessary on medical grounds. It is then possible for a doctor to find himself recommending longer sentences than retribution would require' (Gunn, 1971). To protest that this is gross unfairness can be met by the retort that 'unfairness' is essentially a reaction from those supporting punishment. It has no place in the affairs of those supporting treatment.

The flexibility in the juvenile justice system raises the spectre of semi-indeterminate sentences and release by executive decision. Take for example the youth treatment centres, which are closed units intended to act as institutions for young people who require 'care and treatment in secure conditions'. Originally they were intended for the reception of children subject to Approved School Orders (under the 1933 Act), but later they were extended to cover care orders under the 1969 Act. The care order incorporated a much wider range of children, and by 1979 youth treatment centres were taking children who had been committed to care by voluntary agreement. Almost a third were in care as non-offenders (DHSS 1979a, p. 66). In a pointed attack on the youth treatment centre the DHSS researchers argue that the starting point for their criticisms 'probably lies in the influence of the medical or disease model of social work practice'. The report goes on:

> The product of the medical model . . . seemed to be the constant passing on of children to others considered more 'expert' or 'specialized'; the perpetuations of myths about 'diagnosis', 'treatment' or 'cure' at the expense of 'care'; the justification of a control and containment decision — a practice which we deplore when it happens on the other side of the Iron Curtain — and the use of therapeutic euphemisms which indicate unwillingness to face the reality that children were being locked up for extended periods occasionally in solitary confinement. [DHSS, 1979a, pp. 228-9]

It is perhaps this 'unwillingness to face the reality' that constitutes the most serious criticisms of rehabilitation within the juvenile justice system, although in the quote above it is the 'constant passing on of children to others considered more expert', which creates the movement towards extending closed institutions. Yet punishment, judicial or otherwise, relies on an awareness that suffering is being inflicted for a wrong done. And because it involves inflicting suffering it requires justification. It does not mean that people, whether they be children or not, should be dealt with as if they were capable of manipulation. It is a great pity that the very qualities of our society that include liberty and respect for others are weakened by our eagerness to provide children with expert help — and at the same time fail to appreciate the dangers of so doing. Juvenile offenders may not always be responsible for their actions in the same way that adults are, but they are entitled to similar respect. Too often 'treatment' reduces their dignity by making them capable of manipulation and at the same time making them unable to retaliate against an enveloping bureaucracy whose outward aim is to offer and provide help. It is difficult enough for adults to show the weakness of this doctrine, but how much more so is it for children unaccustomed to the nuances and hidden meanings that this entails? This is not an argument or plea for a particular philosophy of punishment, but a demand for a candid recognition of the 'serpent-windings' of treatment and the dangers of constantly proclaiming that rights are synonymous with therapy.

However, the position of the juvenile offender is a good deal less complicated than that of the endangered child — a term used here in preference to the more common one of 'beyond control' or 'exposed to moral danger'. The term 'endangered' is a catch-all term covering those whose appearance before the juvenile court is a civil rather than criminal nature.

THE ENDANGERED CHILD

Phylida Parsloe notes that the endangered child was already subject to legal controls before the modern juvenile court system was introduced (Parsloe, 1978, p. 121). The civil side of the British juvenile court dates from the Industrial Schools Act of 1854, which applied to Scotland, and the 1857 Act, which applied to England and Wales. These and later Acts empowered magistrates to commit vagrant children and young persons to industrial schools if their parents regarded them as incorrigible; the Act also gave powers to commit those who associated with criminals, or were themselves criminals and convicted of criminal offences (Parsloe, 1978, p. 121). These Acts incorporated and extended powers previously contained in the Poor Law.

Status offenders, or endangered children, are controlled by existing legislation and broadly speaking can be divided roughly into two groups: those who are victims of adult offences, such as the victims of family cruelties, and those whose behaviour is likely to lead to immorality, such as being away from home and/or mixing with adult criminals. Children who fail to attend school are included in the second category. Few of us would, I think, wish to remove all forms of legal protection, as some children may require assistance against those who are cruel or exploit them. The problem is how to deal with them once protection is given.

All modern juvenile justice systems have included the endangered child. Definitions of endangered vary; in Britain they are relatively narrow, but in North America they are wider. Generally, the endangered child can be seen as having *his* rights violated in contrast to the offender, who violates others. This definition is not complete, for there are some instances where endangered children have violated others' rights (i.e. offenders below the prosecutable age), and some where no rights have as yet been violated (i.e. those children who have run away from home). For these purposes, however, the definition is adequate as it conveys the major distinctions between the two groups.

In the more serious cases endangered children are taken away from their homes and placed in institutions under a care order or its equivalent. Regrettably, they may see this as punishment, and the stigma attached to institutional life as a 'state-raised kid' is a further price to be paid for protection. And yet I do not see how these particular problems can be readily avoided. Some children would be in serious danger unless the State intervened, and although children may dislike intervention, I cannot see how any society can stand by and ignore them.

Of itself, the plight of these children is bad enough, but it is not helped by modern thinking which insists that there is no qualitative difference between the deprived and the depraved. Originally the link was established by Mary Carpenter in the nineteenth century, who argued that no worthwhile distinction could be made between pauper and penal children. She preferred to concentrate on current behaviour than dwell on past excesses. Her aim was to produce 'character' where punishments were the natural consequences of present disobedience. Mary Carpenter's views were an extension of her religious beliefs, which saw all children as 'God's children capable of leading useful lives', provided that is they were given the appropriate training.

The modern view is founded on the assumptions relating to the aetiology of delinquency. Joel Handler calls this the 'unified theory of deviance', whereby all behavioural problems can be traced back to defective relationships in early childhood (Handler, 1973). It matters not that the problems can be as varied as attempted suicide, broken marriage, criminality or truancy, for the roots are all to be found in early childhood experiences. On this basis 'the depraved' and 'the deprived' are said to have the same aetiology.

The White Paper preceding the 1969 Children and Young Persons

Act gave official approval to the unified theory of deviance. Endangered children and criminal children were to be classified as 'in trouble' (HMSO, 1968). 'Trouble' was an indication of maladjustment or immaturity, or a symptom of a damaged or abnormal personality. According to the White Paper, juvenile delinquency has no single cause manifestation or cure, for 'at some point it merges almost imperceptibly with behaviour that does not contravene the law' (HMSO 1968, para. 6). The Kilbrandon Report adopted a similar position when it saw the offences as having significance only as a pointer to the need for intervention (HMSO, 1964, para. 71).

The 1968 White Paper was reiterating an argument by the Departmental Committee that preceded the 1933 Act:

> In many cases the tendency to commit offences is only the outcome of neglect and there is little room for discrimination either in the character of the young person concerned or in the appropriate treatment. [HMSO, 1927, para. 71]

Not everyone saw it that way. Phillida Parsloe cites evidence given to a committee on criminal and destitute juveniles where it was suggested that the deprived and depraved should be kept apart. Without separation there would be 'a tendency to provoke most injurious comparisons between both parties'. This would lead to 'a risk of lowering the general standard of moral feelings as to crime and the necessary punishment of crime among the workhouse children if they were to be associated without any restriction with those who had been sent to prison and punished' (quoted in Parsloe, 1978, p. 122). In an earlier paragraph the same witness drew a distinction between depravity and deprivation on the grounds that the former had been convicted for offences, mainly dishonesty.

A few modern critics would agree. Richard Sparks asserts that differences between offenders and endangered is that one commits offences and the other does not (Sparks, 1969). In a similar vein Rod Ryall wishes to preserve differences by regarding law-breaking as having distinctive features (Ryall, 1974). Ryall's basic point is a challenge to the assumption that delinquency is a symptom of underlying personal maladjustment. While some delinquents may exhibit signs of emotional disturbance, and some endangered children have committed delinquent acts, to bracket both groups is to Ryall to take an unjustified conceptual leap. Delinquent behaviour can be a habit, with its own rewards of excitement, peer group status and material gain, which may generate the inclination for further offences. The endangered child has no such rewards. If Ryall is right, the type of care offered may be inappropriate for the endangered child if care is aimed at frustrating criminal values — and, if not, then inappropriate to the criminal child.

Unlike their nineteenth-century counterparts, modern writers are rarely concerned about 'lowering general standards of moral feelings'. However, the earlier point remains, for once the endangered and the offenders are placed together it is difficult for either group to assess the reasons for being there. How are they to view a situation where children are placed in the same institution for different types of behaviour, and where it is possible that one — the endangered child — remains longer than the criminal? The system becomes patently unfair. Of course, if the aim is to devise treatment to meet the child's 'needs', then, again, fairness is of less importance, and if both groups exhibit different symptoms with the same 'disease', then fairness is also inappropriate.

Can it be so unimportant? It will not do to say the distinction between the two groups is accidental, or that the endangered child may only be lucky enough not to have been caught committing an offence (*Hansard,* 1932, vol. 261, p. 1179). Even if it were true, we do not deprive people of their liberty because some are lucky enough not to get caught. It will not do either to assert that the final treatment outcome is the ultimate consideration, or that questions about punishment are irrelevant to the endangered child. While it is true that the juvenile court sits as a civil rather than criminal court, the sentences are similar and the endangered child is placed *within* the prison system even if we call it by a different name. Moreover, the 1969 Children and Young Persons Act provides facilities for the endangered child to be removed to borstal. Section 31(2) states that the court may, if it is satisfied that the child's behaviour is such that it will be detrimental to the persons accommodated in any community home, order the child to be removed to a borstal institution. Borstals are run by the Prison Department and intended for the recovery of young adult offenders from established criminal habits. The child may also go to a youth treatment centre, with a maximum security system more imposing than most prisons, and yet need never have been convicted of an offence.

We can readily acknowledge Francis Allen's point that there is no distinction between a court that directs its efforts to doing something *to* a child because of what he has done and a court concerned with doing something *for* a child because of what he is and needs (Allen, 1964, p. 19). In an authoritative setting doing something *for* a child is also doing something *to* him. Nor can we easily ignore Garafolo's comment that the mere deprivation of liberty, however benign, is undeniably punishment. When those provisions are replicas of prisons we are involved in an acute form of punishment.

PROPOSALS TO AMEND THE CRIMINAL SYSTEM FOR JUVENILES

From the British standpoint, interest in juvenile justice has, until recently, been regarded as peripheral to the criminologist's task. The Children and Young Persons Act changed this and drew together a number of disparate critics, all offering specific solutions. The proposed solutions are varied. Some are pragmatic, concentrating on specifics such as youth treatment centres and calling for a limitation on the number of places available. Others suggest that custody ought never to be inflicted unless it is necessary for the protection of the public and where a clear advantage can be secured by removal from the community. Still others, such as the Justice's Clerks Society, call for increasing power to be given to the courts for example to provide sanctions for the supervision order, thereby making it more like the older probation order; or for amending the care order to allow the courts to decide on the institution in which the offender should reside (HMSO, 1975b). Others want the range of sentences to be increased, i.e. many that exist only for adult offenders to be made available for juveniles too. The community service order is the obvious example here.

The ever-increasing clamour for change is part of a growing sense of dissatisfaction with the modern form of juvenile justice. As it stands, juvenile justice has few supporters except social workers or their representatives, who reply to their critics by blaming the defects on the lack of resources and the shortage of staff. The Association of Directors of Social Services (ADSS) tenaciously cling to the treatment model and are opposed to proposals that:

> (a) differentiate further between those young people who offend and those who do not because experience is that it is often a matter of chance which young people come to the notice of the social services

because of delinquency, emotional problems, or family and personal problems

(b) focus on lines of demarcation between agencies rather than concentrating upon providing a network of services for young people and maximising the opportunity for inter-agency cooperation. [ADSS, 1980]

One of their proposals is to introduce a Youth Contract Order lasting between one and three years. This order would operate in a similar way to the Scottish system. Their proposals illustrate an obdurate refusal to acknowledge that punishment is imposed by an authority for an offence on an offender.

The Association gives details of the Youth Contract Order:

> The necessary individual and specific nature of the contract implies that once the magistrates have indicated their desire and intention to make such an order the family, young person and services involved would need to meet to prepare a draft contract. There would then be an adjourned hearing of the court at which the Branch would consider and amend the contract as necessary; having secured the agreement of all parties to the contract they could 'seal it' so that it takes the effect of an order. [ADSS, 1980, p. 5]

More theoretical solutions are proposed by Phyllida Parsloe, who wants 'a continuous debate where those involved in the juvenile justice system recognize and balance the competing and important demands of the criminal justice, welfare and community approaches' (1978, p. 282). Others demand a less ambiguous system, where the court is committed either to welfare or justice but not to both, for this is said to produce confusion. In a manner that hints almost of desperation, some writers have argued that a child has a right to be punished (Fox, 1974). This argument was earlier proposed by the President's Crime Commission, who wanted treatment 'to descend from its monopolistic position in juvenile justice and be incorporated with other goals of the system' (US President's Commission, 1967). Sandford Fox wants to extend the argument to include 'the complete banishment of treatment in juvenile justice and substitute it for the right of the child to punishment'. Fox's position relates directly to Hegel, who thought the criminal was 'honoured as reasonable because punishment was regarded as containing his own right' (Hegel, 1967, para. 100), and to Bosanquet when he said that penal action upon a criminal should be regarded as an expression of his own will since it is entailed in maintenance of a system to which he is himself a party and in which he has a vital interest. Under those conditions, said Bosanquet, punishment is his right which must not be defrauded (1965, p. 211).

Yet Fox, it seems, is not so much advancing the case of the child's right to receive punishment as arguing that the child should avoid treatment. Fox also wants a further right that no child may be subjected to punishment, or other forms of deprivation, for refusing to accept treatment. This is a right that Fox insists must be accompanied by adequate institutional means of enforcement. But if Fox means that children ought to be punished rather than treated then so be it, although it is not the same as saying that children have that right to punishment. Once he asserts they have this right to punishment he is pushed back to a Hegelian view that punishment is preferable and of some value; that it gives the child the possibility of maintaining standards that he has transgressed. Why then did he not suggest a retributive position, which would have led him to the Kantian view that 'no one undergoes punishment because he has willed to be punished, but because he has willed a punishable action' (Kant, 1897, p. 201)?

Other solutions have focused on a Bill of Rights for children which would place limits on the intervention permitted in children's lives. Sanford Fox has been prominent in this debate also. He greatly fears behaviour modification programmes, including the so-called 'aversive conditioning' programmes, which he says punctuate learning experience with 'just the right amount of excruciating pain' (Fox, 1974, p. 4). He also fears the later technologies which use brain implants, which interface directly with the computer to programme behaviour patterns. (These operate in such a way that, should the offender show a pattern of electrical brain activity characteristic of a sexual or aggressive urge, space-age telemetry automatically provides him with a disabling headache, or a paralysis, or unconsciousness. 'Choose your programme', says Fox, 1974, p. 5.) Treatment, according to Fox has no theoretical limits imposed on the type or use of such methods. He argues that limits ought to be imposed. In Britain the movement has included a charter which has been drawn up by a group of children in care where they 'claim the right to choose those who will offer representation whether it be legal or otherwise' and 'the right to be as much a part of society as the next person and not to be labelled in any way. In short to live' (National Children's Bureau, 1977).

Others advance the argument for a general Bill of Rights for children. The White House Conferences on Children recommended the right to have healthy and employed parents and the right to a competent school and to decent nutrition, etc. In Canada, section 39 of the Quebec Charter of Human Rights and Freedom states that 'Every child has a right to the protection, security and attention that must be provided to him by his family or the persons acting in their stead.'

The Canadian Charter, like many of the United States charters, possess symbolic significance but does not contain rights that are readily enforceable. These charters contain rights of a high order of generality, which at best provide an ethical requirement on governments to maintain standards. The Children's Rights movement contains many strands of opinion varying from those who wish to provide rights of a high order of generality to those who wish to grade rights according to the child's capacities to make decisions. Finally, there are the permissive group: those who wish to advance children's rights to the point where they are not distinguishable from that of adults. Here the aim 'is to maximize freedoms and liberties for children according to the child's own wants and desires' (Leon, 1978, p. 6).

The Children's Rights movement follows a wider movement in modern society to produce a Bill of Rights aimed at protecting the individual from the incursions of the State. Lord Hailsham has proposed a Bill of Rights for Britain, and, more specifically, N. N. Kittrie has proposed a Therapeutic Bill of Rights for mental patients (see Bean, 1980). However, the problem for children is that a Bill of Rights does not stop them being dependent on adults. Any code devised to support children's rights must involve adults who are capable of seeing when rights are violated and advising and representing them in any disputes. So children remain dependent on adults to make their important decisions.

In making this criticism I am avoiding the more delicate arguments about Rights, that is about whether the movement is about natural rights of children or legal rights. They differ; the former involving the debate about the existence and nature of natural rights, the latter involving the question of rights related to legal procedures. And yet the Children's Rights movement contains within it an important moral question. 'What are the legitimate justifications for giving one human being power over nurture, training and experience of another?'

(Coons and Mnookin, 1978, p. 392). Furthermore, what ought to be the nature of that power? And, should the child commit offences, what ought to be the limits of intervention within which adults operate? The Children's Rights movement have asked these questions and it is to their credit that they have done so.

SOME PROPOSALS FOR CHANGE

Here I wish to produce some personal suggestions for change. Obviously, given the nature of this enquiry, the overriding assumption is that the debate must be about punishment. From this assumption, a number of general principles emerge. First, there is to be recognition that juvenile justice for offenders *means* inflicting punishment. Once this is accepted certain others automatically follow; for example, there will be no further attempts to deceive; there will be a constant demand for justifications; there will be a recognition that punishment in Ross's terms involves a threat and not a promise of future rewards (Ross, 1930, p. 63). Furthermore, there will be no other attempts to link juvenile justice to a family-based service, for this avoids or obscures the nature of the courts' authority and the imposition of suffering.

Second, punishments are for an offence, actual or supposed. This means the *offence* is the major criterion for imposing suffering, and not the background or the needs of the child. It means also that punishments are always methods of establishing social control and that law is an instrument designed to that end. If the offence is considered to be the major criterion, then punishments must be fair, and above all must be seen to be fair.

Third, and following from this, there should be no situation in which the punishment of a child should exceed that likely to be given to an adult. If children are less responsible for their actions, then they should be punished less, not more. I am not suggesting that children should receive the same types of punishment as adults, for that would be a retrograde step. Clearly, children ought not to be kept in the same types of institutions as adults; what I am saying is that, where an adult would have received a custodial sentence of (say) three months, children should not receive more.

Fourth, there is the thorny question of responsibility. As the legal position stands at present, responsibility is accorded to age. *Prima facie,* this seems reasonable. Yet I have the impression that juvenile courts rarely attempt to assess responsibility although it seems to be of some importance. To do so would place more emphasis on the nature of the offence and less on the punishment.

These four principles should be seen in relation to the other tentative conclusions given in the final chapter. They have been suggested here because they apply specifically to children and operate over and above those suggested later. We now come to the other thorny question of the endangered child, which seems to be the most intractible problem of all.

We can begin by noting that endangered children often require protection but sometimes are reluctant to leave a hostile family even if they are in danger. Most children will see protection as punishment, particularly if the child is taken from home by order of a court. It may not be punishment in the strictest sense of the term — suffering imposed for an offence committed — but it approximates to it. Lawyers such as Francis Allen would argue that doing something *for* a child is to do something *to* him, which is punishment, albeit in a weakened form. Over and above this, the problems of the endangered child are age-related; by that I mean that endangered children under the age of 10 pose different problems from those aged 14 or above. The older age group are more likely to view court orders as punishment, although provisions for all age groups involve the same test; that is to say, we are still doing something *to* them.

Various possible solutions arise. One is to retain the present system or even extend it. So if the unified theory of deviance is so attractive why confine it to children? What would be wrong with (say) detaining the mentally ill or attempted suicides in institutions where they could be transferred to prison if their behaviour was incorrigible? Why not make it a general rule that all deprived equal depraved — and extend the system to adult courts? We would rightly view such a suggestion as ridiculous — but not apparently for children.

Another possibility is to insist on a separation between endangered and criminal. If that were to occur it would need to take place at two levels: in the courts and in the penal institution. At the court level it would involve separating the offender from the endangered, possibly by way of a family court system where the juvenile court was left to deal with offenders. If there were no family court then the court sitting as a criminal court would be geographically and institutionally separate when it sits as a civil court. In the penal system the endangered would be separated from the criminal.

Consider now the case of a young child aged (say) 13, charged with an offence and coming from a deplorable background. If the system involved separation then that child would be dealt with for his offence. The sentence would be based on the assumptions mentioned above. What then does the court do about the child's background? The answer would be that the background would be irrelevant to the sentence for the offence, so if the child was endangered he would need to be recalled to the court, sitting as a civil court this time, to have his case heard as an endangered child. This would produce a distinction between punishment for an offence and a recognition by the court of its own aims and methods.

There are of course disadvantages. Suppose the child was fined for his offence and later taken away from home for being endangered. This would give the impression that the background was a more important feature and the distinction between punishment for the offence would then become blurred with perceived punishments for the background. Then there are the institutions themselves. It may not be possible or practical to provide two types of institutions offering qualitatively different regimes. There is likely to be a levelling effect where one becomes hardly distinguishable from the other in terms of personnel, facilities, etc. The child may be bemused when transferring from one to another seeing no difference.

Yet in spite of the disadvantages, the proposed system would be preferable to the current one, if only because it clears up the existing confusion. Inevitably there will be disadvantages, as no system dealing with children can ever be without them. We should not ask for a flawless system but should approach the question from the perspective of doing least harm.

Would it ever be possible to return the juvenile court to a court that emphasizes retribution or deterrence and minimizes treatment? Could children be sentenced for retributive or deterrent reasons? In the strictest sense, no, for there is always the problems of levels of responsibility, and as we have said before retribution and deterrence depend as theories on responsibility. But this would not prevent a partial system being introduced. By 'partial' I mean an emphasis on procedural forms rather than content. A number of examples will clarify the point.

First, consider retribution. It was stated earlier that some measures of retributive justice have been retained, such as the principle that the court must first try the case and determine whether what is alleged is proved. If a case fails for want of proof the court cannot act. In Britain juvenile courts have also retained some forms of procedural rules. It seems reasonable therefore to suggest that they be extended in such a way as to give the child the protection of retributive justice. So, for example, the tariff would determine the length of sentence and the procedural rules would determine guilt. Were these to be fitted into the suggestions made earlier a form of protection would be given. It would not be a fully retributive system, for the notion of 'deserts' would be adjusted according to levels of responsibility.

Consider also a utilitarian system. Here the emphasis would be placed on the law as a means of preventing mischief. To those objecting to such a view I would return to the example given earlier of the boy involved in blackmail. Would not a strong deterrent system help the child by deterring him from blackmail? Of course it would, but it is not fashionable nowadays to talk of prevention in this manner. If the deterrent argument were re-introduced it would be only 'partial deterrence', recognizing that those who were not deterred ought not to be judged in adult life for offences committed as children.

I would not advocate a rapid return to retribution or deterrence, but rather a slow step-by-step approach to assess the impact of the changes. The Gault decision began the process.[8] We still have a long way to go yet some changes are already being made. In Britain a White Paper on *Young Offenders* (HMSO, 1980) stated that 'the Government agrees with those who hold the view except with special circumstances of the life sentence (including detention under Section 53(1) of the Children's and Young Persons Act 1933) all sentences should be determinate so that the courts can mark the seriousness of the offence by the length of sentence they impose' (para. 11). This public acknowledgement to the strength of retribution was not always followed by certain subsequent proposals, which remain heavily steeped in the rehabilitative tradition (for example the use of intermediate treatment), but at least the White Paper makes a start. A cautious approach is to be welcomed, and a public affirmation of the move towards determinate sentences is in line with that cautious approach.

NOTES

1. The notes by Leo Goodman in *Clarke, Hall and Morrison on Children* (1972, pp. 14, 469, 981) provide an excellent account on this and other features relevant to legal provisions of punishment. For those wishing to pursue the legal position further see also Henston (1977, pp. 23-4, 348-59); Cretney, (1979, ch. 17); and Bromley (1976, ch. 10 (d)).
2. In this remarkable section of Kant's *Ethics* he asks how far has the human race progressed on the road to perfection? 'If we look at the most enlightened portion of the world, we see the various States armed to the teeth, sharpening their weapons in time of peace the one against the other. The consequences of this are such that they block our approach to the universal end of perfection' (Kant, 1930, p. 252). Kant argued that no prince has contributed one iota to the perfection of mankind, to inner happiness, or to the worth of humanity; all of them look ever and only to the prosperity of their own countries, making that their chief concern (p. 253). The hope for that better world, said Kant, was still distant. 'It will be many centuries before it can be realized.'
3. There is an active move to stop corporal punishment in schools, justified on the grounds that it is both degrading and ineffective. (STOPP, undated). While the methods of punishment may be an important area for discussion, few of those opposed to corporal punishment oppose all forms of punishment for children. Generally, opponents of corporal punishment wish to substitute less severe forms.
4. Bradley (1927) extends this argument in a section entitled 'Notes to Essay 1 (pp. 42-57), where Section A of those notes deals with 'Compulsion and Responsibility'. This section and ch. 1 repay careful study, even though the style is often irritating by Bradley's polemic and use of language. For a more updated argument see Ross (1975).
5. Phyllida Parsloe quotes Section 3 of the Illinois Act which gave the courts their name.

> In counties having over 500,000 population the judges of the circuit court shall, at such times as they shall determine designate one or more of their number whose duty it shall be to hear all cases coming under the Act. A special courtroom to be designated as the juvenile court room shall be provided for the hearing of such cases, and the findings of the court shall be entered in a book or books to be kept for the purpose and known as the 'Juvenile Record' and the court may for convenience be called the juvenile court. [Parsloe, 1978, p. 53]

While the first juvenile court began in England and Wales in 1908, the appropriate Act consolidated previous legislation for many features of the Act had already been implemented (Parsloe, 1978).
6. Many of the accounts make harrowing reading. See particularly HMSO (1979).

7. The juvenile liaison schemes which operate a formal cautioning procedure do much to decriminalize juvenile justice. Currently (1980) about one in three of all boys and one in five of all girls are formally cautioned. Yet the courts still deal with large numbers of children prosecuted for minor offences. It is not clear why this should be so.

8. The Gault decision is fully reported in US Presidents Commission on Law Enforcement (1967, pp. 57-76, Appendix A). The US Supreme Court stated that the juvenile court has virtually unlimited discretion in which the following basic rights are devoid: (a) notice of charges; (b) right to counsel; (c) right to confrontation and cross-examination; (d) privilege against self-incrimination; (e) rights to a transcript of the proceedings; and (f) right to appellate review (p. 59).

5

Modern Trends

Recent decades have been dominated by a belief that something could be done about the problem of crime. The assumptions underlying that belief stem from an optimistic view of the nature of society generally, and a similar view about human capacities. The growth of the social and behavioural sciences has assisted, or run parallel with, that belief. Whether it be the extreme optimism of Marxian theoreticians or the more muted optimism of social problems theorists, the belief has been sustained. Rehabilitation encapsulates that belief, but so too in its way does Benthamite philosophy. A strength, it seems to me, of retribution is that it is not always optimistic.

The search for solutions has led to some unexpected revelations. First, it has been found that the solutions themselves have become part of the new problem. The 1969 Children and Young Persons Act has not, as was hoped, reduced the levels of juvenile crime; rather, the Act itself and the methods of implementation *are* the new problems. It is not that the 1969 Act has made the situation marginally worse — for by any standards that is true — it is that the Act has become a problem in its own right. So too have similar pieces of legislation aimed at producing betterment, the 1959 Mental Health Act being the most obvious example (Bean, 1980).

Second, the search for solutions implies that solutions are obtainable and desirable. Yet Durkheim warned us that crime was normal and that levels of crime should be expected. He saw no solution as such, except the possibility of reducing crime from abnormally high levels or increasing it from abnormally low levels, although with uncharacteristic ingenuity he did not tell us what the normal levels were. However, he saw no possibility of a society without crime. Had the optimists addressed themselves to Durkheim's question, their arguments might have been realistic. Typically, they have sought to produce a society where there is no

153

crime, or to believe that all offenders are capable of personal regeneration. It will take a long time for criminologists to accept an alternative position, that penal institutions are not there solely to help offenders; de Tocqueville made the same point:

> I say it boldly: if the penitentiary system has no other purpose than reform the law giver we must abandon the system, not because it is not admirable but because it is too rarely attained. The moral reform of the individual is a great thing for the religious man but not for the statesman . . . [quoted in Moberly, 1968, p. 127]

It will also take a long time to abandon the view that every offender is a candidate for therapy, and to substitute it for an alternative — that all offenders are candidates for justice. Were this to be so some basic changes would be required in our thinking, not the least of which would be a candid recognition that the penal system may have little to do with the crime rates generally. But this is to anticipate a number of points to be made later. We can begin by looking briefly at some of the difficulties involved in using philosophies of punishment to examine the penal system.

DIFFICULTIES IN APPLYING PHILOSOPHIES OF PUNISHMENT TO THE PENAL SYSTEM

In spite of any scepticism one might have about the role of the penal system as a means of reducing the crime rate, at least to any significant degree, this scepticism has not been shared by the legislators. The period since 1945 has produced an unprecedented expansion in the number of sentences available to the courts, and between 1965 and 1980 the rate has accelerated. Deferred sentences, suspended sentences and community service orders have been introduced, among others. So also has parole. Not all have been aimed directly at reducing crime, except in the most general way. Sometimes economic pressures have dominated where the search has been to find cheaper methods of dealing with offenders, while sometimes a new sentence has been introduced to ease a specific problem such as the high levels in the prison population. But others have been introduced with greater expectations and more often than not have been followed by disappointment when the success rates failed to live up to the earlier optimism.

Even so, this has not stopped governments introducing new

measures or trying to refashion existing ones, according to a specific penal philosophy. But this is to oversimplify. The modern penal system, like the juvenile court is an institution of great complexity, where the sentences available to the courts contain within them a number of differing philosophies. It is no easy task to identify them. Some sentences may have been introduced under specific philosophical banners but have changed over time and incorporated new ones as they evolved. Then there is the task of identifying philosophies in the first place. The pronouncements of judges will not help. A judge may sentence an offender for (say) retributive reasons, but the organization to which the offender is committed has reduced retribution to a minimum and now emphasizes rehabilitation. Some sentences may have competing philosophies where one or perhaps two may dominate. Rarely does one find a sentence of the court that reflects one to the exclusion of others. Most people would, I think, agree that probation was reformist, but could not a probation order be a deterrent and perhaps retributive in part? What are we to make of community service orders or parole? Finally, there may be differences between the intended philosophies of an organization and the pereceived philosophies of the offender. The probation officer may see his contacts with the offender as reformist but the offender sees the requirements of the probation order as retributive. As there are no objective criteria to assess sentences, we have to resort inevitably to officially stated aims and research findings, and to interpret these as best we can. However, others may see it differently.

The aim in this chapter is to determine some of the effects the major philosophies of punishment have had on the modern penal system and to point to some future trends. We can begin by examining the impact of rehabilitation, for this has produced some of the most interesting results. The reaction against it, which often implies a return to retribution, will be discussed afterwards. This approach reverses the previous format where (as in Chapter 2) retribution was discussed first.

REHABILITATION AND THE MODERN
PENAL SYSTEM

The major contribution of rehabilitation has been towards the promotion of indeterminate and semi-indeterminate sentences, which for these purposes includes all those sentences that are individualized, and that are based on an assessment of the offenders' needs prior to sentence, and where the decision to end the sentence is based on an assessment of the offenders' personality and progress. Where indeterminate and semi-indeterminate sentences involve a period in custody, statutory after-care is provided; where they involve non-custodial measures, provisions are made for early discharge based on good progress.

Indeterminate and semi-indeterminate sentences are the logical extension of the rehabilitative philosophy. Indeed, the terms are synonymous. In Britain the movement towards indeterminacy reached its peak with the proposals of the Younger Committee, which recommended the abolition of all existing custodial sentences for young adult offenders, to be replaced by a semi-indeterminate custody and control order. The Committee also proposed a stricter supervision order with powers of short-term detention for supervised offenders *likely* to commit further offences (HMSO, 1974). These proposals have not been implemented.

The indeterminate sentence is a rarity in almost all penal systems. In Britain it takes the form of a life sentence which is confined by law to murder, for which it is mandatory, and to a few other serious offences, involving personal violence or sexual molestation (Walker, 1969, p. 127). Under Section 53 of the Children and Young Persons Act 1933, entitled 'Punishment of Certain Grave Crimes' (which includes murder), a juvenile may be 'detained during Her Majesty's Pleasure' (S. 53(1) as substituted by the Murder (Abolition of Death Penalty) Act 1965), which is in effect an indeterminate sentence.

Nigel Walker argues that 'there is no obvious theoretical reason why the indeterminate sentence should not be used for ordinary offences, such as theft or assault, but there are practical dangers' (1969, p. 127). Indeed there are. There is the obvious danger of its use for political purposes, and a further danger of an offender who has misbehaved in prison, or merely antagonized the staff, being kept longer than was justified. Indeterminate sentences have the effect of placing the offender in a more vulnerable position than under the determinate system. They also produce a grave sense of insecurity when the release date is not known in advance.

The justification for indeterminate sentences has varied over time. In the eighteenth and nineteenth centuries in continental Europe it was justified wholly on political grounds: that is, to incapacitate

certain dangerous political opponents. Similar justifications are use
today in some countries where the penal codes place special emphasis
on offences against the State. Indeterminate sentences have always
been a useful totalitarian device. In modern democratic societies they
are invariably linked to the concept of dangerousness, where
dangerousness may mean danger to self or to others. In the criminal
law 'danger to others' in the forms of violence or sexual assault is the
only justification for indeterminate sentences, although the 1959
Mental Health Act uses 'danger to self' as an acceptable criterion.

The American system, of indeterminate sentences linked to the
demands of treatment, has fortunately not been copied in Britain.
Had it been, the parole boards would have assumed a more dominant
position. In New York State, for example, the twelve members of the
parole board have jurisdiction over all prisoners serving more than
ninety days — a total well in excess of 20,000 — and can, among
other things, decide when and where to release a prisoner who is
serving any indeterminate sentence (Wilson, 1975, p. 171).
Conversely, the courts assume a less dominant position when
indeterminacy is strong.

In Britain the semi-indeterminate sentence is more common. By
semi-indeterminate I mean where a maximum and minimum period
is fixed by the court, but the decision to release is made by an
executive board within the allotted time span. A sentence of borstal
training is semi-indeterminate; it is for a period of between six
months and two years, and the offender is released some time during
that period, depending on training achievements. Parole as it operates
in Britain, is not part of a semi-indeterminate sentence strictly
speaking, but an administrative measure to provide early release for
offenders who were given specific sentences by the court. However,
the care order for juvenile offenders is clearly semi-indeterminate
(Sec. 1(3) of the 1969 Act).

Semi-indeterminate sentences have been largely confined to young
offenders up to the age of 21, although some measures of semi-
indeterminacy exists in the adult court (see Powers of the Criminal
Courts Act 1973, S.28). Juvenile justice is, and always has been, the
favoured area of semi-indeterminate sentences, which under the
Children and Young Persons Act 1969 includes the care order.
Supervision orders are weak forms of semi-indeterminate sentences
but are included because they contain provisions to discharge the
orders on the grounds of good progress.

Semi-indeterminate sentences have the following features. First, a minimum and maximum period of sentence is provided by the courts, but the decision to release within that time span is taken by an executive body. Second, unless the sentence is itself a form of supervision, semi-indeterminate sentences invariably contain after-care, which may or may not be part of the original sentence; thus, a sentence of borstal training includes a period of after-care which begins on the date of release from the institution. Third, semi-indeterminate sentences also invariably contain periods of recall which operate when the offender breaks the condition of his licence.

Unlike the indeterminate sentence, which is strictly confined to prison, the range of semi-indeterminate sentences includes custodial and non-custodial orders (i.e. borstal and probation), with differences throughout the custodial range (i.e. borstal and care orders). These differences allow competition, or rather preferences, to exist, where the courts choose one sentence rather than another. Preferences exist according to the perceived nature of the regimes, rather than the time spans allotted. So, with the introduction of the care orders after the 1969 Act, the proportionate use of borstal sentences increased for the younger age group because borstals were seen as more secure institutions than those being offered by care orders. Parole has been included with the indeterminate sentences but is in a category of its own, being neither determinate nor semi-determinate. It is, as Donald West defines it, 'a procedure whereby a sentence imposed by the court may be varied by administrative action' (West, 1972, p. 11), in other words, where the executive is granted power to release a prisoner before the end of a sentence originally specified by the judiciary. In Britain, or more accurately in England and Wales, parole was introduced by the Criminal Justice Act 1967. On 1 April 1968 the first prisoners were released on licence. Out of 4,347 prisoners eligible for parole, 406 were released (i.e. 8.5 per cent). By 1977 over 50 per cent of prisoners eligible who did not opt out were being paroled — more than 5,000 out of 10,000 eligible cases. Put another way, a daily average of 2,700 prisoners are out of prison who would otherwise be inside.

The American parole system developed much earlier. It began as part of the juvenile justice system in New York at Elmira Reformatory in 1869, and was extended to other states where it was used for adult prisoners. Linked as it was to the juvenile system, it began as a reformist measure and was used in conjunction with indeterminate sentencing. However by the 1930s commentators began to note that, irrespective of its reformist origins, it had reverted to its earliest form as a means of controlling and managing convicts within the prison system and outside while on licence. Keith Bottomley talks of 'reverting' because he traces the origin of parole back to the 'ticket of leave' system developed alongside the use of transportation in England during the seventeenth and eighteenth centuries. Bottomley also points out that it was not long before parole began to introduce indeterminacy into the American system; and, indeed, he argues that there is an inevitable connection between the two so that the same issues and problems surround the discussion of the theory and practice of parole as of indeterminate sentences (Bottomley, 1973, p. 195). Whether the parole system will produce indeterminacy in Britain is a moot question. I would suggest that it would be more appropriate to say that rehabilitation produces indeterminacy, of which parole is a part. It would have been more appropriate if Keith Bottomley had made the connection in this form rather than in the form that parole produces indeterminacy. He has, I think, missed the important link and misread the antecedents.

In Britain, parole can be granted only to those serving a term of imprisonment of eighteen months or more and to those on life sentences. So acting on the basis of one-third remission, a prisoner is eligible for parole twelve months after sentence or one-third of the sentence, whichever is the longer. Briefly, there are two stages of the procedure: the first relates to the Local Review Committee (LRC), which acts primarily as a referral agency to the second stage, the national Parole Board. The Parole Board's recommendations go to the Home Secretary, who may intervene and ask for the case to be reconsidered. (Only four cases were referred by the Home Secretary in 1976.)[1]

Semi-indeterminate sentences, including parole, introduce new dimensions into a penal system. Again, de Tocqueville made the important point when he said the pursuit of worthy goals increases the bureaucracy of centralized and local government. To operate semi-indeterminacy a bureaucracy is required to produce the necessary reports prior to sentence, to oversee the treatment during sentence, and to determine the appropriate time for the offender's release — as well as to control supervision during the period of after-care. The probation service, the social work departments and the parole board have provided the necessary bureaucracies in Britain.

Elsewhere similar bureaucracies exist under a different aegis.

More specifically, semi-indeterminate sentences affect the position of the courts. The effect is not straightforward, although were semi-indeterminate sentences to have a monopoly in modern penal systems the courts' influence would cease, and would be replaced by sentencing panels; for courts have only a minor part to play in a fully fledged reformist system. When reform operates alongside other philosophies courts have to accommodate to it, and they do so in various ways. There is some evidence to suggest that judges increase the sentences for certain offenders who would be expected to receive parole, by adding on the likely period of parole supervision — although this is hotly denied by the members of the judiciary. Where this occurs the aim is to by-pass or neutralize the parole procedure.[2] It becomes a defiant gesture against a perceived limitation on the courts' influence. Complaints and representation by pressure groups such as the Magistrates' Association, protesting against their impotence in the juvenile court, are similar attempts to retrieve power removed initially by legislation under the 1969 Act. This much is obvious: that the growth of semi-indeterminacy produces a reduction in the powers of the courts and an increase in the powers of the reformist.

Yet this is only part of the picture. We need to distinguish between the earlier and later stages of reform. In the early stages probation officers and social workers do the courts' work by gathering and disseminating information about the offenders' personal lives. Welfare workers become part of an extended court team whose head is the magistrate or judge. Only at the later stage — when the reformists begin to replace the courts — does conflict arise. Until then the courts are understandably reluctant to lose the services of so many extra professionals who willingly act as their agents. The first stage of reform is marked by an increase in both legal and welfare bureaucracies, followed at the second stage by a greater increase in welfare bureaucracy.

During the first stage of reform, information provided to the court produces, I think, two major but unintended consequences. The first is to influence the courts in such a way as to lead them to believe many of the rehabilitative arguments, and make them act as if their main task were not to punish but to assist offenders. Many criminologists have appeared to follow their lead, for they too have become preoccupied with the welfare functions of the court and seem to have forgotten its major task. The second consequence is to shelter the courts and protect them. Almost alone among modern criminologists, Nils Christie recognizes this:

> The courts have for a long time been drifting in a stagnant lagoon protected by the belief that they are through expertise striving to reach attainable utilitarian goals. It is time they were forced out of this into the flowing waters of a clearly expressed and exposed morality. [Christie, 1974, p. 296]

To force the courts out of their 'stagnant lagoon' would require a reduction in rehabilitative personnel and a new way of looking at the courts' task. The change would not be easy. It would mean a return to discussions about punishment accompanied by a debate about the position of courts generally. This is unlikely to happen unless and until other factors become recognized. One such factor is a greater understanding of the methods employed under a rehabilitative regime. Semi-indeterminate sentences provide the most profitable examples.

The nature of semi-indeterminacy requires that the offender's behaviour during his sentence be considered in any decision to release. This is what Roger Hood calls 'double sentencing', where the original sentence is based on the offence and the personality of the offender up to that offence, while release is granted on this plus subsequent behaviour. Over and above 'double sentencing' there are political decisions that can dictate release. I do not mean by this that offenders who commit political crimes are detained longer than non-political offences, or that the State interferes in the judiciary; rather, general release dates can easily be determined by the pressure on places. The average release date for borstal sentences is highly correlated with the numbers detained — the greater the pressure on places, the shorter the average length of time served.

Second, the decision to release is by the executive. The arguments surrounding executive release need not be rehearsed here, except to state in the broadest terms that executive release grants power to a board to make decisions, often in secret, about the future containment of offenders based on criteria with little or no proven validity. Attempts to improve the quality of predictions have usually been made with the aid of sophisticated statistical techniques which select variables having predictive qualities. Unfortunately, as yet these techniques are unrefined and produce ethical problems greater than before. First, there is the ethical issue of subjecting offenders, and perhaps non-offenders, to these techniques; then there is the problem of 'false positives'. Albert Rosen puts it this way: 'Our chance of accuracy is less the rarer the action we are attempting to force' (Rosen, 1954). Assume, therefore, that we were attempting to predict the outcome of certain violent criminals. Statistically we may be able to show that selected variables have a predictive value, but for every correctly predicted violent criminal, we must include a number of 'false positives', that is, persons who are equivalent as regards every measurable characteristic, but who will not commit any violent crime. The more serious the crime the greater the increase in false positives. Those who argue that prediction could be used to assist executive decisions must face the inevitable consequences described so accurately by Nils Christie: 'We are usually willing to let ten guilty persons go free in order to avoid condemning an innocent person. But if we want to resort to incarcerating possibly dangerous criminals we must lock up several who are not dangerous in order that a few should not get an opportunity to commit a fresh offence' (Christie, 1974, p. 287).

With parole the arguments are no less complex. The same questions can be asked of parole as for semi-indeterminate sentences generally, for parole contains release by executive decision, the use of predictive techniques, etc. However, the major difference is that parolees are released through a formally constituted parole board comprised of selected personnel appointed by the Home Secretary, whose task is to review each application and make a recommendation.

What is the nature of this review? How does it compare, for example, with other procedures followed by similar bodies outside the penal system? First, the process is obviously both bureaucratic and secretive. Second, the prisoner has few rights, prior to and during his licence period. He is, as Lord Hunt once observed, a person who continues to serve a prison sentence in open conditions. Third, the prisoner does not appear at the hearings, nor is he represented. There is no opportunity to appeal against the parole board's decisions, and there are no reasons given for the refusal of parole. The parole licence can be revoked if the parolee fails to report to his supervising officer, or fails to conform to any of the conditions of his licence. The parolee has no opportunity to appear at the hearing or appeal against the decision. The prisoner's position is accurately described as someone who is receiving a privilege, not a right.

If the aim has been to grant privileges to the prisoners, there can be no dispute about the way the Board operates. But these privileges are tied up with other issues which cannot be so readily dismissed. Of itself, a privilege does not usually require a reason to be given if it is withheld, and it probably does not require conditions of fairness related to those privileges. Nor does it require a right of appeal. Yet when privileges are linked to a general system of punishments, the situation becomes more complex. With privileges generally we can say that, if X has a privilege to Y, then the acceptance of that privilege will be beneficial to X and in the normal course of events will probably not drastically affect his life if it is withdrawn. But when X's privileges relate to the reduction in some measure of suffering, and where the withdrawal of that privilege means that suffering continues as before, it becomes quite a different matter.

As a method of granting privileges the Parole Board operates more on the administrative model than the judicial one (Barnard, 1976). Principles of equity do not apply, nor do principles of due process. Questions of 'public interest' affect decisions such as the current offence and past record of the offender, the risk he poses to the public, and his personal and social circumstances. Some writers, notably Keith Hawkins, have called the Board 'a *quasi* judicial process' (Hawkins, 1973), although '*quasi*' in this instance refers to the factors taken into consideration, not the method of operation. But whether it is administrative or quasi-judicial, the courts have imposed an obligation on all statutory bodies to act fairly. Lord Denning made this clear in *Breen* v *Amalgamated Engineering Union* (1971):

It does not matter whether its functions are described as judicial or quasi-judicial on the one hand, or as administrative on the other hand, or what you will. Still it must act fairly. It must in a proper case give a party a chance to be heard.

And in another judgment, *R*. v. *Gaming Board for Great Britain* (1970), Lord Denning also said the Board must let their impressions be known so that they can be disabused. The Gaming Board's duties are to investigate thoroughly the applicants who apply for Gaming Licences:

Without disclosing every detail the Board ought in every case to be able to give sufficient indication of the objections raised against him such as to enable him to answer them.

When Lord Denning insists that tribunals should be 'fair' they cannot also provide privileges, for privileges are special advantages gained, and are freedoms from burdens endured by others. Privileges invoke special rights granted according to selective definitions; fairness involves comparability, or the antithesis of privilege. Fairness also implies openness, while privileges are more akin to secretiveness.

Then there is the question of the purpose of parole. Hall-Williams sees it in pragmatic terms, as a means of allowing prisoners to be on licence in the community rather than remain in prison (1978, p. 2). He recognizes that parole schemes are invitations to judges to adjust their sentences but believes there are sufficient official discouragements to keep the system in check. Others have taken a stronger rehabilitative position, arguing that parole allows a board of experts to identify 'a peak' in the prisoner's treatment programme. The subsequent period of licence continues the treatment in the community. When parole was first introduced there was much discussion about the 'peak' in training, and a major reason for establishing a Parole Board was that it would be composed of experts who knew about offenders. Civil servants were thought to be inappropriate, having administrative rather than criminological experience.

It is interesting to note how these reformist arguments have lost their impact, to be replaced by the pragmatic approach adopted by Hall-Williams. It is possible to account for the change by relating it to the decline in rehabilitation generally, but I think the decline is coincidental. The percentage of prisoners released is, I think, the important factor. We can see it in these terms. Prisoners can be divided into two categories: those granted parole and those not. When parole was introduced the numbers released were small, only about 10 per cent. They were seen as a select group, almost an elite. Those not granted parole, i.e. the large majority, were simply viewed as ordinary prisoners, perhaps even run-of-the-mill. But once the scheme became established and the percentage of released prisoners rose about 50 per cent, parole became an expectation for all. Those granted parole began to see it as a right, those not granted, as an injustice. Initially the scheme rewarded the good and ignored the bad; later it merely punished the bad. Initially it was a rehabilitative technique, for those capable of taking their place in the community; later it became a technique for keeping incorrigibles in prison.

The decline in reformist aims had, I am suggesting, more to do with the increased numbers of paroles than with any doubts about reformist thinking. Of course doubts about reform may have contributed to a more open approach about the nature of parole, but they did not promote the change. Had reformist aims still been fashionable, as in the United States, they could have been preserved in spite of changes that were undermining them. Parole would then have been open to a different set of criticisms, and in fact reformists may count themselves fortunate, if the American experience is anything to go by, to have avoided these. John Conrad argues that parole boards in the United States have a share in the sentencing process which determines punishment on the basis of an appraisal of the success of treatment adjusted to the impression of the tolerance of the community. He points out that both considerations are subjective and based on assumptions that derive little from theory or principle. The net effect, says Conrad, is to reduce the credibility of treatment. 'The semi-indeterminate sentence as at present administered not only contributes to the great length of American sentences but also to the essentially anti-therapeutic culture which prevails despite the increase in services' (Conrad, 1965, p. 52). All reformist schemes, of which parole is the most striking example, are affected by the manner in which they cease to be regarded as a privilege and become a claimed right. Parallels with semi-indeterminate sentences such as borstal training are not exact, for *all* borstal offenders are eventually released, whereas parole remains a method of administrative procedure to vary the initial sentence of a selected few. None the less, there are sufficient similarities to bracket them together for these purposes.

I have not said anything about the many criticisms of parole, for example the way in which the rates of parole from different prisons may vary in ways that imply idiosyncratic decisions by the LRCs; nor have I said much about the criticisms of some commentators who insist on reasons being given by the Parole Board to all eligible prisoners. The debates lie outside the main area of interest, which is to relate parole to the question of punishment. Here, we are more concerned with the way in which the nature of semi-indeterminate sentences permit changes to occur without apparently affecting the regime or original justification for the sentence, in other words produce label-swapping.

The most obvious and crude example of label-swapping that occurred in its most acute form was in the juvenile justice system. Prior to 1969 offenders were sent to approved schools under the Approved School Order, but after the 1969 Act offenders went to community homes, which were new names for the old approved schools. The staff remained largely as before, as did the regimes. The major difference was the name of the sentence: a care order. I am, of course, making a slight exaggeration, but the point remains that modern systems are adept at label-swapping while retaining the regime. This was most striking in the British mental health system of the 1930s, when 'asylums' became 'mental hospitals' and patients were no longer 'incarcerated' but 'compulsorily detained'. The labels were changed by Act of Parliament (the 1930 Mental Treatment Act), but there were no changes in the patient's objective reality (Bean, 1980).

More subtle are what Conrad calls the 'differential scales of retribution' that exist with semi-indeterminate sentences that become dominated by internal and external considerations of sanctions and control. The concept of dangerousness has begun to emerge as a paramount consideration in Britain, leading to an increasing distinction between the dangerous offenders and the rest. Elizabeth Barnard points out that parole intensifies this distinction, 'the more so the higher the paroling rote, and especially because all the factors influencing the original sentence are considered again, when parole is an issue' (Barnard, 1976). From its inception the parole scheme in Britain has had a low parole rate for dangerous offenders, particularly long-term prisoners applying for parole at first review. 'Dangerousness' can be readily justified as a means of protecting society, but it can be easily transformed into new and more generic forms. James Q. Wilson, for example, talks in terms of increased sentences for what he calls 'repeaters', and since most repeaters are blacks it is clear that he is implying that these sentences should operate on the basis of class dangerousness (Wilson, 1975). Wilson is not of course directly advocating semi-indeterminate sentences; the example is of value if only to show how differential scales of retribution may operate within a semi-indeterminate framework and how they can change according to requirements that operate outside the offender's control.

The second important consideration relates to the debate

surrounding parole. Some commentators have wanted parole to be abandoned because they say it produces injustice and because of the insecurity created among prisoners. I do not wish to disagree with those criticisms; my point is a more general one: why restrict the arguments to parole? As the system operates at present parole has more favourable aspects than many other forms of semi-indeterminacy. A Parole Board gives careful consideration to each application, and whatever criticisms have been made of the methods of the Board no one has doubted its integrity. Regrettably, the same cannot be said for some other review boards. In our own examination of the statutory reviews of children in care we found marked variations in the quality of those reviews, where some were exhaustively conducted and others were perfunctory. Sometimes the children themselves were active participants; at other times they were called in to agree to decisions already made. Little or no research has been conducted on the decision to release offenders from borstals, nor on the decisions of probation officers to bring offenders back to court on breaches of probation, but the results may be instructive — although in the latter case the offender has his case heard by the court. I am not suggesting that a formally constituted board be appointed for all borstals and all probation officers and social workers but merely suggest that we have become overconcerned with parole to the detriment of other forms of semi-indeterminacy.

Finally, there is the position of the probation service to be considered in semi-indeterminate sentences. The probation service's position is affected in two ways: by the use of a probation order which is a semi-indeterminate sentence in itself; and by the supervision of offenders on licence or statutory after-care. As a semi-indeterminate sentence probation is unique in that there are provisions in England and Wales for the offender himself to apply to the court for the probation order to be discharged on the grounds that he has made good progress. A similar provision is granted to the probation officer. However, the offender rarely makes the application. Unlike the probation order, the statutory after-care system has fitted uneasily into the probation officer's vision of himself as a social worker in the courts. The service has always insisted that there was a voluntary component to its method of treatment, and offenders have to agree to be placed on probation. The voluntary component might be illusory but it is maintained, and there is much discussion in the probation literature about 'contracts' being established between probation officers and their clients (see Chapter 4). The importance of statutory after-care and parole is that it exemplifies surveillance. Statutory after-care did not introduce surveillance; it merely confirmed it.

Surveillance has not been introduced because of the type of offenders on after-care; indeed, they are probably no more nor less criminal in their antecedents than the typical offender on probation. Nor does it appear that the extent of probation contacts with the after-care offender is different in amount from those offenders placed on probation. However, the statutory requirements and the social expectations surrounding statutory after-care can make it a qualitatively different method of supervision, for there is likely to be more public outcry when parolees are reconvicted than for those on probation. I have used the term 'surveillance' deliberately because I wish to argue that statutory supervision has a limited set of aims and objectives. Statutory or compulsory after-care promotes surveillance. It is not difficult to believe that the offender also sees surveillance as the method used and is encouraged to do so by the conditions of his licence relating to recall and the warnings given by the probation officer.

Statutory after-care has not been grafted on to the probation service, or juxtaposed with the traditional form of supervision of the probation order. It is, and always has been an integral part of the probation officer's work, being another form of probation order. Moreover, surveillance is being extended more and more into the probation officer's task. We already have supervision linked to the suspended prison sentence and the deferred sentence, together with the community service order introduced under the 1972 Criminal Justice Act. The Home Office has recently resurrected proposals originally formulated in the 1960s to provide compulsory supervision for all ex-prisoners, thereby extending parole and presumably reducing the prison population (HMSO, 1977b). While the probation service is seen as a resource to help reduce the numbers sent to prison, and incidentally as a means of providing a publicly acceptable face to that resource, it will I think be drawn further into the world of surveillance. Statutory after-care introduced that dimension; parole increased it. It is now a matter of time, given present trends, to see how far the probation service will go in that direction.

I would suggest therefore that future questions ought not to be about whether the probation service should or should not be involved in surveillance, but about what sort of surveillance is required. Are some sorts of surveillance qualitatively better than others? Do those countries that separate parole and probation departments produce different types of surveillance for each department, and if so which is to be preferred? For the probation service is the other half of indeterminacy; no such sentence could operate without the corollary of supervision in the community. The probation order itself is an integral part of the wider question of semi-indeterminacy. Were the probation service to opt out of (say) parole or statutory after-care, then another service would have to be found, for semi-indeterminate sentences require non-custodial surveillance. There would however be little to be gained from such a move — for the offender, the probation service or the State. What is required is a candid recognition that the future of probation is bound up with the future of indeterminate and semi-indeterminate sentence.

THE FUTURE OF REHABILITATION

Were we to look in very general terms at changes in the modern penal system, we could notice that deterrence and retribution have lost ground, the latter more so than the former, while rehabilitation has surged ahead — at least, until recently. The pattern has been uneven, rehabilitation being most dominant in the juvenile court while retributive sentences still exist in the adult courts (Thomas, 1979). Since 1975 however it has become possible to talk of a demise of rehabilitation. I do not mean by this that rehabilitation is no longer practised in the court, or in penal sanctions, for that would be patently untrue; rather, I mean that rehabilitation no longer commands the moral force it once had. As a philosophy it had always attracted support from the liberal social democrats, who saw it as a hallmark of humanitarianism and a way of improving the quality of life in society. Conversely, the extreme political right have always remained sceptical, seeing it — wrongly, in my view — as a soft option which offered too much sympathy and too little discipline for the offender. The extreme left were equally sceptical; they saw it as a method of tidying up 'the social junk of capitalism' and as such prolonging an unjust economic order. When the liberals began to see it as theoretically faulty and capable of producing its own form of injustice, the basis of its support began to wither.

Nowhere is the demise more clearly shown than in a comparison of two Home Office documents, one published in 1959, the other nearly twenty years later. In 1959 the White Paper, *Penal Practice in a Changing Society* (HMSO, 1959), based its thinking on Rule 6 of the Prison Rules made under the 1948 Criminal Justice Act, which states:

> The purpose of training and treatment of convicted prisoners shall be to establish in them the will to lead a good and useful life on discharge, and to fit them to do so.

To this end the 1959 White Paper noted with satisfaction that 'methods of training have been progressively extended and improved, notably in the application of psychiatry and psychology' (para. 46). Research had an essential place; its aim was to identify 'those characteristics of an offender that indicate whether a particular level of treatment will be suitable for him' (para. 20) and for the recidivist, 'to learn more of its causes'. So, through more precise methods of classification the White Paper thought we could reduce recidivism by more effective personal training (para. 51).

By 1977 that had changed. In almost twenty years reform had lost its earlier prominence. The later document (HMSO, 1977b) described the 'causes of crime' as multi-faceted, and the new aim of the penal system is not to be the recovery of offenders, but:

(1) to maintain public order;
(2) to maintain confidence in the rule of law;
(3) to reduce the incidence of crime through the deterrent, containment and rehabilitative effect of the criminal justice system.

In this new scheme, rehabilitation was placed low in the order of priority.

The policy objectives at the level of the criminal justice agencies were (HMSO, 1977b):

(1) to detect offenders and bring them to justice;
(2) to try accused and sentence convicted persons speedily, fairly and without discrimination;
(3) to exact penalties economically, effectively and humanely;
(4) to maintain and improve professional standards of the criminal justice agencies;
(5) to secure that the scope and content of the criminal law are acceptable to contemporary society.

The new policy document adopts a much wider stance, recognizing claims that it ignored in 1959. It did not mention retribution as one of its aims but emphasized deterrence and justice. The interesting question for criminologists is the likely effects of the document. Is it reflecting a trend or producing new policy? Or perhaps both? Is it helping to remove rehabilitation from the penal system and unwittingly produce a vacuum which will be difficult to fill? No one can say as yet, but a likely effect may be to encourage a pragmatic approach where the aim is to deal with issues as and when they arise without producing a general philosophical framework. So, for example, where there is pressure to reduce the prison population solutions would be sought in ways that restrict the courts' powers to send offenders to prison, or restrict the types of offenders to be sent to prison, or even remove certain types of offences from the statute book. In the pragmatic approach a specific task is set and measures are taken accordingly. Its strength is that it deals with problems as and when they arise, and it fills a gap while a more coherent philosophy arises. Its weakness is that it becomes a poor substitute for a philosophy and may allow official manipulation to take place according to incremental demands. Pragmatism can easily lead to a view that the system is dominated by immediate demands which are solved by tinkering with certain segments.

RETRIBUTION AND THE MODERN
PENAL SYSTEM

In spite of the abundant criticism directed towards retribution, it has managed to survive within modern penal systems. This is confirmed by the presence of the 'tariff', which is, according to David Thomas, a basis for maintaining consistency in the sentencing of different offenders (Thomas, 1979). The object in determining a tariff sentence is to reflect the culpability of the offender, or, in Thomas's words, 'for the sentence not to be more severe than is justified by the gravity of the offence for which it imposed' (p. 29). Tariff sentencing appears to be more common in the High Courts than the Magistrates' Courts but is present there none the less. Indeed, it operates whenever the court wishes to assert an overriding principle of proportionality. It contains more than retribution, for it is a complex of philosophical arguments of which retribution is only one; deterrence also exists within tariff sentencing.

The maximum penalty fixed by statute has a strong retributive flavour. While maximum penalties play a limited part in the process of defining the scale of the tariff, their presence reflects the legislator's determination to restrict sentences to the most that is deserved. Adjustments in the maximum sentences over time (rape, for example, was a capital offence until 1840 — Thomas, 1979, p. 30) reflect changes in the notion of deserts as surely as do changes in the tariff. Maximum sentences are based on the old retributive principle that some offences deserve certain penalties; others deserve less. They are also based on the retributive presumption that justice must be equated with a scale of sentences. Justice would not be served if (say) the maximum punishment for speeding offences would be the same as for (say) robbery, rape or murder.

Modern interest in retribution has developed as a reaction against rehabilitation. In its modern idiom it is usually called the 'justice model', although again the justice model is used to cover many different positions. Keith Bottomley informs us that David Fogel is usually credited with coining the phrase 'justice model'. (Fogel was Commissioner of Corrections in Minnesota, from 1971 to 1973 and developed his ideas at the practical as well as the theoretical level in the day-to-day running of prisons in Minnesota.) Bottomley notes that a major focus of advocates of the justice model was, and is, at the procedural level, where it is argued there is a need to control the exercise of discretion and to introduce a greater degree of openness and accountability in criminal justice decision-making. There has been, says Bottomley, an almost total rejection of the individualized treatment model as a basis for penal policy, but less unamity on what should replace it as the basic penal objective (Bottomley, 1979, p. 138). Sometimes it appears as if the justice model should be juxtaposed or added on to treatment by increasing attention to procedural rules. If so, then it is not easy to see how this would be achieved, for the two approaches are incompatible (Bean, 1980). Justice may impose external control on the treatment officials in the form of requirements to abide by certain procedural safeguards, but it cannot control the methods or the aims of treatment. At best it provides a limitation on the reformist's activities. Yet some advocates of the justice model wish to go only as far as this, and many suggestions for the improvement of juvenile justice, go no further than providing limited requirements on treatment officials by increasing the role of the courts (*The Times*, 12 April 1980).

On the other hand, some commentators have wanted to go further. An American Committee for the Study of Incarceration under the chairmanship of Andrew von Hirsch argued for what they called the principle of 'commensurate deserts', which they considered should have priority over other objectives in decisions about how to punish.

> The disposition of convicted offenders should be commensurate with the seriousness of their offences, even if greater or lesser severity would promote other goals. For the principle we have argued is a requirement of justice, whereas deterrence, incapacitation and rehabilitation are essentially strategies for controlling crime. The priority of the principle follows from the assumption . . . [that] the requirements of justice ought to constrain the pursuit of crime prevention. [von Hirsch, 1976, pp. 74-5]

Commensurate deserts are, say the Committee, based on commensurate notions of fairness. By 'commensurate' the Committee meant 'proportionality' or 'just deserts'. Only grave wrongs required severe penalties, said the Committee; minor wrongs deserve lenient ones. In fact, the principle of commensurate deserts turns out to be hardly distinguishable from retribution. We find similar arguments used by Norval Morris, who placed the concept of desert at the centre of his proposals for the justification of imprisonment. No sanctions, said Morris, should be greater than that deserved by the last crime or crimes for which the offender is being sentenced (N. Morris, 1974, p. 75). In Morris's view, no prison sentence should exceed the deserved maximum: as such the argument becomes another form of limiting retribution.

The American Committee's report was greeted with little enthusiasm by some of its members. Leslie Wilkins, for example, hoped that a different model would apply — economic/rational or even humanitarian/therapeutic — although he recognized that they had proven even less appropriate. However, he could not accept the main principle as a declaration of desirable policy but thought 'it was less unacceptable than any others which were considered at the time' (von Hirsch, 1976, p. 178). Why should this be so? The answer I think lies in the last paragraph of the report:

> But it should be only small comfort that our theory of punishment deals somewhat less unfairly with deprived persons than traditional utilitarian theories do. As long as a substantial segment of the population is denied adequate opportunities for a livelihood any scheme for punishment must be morally flawed. [von Hirsch, 1976, p. 149]

The Committee was interested in linking punishment to social justice. Herein lies the weakness, and one that has bedevilled the criminological subject matter as well as dominating the practice of the court. It has also helped produce the injustices of the treatment model. We may have to consider that it is not possible to link punishment to social justice since they operate within different conceptual frameworks. It may be possible, and indeed it may be highly desirable, to link the formation of law to social justice. In retributive terms, if we think the poor or the disadvantaged should not be punished then it is up to the legislators to determine that. It is not the duty of those involved in the punishment to make that decision.

This point can be clarified by examining more closely the retributive influence on the penal system. What would a full-scale retributive system entail? We can see the answers in terms of principles rather than specifics. Obviously, it would contain all the elements of retribution noted earlier, i.e. proportionality,desert, etc., and we can take these as accepted. To proceed further we need to extend the debate, yet return to more orthodox philosophical theories of punishment. Here I find myself strongly in agreement with Professor Mabbott's view, although agreement came by quite a different route. Mabbott believes that a connection must be made between punishment and crime, not between punishment and moral and social wrongs or, for our purposes, between punishment and social justice. His view, he says, helps us meet many of the objections to the retributive views as ordinarily stated, and helps also to meet the point made by the American Committee. Professor Mabbott gives the example of the authority who believes the law in question is a bad law. As mentioned earlier, he describes himself in such a position:

> I was myself for some time disciplinary officer of a college whose rules included a rule compelling attendance at a chapel. Many of those who broke the rule did it on principle. I punished them. I certainly did not want to reform them; I respected their characters and their views. I certainly did not want to drive others into chapel through fear of penalties. Nor did I think there had been a wrong done which invited retribution . . . My position was clear. They had broken a rule; they knew it and I knew it. Nothing more was necessary to make punishment proper. [Mabbott, 1939]

Professor Mabbott objects to the application of the reform theory for as he says, a man who commits a wrong before the date on which a law is passed is as much in need of reform as a man who commits it afterwards. Nor is deterrence likely to suffer because of additional punishments for the same offence. The orthodox retributive theory is equally at a loss, for if punishment is for wrongdoing the wrongdoing existed as certainly before the passing of the law as after it. Punishment then is for a crime and only for the crime: it is not aimed at producing benefits for the offender.

A purely retributive theory is exclusive. It omits considerations of all matters other than those of the offence and the punishment. Professor Mabbott is quite clear on this point. In the example given above his students had broken the law; they knew it and he knew it, and he says nothing more was necessary to make punishment proper. At first sight this must seem an odd position to adopt. The law itself was clearly archaic and not one meeting with Professor Mabbott's agreement, yet he enforced it none the less. The temptation to do otherwise must have been great, for it raises those age-old questions of what to do about bad law. It also commits Professor Mabbott to the view that where the law has been properly administered justice has been done, no matter what the law is like. He did not, as did the classical utilitarians, distinguish between a law being justly administered and a law itself being just. Justice in Mabbott's terms does not involve a debate about the nature of law: that much he accepts.

Mabbott's position also has the merit of delineating the boundaries of the subject matter. W. D. Ross argued, rightly in my view, that there were two stages to the debate on punishment which are not usually kept apart. 'The infliction of punishment by the state does not, or should not, come like a bolt from the blue. It is preceded by the making of a law in which a penalty is affixed to a crime. We must I think distinguish this stage, that of affixing of the penalty from that of its infliction . . .' (Ross, 1930, p. 61). Law, in Ross's terms, is a system of promises that the offender has not escaped scot-free, and a promise to those who do not commit crime that they will not be punished. The selection of law, says Ross, is a matter of expediency. Justice occurs after selection. I think this must be right, and so presumably would Mabbott. Ross also points out that we do no claim that laws should be made against all moral offences, or against groups, even though we may wish to exclude that behaviour. Legislators have to consider such questions as whether a given law should be enforced if it were made, and whether a certain type of behaviour is important enough to make it worthwhile to set the elaborate machinery of the law at work against it. It may be better left to the injured person to seek his own solution, or left to public opinion (Ross, 1930, p. 62). For these reasons sociologists attempting to produce theories of law creation enter a field clouded by variables that are difficult to define and more difficult to calculate. Often legislation becomes a matter of expediency.

If we use the term 'expediency' to suggest that the process of law creation is highly complex, then the point can be accepted. It becomes a matter for the law-creators to determine the legislation required. It also becomes a matter for the law-creators to predict the type of person likely to be caught up in the control machinery. If they believe that the mother who steals bread to feed starving children is not committing an offence, then so be it. If they believe that the poor or disadvantaged ought not to be regarded as breaking the law, then again, so be it. So if the law-creators' interest is in social justice, they must decide which categories to exclude should the law be broken.

In these circumstances the legislator would be faced with a number of basic tasks, one of which would be to exempt certain categories of offenders at the time of law creation; another of which would be to be more careful about the types of laws enacted.[3] If the first, then it would be argued by some that I am making a distinction that is against the principle of law-making in Britain, i.e. selecting certain social groups as warranting special attention and being allowed to behave in a way for which others are punished. But there are already precedents for this. The Infanticide Act allows a mother to be guilty not of murder but of manslaughter if she kills her child within twelve months of its birth if her conduct can be attributed to the effect of giving birth or lactation. We already make special defences for children and the mentally ill, whose actions are deemed to be of a qualitatively different nature. These specially selected groups are granted their status according to precepts that include social justice. If social justice is required, then it becomes a matter of extending those groups.

We may not of course want to grant selected social categories exemption, believing that it is neither practical nor desirable to do so. This would be acceptable to the retributivist, who may question the validity of granting existing exemption anyway. But that may not matter. As long as the basic principle is retained the argument remains intact. And that principle is based on the distinction between law creation and law infliction where the latter operates from retributive principles.

Where this basic principle is to be accepted a number of secondary principles follow. We cannot, or ought not, attempt to punish in order to improve the offender's position. We are rarely able to do so, and often through the best of intentions we make the position worse. Yet how often do we hear that 'prison does no good' as if the only basis on which prison can be adjudged is on grounds of betterment. We are still dominated by Patterson's dictum that the aim of imprisonment is to encourage the offender to lead a good and useful life on discharge. In retributive terms, nothing could be further from the truth: the aim of prison is to punish a person because he has broken the law where the length of that sentence is to be determined by principles of commensurate desert or retributive controls along the lines suggested by Mabbott.

What then is the future of penal reform; or, rather, has reform a future within the retributive framework? The answer is, of course, yes. Mabbott rightly says that penal reformers would meet with more support if they were clear that they were attempting not to alter the system of punishment, but merely to give its victims 'fair play' (Mabbott, 1939). We have regrettably confused those issues over the years. Special privileges for prisoners have been advanced under the realm of treatment when they were nothing more than humanistic devices, and special rules for prisoners have been justified on similar grounds. Our interest in prisons has produced a confusing pattern of changes, but not I think as far as the prisoner is concerned. We have introduced prison welfare officers for reformist reasons, but the prisoner knows that the presence of the prison welfare officer does not diminish his punishment, although it may remove an indirect and regrettable consequence of it. We have also adjusted the periods of punishment in the prisons to relate to the offender (e.g. extended sentences), yet we have no more right to keep prisoners in prison for long periods for therapeutic reasons than to imprison anyone else for such reasons. Nor have we any more right to grant prisoners privileges that we call therapeutic which can be withdrawn for therapeutic reasons. If justice is to be about fairness, then that fairness must extend to prisons as to elsewhere.

Arguments about fairness are not confined to prisons. In retributive terms they extend throughout and include the semi-indeterminate and determinate sentences. For the reasons given above we have no right to detain people, or to control people on probation for relatively long periods on treatment grounds because we think they require lengthy periods of control. Nor, on retributive grounds, do we have any right to suggest that some individuals are less responsible for their actions than others because they come from different social backgrounds. Mabbott is right when he says he wishes to establish the theoretical importance and the practical value of distinguishing between penal reform that alters the accompaniments of punishment without touching its essence and those attacks on punishment made by reformers who see criminals as in need of treatment. His criticisms would be directed towards every judge who answers that he is punishing a man to deter others or to protect society, and to every juryman who is moved to his decision by the moral baseness of the accused rather than by his legal guilt.

Following on from this, we can now make a closer examination of mitigating circumstances, for this is another area closely associated with the retributive position. It is not the only one, but it is illustrative of an important area of confusion. We would need to ask which mitigating circumstances were relevant. Obviously, there is the extent of complicity in a crime; for example, the person who stands apart from others who are breaking windows — and may even try to remonstate against them, albeit in a half-hearted way — cannot be seen to be as the others, although all were (say) convicted of criminal damage. But how about previous convictions or social background? Clearly, social background is of little relevance to our argument except in the most extreme circumstances, such as age of responsibility, but previous convictions are more difficult. The present justification for including them is a deterrent argument derived from Bentham and sustained on the basis that they are an indication of the offender's previous life-style and complicity in the current offence. At their worst they tend to produce arguments for extending sentences such as preventative detention or corrective training as established in the 1948 Criminal Justice Act and the Extended Sentences, where severe sentences can be introduced on the grounds of incorrigibility. If punishment is for the present crime and not for past excesses, then previous convictions can have little value.

To expand the point, we can return briefly to the American Friends Committee. A closer look at their arguments show that they were confused on two basic points. Their demands for a return to a retributive system of sentencing turns out to be something quite different and largely unworkable; and, one could add, it is almost as if the Committee did not understand the basis on which a retributive system would work — in spite of quoting Kant with approval. This confusion stems from their insistence that they were social reformers, and as such they fell into a trap as assurably as other reformists have done. The constant hankering for betterment to be part of punishment has, I think, made them see the problem the wrong way round. Betterment is appropriate to the legislative stage, not to the punishment stage. The justice model, as formulated by the American Friends Committee, becomes no more than an attempt to reduce excesses in the present system and then smuggle in some form of betterment later. As such the position is doomed to failure, for it can only lead to further excesses. The Committee says that they do not want a sentencing system to aggravate the biases existing in society, but in retributive terms it is no part of punishment to deal with existing biases or to help reduce them. Punishment is punishment because a person has broken the law.

Second, there is confusion about mitigating circumstances. All modern systems of justice allow consideration to be given at the sentencing stage to include the character of the offender, previous criminal record and the circumstances in which the offence(s) was committed. The American Friends Committee talks of a 'presumptive sentence' (1976, p. 99), i.e. a specific penalty based on the characteristic seriousness of the crime, to allow the judge to lower the penalty below the presumptive sentence if mitigating circumstances exist, or raise it according to the circumstances and previous record of the offender. The confusion stems from their insistence that 'mitigating circumstances' can be extended to include the background of the offender, which for these purposes means the offender's criminal record.

> The seriousness of the offence to which the commensurate deserts principle looks embraces the defendant's prior criminal record: the number of his previous convictions and the seriousness of the crimes involved. A first offence in our view is deserving of less punishment than a second or third. [von Hirsch, 1976, p. 84]

But why? The Committee reject predictive arguments to justify this practice (in other words, the more often someone has offended in the past, the more likely he is to do it again); and they reject deterrence arguments (that, having continued to commit crimes despite previous punishments, recidivists might as a class require a greater penalty to induce them to desist). They then argue that second and subsequent offenders should be dealt with by a heavier punishment 'because repetition alters the degree of culpability that may be ascribed to the offender' (von Hirsch, 1976, p. 85). But it cannot alter culpability if the term 'culpable' means complicity in the offence; nor can it be affected in terms of moral blameworthiness, unless of course moral blameworthiness is assessed in terms of past character. And that, it seems, is what the Committee wishes to do: they wish to substitute moral blameworthiness for 'personality' or 'social background', and so are led to a moral version of the treatment model they appear to reject. Alternatively, they are subscribing to a deterrence argument in spite of an earlier rejection of it. Either way, the Committee's insistence on including the offender's prior record weakens their argument and produces a confusion that is difficult to avoid. That is why the American Friends Committee was wrong to require a prescribed increase in the presumptive sentence depending on the number and seriousness of the prior crimes, but right to suggest changes in the presumptive sentence where there were special circumstances affecting the gravity of the violation (1976, p. 100), such as in the case of an assault, for example, where the physical injury was more severe than usual or where provocation was excessive. The American Friends Committee never appeared to come to grips with what retribution implies.

I have spent some time on the proposals of the American Friends Committee if only to show some of the implications of a retributive system of punishment within the penal system. In Britain there is a growing interest in the 'justice model' aimed at reducing the arbitrariness of decision-making and directed towards the safeguards of procedural rules. Often, those supporting this model do so without realizing or acknowledging that they are moving towards a form of retribution. As yet their arguments have been presented in a piecemeal fashion, without resort to a full retributive theory. So, for example, parole has been attacked as lacking due process (Hood, 1974a); so too have social inquiry reports (Bean, 1976), but the attack has remained at that level.

Even so, the advantages of a retributive approach are beginning to become clear. More safeguards would be provided for the offender, and the commitment to justice would be paramount. Offenders in penal institutions would be provided with the security inherent in a retributive system. The theory is not without its drawbacks, however. Indeed, it operates almost as if punishment existed in a vacuum and there were no process of negotiation prior to the court appearance. I am not thinking here of the formal requirements for negotiation contained in the Children and Young Persons Act 1969, but of the more informal ones conducted by police when they decide to arrest and charge an offender. These informal negotiations operate in such a way as to affect the decisions of the police, for the decision to prosecute may be based on many factors, one of which is on a trade-off of information between one offender and another. Offender A is not prosecuted for an offence if he gives the police information about more serious offences committed by B. The police have wide established powers of discretion that is permitted by law. Similarly, the Department of Public Prosecutions (DPP) makes decisions about prosecutions that are made 'in the public interest'. Both the police and the DPP operate informal systems which exist on the boundary of the main system. It becomes an oversimplification to say that a person is to be punished because he has committed an offence, for it ignores the reality of informal negotiations.

How can this dilemma be resolved? How can we on the one hand insist on a straightforward connection between crime and punishment and yet tolerate informal judicial procedures? Again, there is no easy solution, and it would be foolish to pretend otherwise. One possible solution would be to view the activities of the police and the DPP in the same way as for law creation generally, i.e. as a separate system, operating subject to its own internal constraints, but subject also to public scrutiny. I do not know if this provides a satisfactory explanation, for it seems that the police will always operate within bounds of secrecy for that may be the only way in which they can work effectively. This being so, we must accept the limitations that their work demands, although not of course uncritically. There is no doubt that the decisions of the DPP could be more widely known. How, for example, is a decision made that is 'in the public interest'?

A retributive system would not claim to remove these ambiguities, nor should we expect it to, but it would go some way towards it. However, this leaves the thorny question of the nature of the punishment under a retributive system. How are prisoners to be punished retributively? It is easier to answer this by defining what a retributive system would not do. There would be no enforced therapy and no attempt to adjust the prisoner's release date according to resistance or acceptance of therapy. There would be no indeterminate or semi-indeterminate sentences, nor would there be statutory licence on release. The period in prison would closely resemble the punishments in ice hockey, where the offender is taken off the ice and remains for a specific period in the 'sin-bin'. No one speaks to him, no one tries to help him; nor do they attempt to change him. Unlike ice hockey, reformist techniques may be available, but where they are the offender's release date is not determined or affected by acceptance of these techniques (Bottoms, 1978).

Of course, there are major difficulties in the application of such a model for a penal system. The game of ice hockey is strangely inappropriate, if only because the player's release from his punishment allows him to be a full participant in the game once his time has been served. The offender coming out of prison is not always permitted to assume a similar place in society. Moreover, the penalty in ice hockey has a more apparent effect on the team's performance than does the offender's period in prison (we are concentrating on prisoners in this model as they offer the most obvious parallels). The third major difficulty lies with those *offering* to help. Throughout the history of reformist techniques the reformist has not been content merely to offer assistance; too often he has wanted to change the offender in some way.

In spite of these disadvantages, the advantages still remain, for above all retribution is not optimistic. Under a retributive system no one asks if the offender has been improved or whether 'prison has done him good'. The question is inappropriate. What matters is that the punishment be proportionate to the crime. This may lead some sceptics to have lingering doubts about a retributive system where the slur of barbarity still exists. I can only reply in terms offered before, and in the certainty that there are some revolutions that are permanent. We can no more return to the barbarity of eighteenth-century prison conditions than we could return to the pre-slavery era. Moreover, as we have said before, the dangers stem less from retribution than from electronic therapy and the new devices such as control units advanced under other theories. Nor will these dangers vanish when rehabilitation disappears, for new dangers are beginning to show themselves. Already we are beginning to see the emergence of the bureaucratic model in our penal system. Here the type of regime and the type of punishment inflicted is dependent on the official in charge of the offenders. The bureaucratic model is career-orientated, for the official establishes regimes in order to further his own success goals. The dangers are obvious; the offender becomes part of the official's plan and the offender's position changes when the officials change. He is therefore offered less overall protection.

The bureaucratic model is already present in North America and exists in a weakened form in Britain. Perhaps it will be transient, operating only during philosophical vacuums and offering a form of control at the local level. On the other hand, once established, it might be difficult to dislodge. Retribution offers a safeguard against that, as it would against other innovations where the basis of the argument lies in the possibility of 'doing something about crime'. We have not yet learned to resign ourselves to the fact that our interventions, albeit from the best motives, may be harmful. Nor have we begun to see the importance of a system that is just.

DETERRENCE AND THE MODERN PENAL SYSTEM

Unlike retribution and rehabilitation, arguments about deterrence have not assumed comparable importance. In this section I wish to show the influence of deterrence on modern penal systems generally rather than specifically. One of the reasons for the lack of interest in deterrence is that it has become intermingled with retribution and rehabilitation. So in the current debate on crime and the penal system deterrence and retribution are sometimes presented as if they constituted a single coherent philosophy. It is not always clear from the various supporters of deterrence/retribution how they would implement new measures, except that they would insist that more unpleasantness should be introduced, and assert that criminals are responsible for their actions and are not victims of circumstances. (The older argument of free will is thereby reasserted in contrast to the deterministic view of the reformists.) The first formal shift towards this approach was adopted in Britain in 1980 when selected detention centres were to be 'stiffened up', to 'act as a deterrent and be retributive for young violent offenders'.

Deterrence has of course remained separate from retribution, but for some the two become bracketed together as part of the general distaste for rehabilitation. Few penal institutions offer pure deterrence — the most obvious exceptions would be the deferred sentence and the suspended sentence — but almost all have a strong deterrent flavour. David Thomas shows how deterrence remains part of the tariff, often coinciding with other theories although occasionally remaining isolated. He says there are many examples in modern sentencing where the higher courts justify a tariff sentence by reference to general deterrence in the narrow sense of inhibiting possible initiators by the fear of penal consequences (Thomas, 1979, p. 14). Serious and grave crimes such as robbery tend to attract deterrent sentences, but so too do other crimes regarded specifically as 'being against the public interest'.

We have already mentioned some of the influences of deterrence on the penal system: the use of previous criminal records, for example, and the methods of determining the length of sentences. Little has been said so far of the major deterrent argument that has dominated the post war period, namely, the debate on capital punishment. Nor do I wish to remedy this, except to note that the results remain inconclusive. For example, in the United States deterrence studies show that legally abolishing capital punishment in those states that rarely imposed it does not lead to any increase in the murder rate, and that states that rarely execute murderers have no more murders than states that never do (Wilson, 1975, p. 192). Wilson goes on to say that 'The crucial question at least for those debating the deterrent issue is whether we can say any more than this' (p. 192). For my part I agree with Wilson, and suspect that there is little more to add except to ask the more sardonic question, which is 'What is there about Anglo-Saxon societies that makes them constantly debate the question of capital punishment?' Beccaria summed it up to my mind when he called capital punishment a 'useless prodigality' and 'ineffectual because of the barbarity of the example it gives to men' (1964, Section 16). But I suppose the debate will continue in some form.

Historically, the use of deterrence has shifted from the ruthless deterrence of the eighteenth and early nineteenth centuries as the sole aim of penal policy. Moberly talks of the more naked deterrence of the Victorian period, aimed at 'terrorization of the criminal classes' as 'avowedly the chief and almost exclusive aim' (1968, p. 269). The possible reformation of the few was merely ancillary, and there was much scepticism about that possibility. The modern method is more subtle:

In so far as the prevention of crime by other than the person dealt with is concerned psychologists agree and history demonstrates that neither fear of monetary amercement nor the physical distress of imprisonment are of material effect. What deterrence there may be springs from more subtle influences; from the fear of public condemnation demonstrated through punishment; from the conduct habits and inhibitions created by open and notorious application in specific cases and of what might otherwise be mere abstract formualtions of right and wrong, from the instinct of individuals to conform with the expressed beliefs and demanded conduct of the herd. [quoted in Moberly, 1968, pp. 260-1]

This view follows on from Paterson's dictum that the loss of freedom, the separation from family and friends, the difficulty of being accepted as a normal member of the community after release all constitute a heavy punishment and will always be a deterrent to potential offenders. Deterrence exists, according to Paterson, in the sentence itself, and this led him to argue that the object of prison treatment should not be to increase the punishment but to reform the prisoner (quoted in Moberly, 1968, p. 260).

The ease with which Paterson links the deterrence of the punishment and the reform of the prisoner suggests a collision of interests between the theories of deterrence and rehabilitation. Nils Christie noted this too when he spoke of the hidden utilitarianism which led to the reformist view that an increase in happiness was the major object of rehabilitation. Christie was able to see how the treatment doctrine was easily translated into a weakened form of utilitarian ethics. Bentham of course would not have approved of the equation, but then he was not able to foresee some of the consequences of his proposals. He was not able to see, for example, that the promotion of the happiness doctrine has the unintended effect of introducing greater control by central and local government and the subsequent interventionist policies that have characterized the treatment approach. Nor was he able to predict that the emphasis placed by the utilitarians on equality could be transformed into a justification for treatment. By this I mean that punishment is socially divisive: it separates the offender from the offended. Treatment, on the other hand, is fostered on the image of social cohesion. When equality becomes the dominating philosophy, or the dominating ethos, it is inappropriate to expect that the penal system will continue to be run on divisive grounds. Treatment then fits into the equalitarian philosophy of state interventionist policies. It loses its force amid conservative politics, for right-wing capitalism emphasizes disparities. Bentham was no socialist, but he helped pave the way for the new radicalism, and indeed for the positivism that has so characterized treatment regimes. Bentham's system of cost accountancy, which weighed up happiness and unhappiness, was eagerly accepted by positivist thinkers with their emphasis on scientific research in the social sciences.

It was stated earlier that deterrence has become bracketed with retribution in modern thinking, but so too has deterrence and rehabilitation. The links noted above are such as to blur the divisions between the traditional philosophies of Bentham and his school and those advocating modern methods of rehabilitation. As such it is becoming increasingly difficult to sift out deterrence influences from others. I am not suggesting that they are indistinguishable, but there are similarities as Christie noted, and as Moberly noted also when he said 'deterrence and reformation are far less distinct and separate than they once appeared' (1968, p. 270). Bentham himself contributed to this:

> It ought not to be forgotten . . . that the delinquent is a member of the community as well as any other individual . . . and there there is just as much reason to consult his interest as any other. It may be right that the interest of the offender should in part be sacrificed to that of the rest of the community but it can never be right that it should be totally disregarded. [quoted in Moberly, 1968, p. 49]

This was the new and revolutionary principle that was radical enough to suggest that the offender had some say in his destiny. The great appeal of Bentham lies in this passage; that is in his respect for values unbridled by the society of his time.

In a more traditional vein the deterrence philosophy has continued to influence the penal systems by Bentham's insistence on less eligibility; that is, the worst condition of the free man must be better than that of the offender, otherwise the free man will be encouraged to improve his lost through crime. The stresses and strains of modern society have resurrected that argument. Under the 1969 Childrens and Young Persons Act the benefits of 'intermediate treatment' have allowed the position of the offender to improve, occasionally at the expense of those not convicted. Intermediate treatment, with its emphasis on outdoor activities, playgroups, etc. (or 'intermediate treats', as one criminologist has called it) has the effect of producing justified resentment among those not so 'fortunate'. The danger is that the pattern of penal reform is likely to outstrip the benefits granted to the population as a whole. More resentment could be produced, and to ignore this is to imply that the legitimate aspirations of non-offenders can be ignored too. Non-offenders have as much stake in the future of society as have the offenders, and more so. But it is no easy task to maintain that delicate balance between the demands of penal reform and the aspirations of others. Bentham considered the problem only from the point of deterrence theory, although it is probable that he articulated the fears of eighteenth-century society as surely as he does now. Those harbouring resentment may forget occasionally that the penal system operates through compulsion, which alone may be enough to dissuade most of us from trying to improve our position through crime. But perhaps that is not the cause of resentment; it may only be sufficient to believe that offenders prosper for resentment to exist, and if this is so we should consider Bentham's arguments with care. In a famous passage Bishop Butler has described the distorting effect of resentment, how 'the whole character and behaviour is considered with an eye to that particular part which has offended us and the whole man appears monstrous without anything right or human in him' (Butler, 1729, p. 112).

I do not wish to make too much of this for resentment is hardly likely to exist against those serving prison sentences — although it may do so against the prisoners families receiving welfare payments. Where it exists otherwise it does so mainly in the juvenile justice field, and we may not consider this too important if a small number of children benefit in an exceptional way. My point is less about the resentment itself, than about understanding the manner of it nowadays, and to show how it has appeared in spite of the strenuous efforts by Bentham to avoid it. In turn, less eligibility provides active discouragement to the active and zealous penal reformer.[4]

But the less-eligibility principle is only a small part of the major utilitarian contribution to the penal system. Deterrence applies to everyone, and those who are not deterred have to pay the penalty. It is the all-inclusive nature of deterrence that makes it indispensible to modern penal systems — and one could add to schools, families and numerous other social institutions. And by 'all-inclusive' I mean that the aims of deterrence are to protect the life, liberty and property of law-abiding people, or to maintain law and order. The achievement of these objects is necessary for the existence of all civilized societies.

Yet while it may be true that deterrence, as a philosophy, has considerable influence on the conventional estimates of the relative wrongness of different kinds of actions, the reverse is not true. Rashdall disputes this, arguing that the penal system influences society by its influence on conventional morality (Rashdall, 1907, pp. 296-7). If influence means 'reflects', then there is no disagreement, although Rashdall seems to be saying more. But in deterrence terms this cannot be so; the aim of punishment is to fulfil the command of the law. The penal system becomes the embodiment of legal commands and exists as an example to those who may feel inclined to break the law. Acceptance of this proposition does not mean that legislation, or the penal system based on the principles of deterrence, is exempt from criticism. The basis of that criticism must come from a different source; for example, from the nature of deterrence itself and the penal system's conformity to deterrent standards. Moreover, as Mundle says, the efficacy of a penal system in promoting the moral education of the community seems much more uncertain than its efficacy in deterring antisocial behaviour through fear of penalties (Mundle, 1954). A penal system under a deterrent doctrine is not directed towards the re-education of the community.

In modern terms, then, deterrence has become submerged by the philosophies of retribution and rehabilitation, and for this reason it becomes difficult to point to the specific contribution of deterrence within the penal system. The modern debate has not included deterrence; the debate about deterrence is largely confined to its affect in crime prevention. Nor do there appear to be any significant changes to alter this. The introduction of deferred and suspended sentences as measures aimed at keeping offenders out of prisons was introduced but then later was changed to incorporate rehabilitation methods; for instance, supervision was introduced for selected offenders. The only other move has been to 'stiffen up' certain selected detention centres, but even then the demands to do so were more often than not retributive. Apart from the length of sentences given by the courts, the penal system has done little to accommodate itself to deterrent thinking. What exists has been well established by earlier legislation. It is almost as if we could talk of the demise of deterrence too if measured against the strength of existing debates and recent changes.

But could such a demise be possible? If so, how could it be checked? It is doubtful if deterrence will ever lose its impact, for it is too strongly rooted in the social order for that to happen. It could of course become neglected or ossified and that would assist its decline. If so, its decline could be checked in two ways: first by a resurrection of distinctions between utilitarianism and rehabilitation and of other distinctions between deterrence and retribution (it is almost a paradox that the great debate of Chapter 2 is no longer a debate outside the confines of a few academic philosophers); and second by a demonstration of the nature of deterrence and its value to a penal system generally. This is the neglected area.

NOTES

1. To appreciate the full significance of parole we must understand how the system operates. What follows is a description provided by a member of the Parole Board.

   Some months before the prisoner's eligibility date, he is invited to make his case for parole in the form of written representation. The prison too begins to assemble a dossier containing the following: (a) a police report on the offence(s) for which he is currently convicted, together with the police antecedents which include previous convictions and sentences, if any; (b) the remarks of the trial judge and appeal court transcripts; (c) the prison reception report, including reports from various sections on the prison, such as the workshop instructor's report, wing managers, etc.; (d) a report on the prisoner's progress which may include a medical report, the prison probation officer's report and a concluding report signed by an assistant governor giving a view about the suitability for parole. In addition the prisoner makes his own representation, either in the form of a written statement or through an interview with a member of the LRC. The LRC then considers the whole matter and refers to the Parole Board those considered suitable. The LRC is composed of five members including the governor of the prison (or his deputy), a member of the Board of Visitors, a senior probation officer, and two independent members drawn from the local community. The Parole Board itself has an independent chairman and a fairly wide membership drawn from the ranks of the judiciary and the legal profession, criminologists, psychiatrists, probation officers and lay members which may include magistrates, schoolteachers, businessmen, clergymen, etc. This Board discusses each case in turn, dealing with perhaps twenty-five to thirty cases each sitting.

2. In this section related to semi-indeterminate sentences I benefited greatly from being a member of a small working party in the Penal Policy

Working Group on Parole which met in June and July 1980. Its members were Peter Banister, Elizabeth Barnard, John Macmillan, Ken Pease, Keith Soothill and myself. See Pease, *et al.* (1980).

3. For those who doubt this, see the 1975 Childrens Act, where some sections were repealed before they became operative, some were contradictory and some were frankly unintelligible.

4. The issue has been resurrected in a curious way in Britain by the Conservative Government in 1980 deciding not to pay the full supplementary benefits to people on strike. The move was criticized for, among other things, providing ex-prisoners with more welfare payments than strikers.

6

Some Tentative Conclusions

Punishment provides the link between rule-making and rule-breaking. Marx captured the essence of it when he said: 'plainly speaking, and dispensing with all paraphrases, punishment is nothing but a means of society to defend itself against the infraction of its vital conditions whatever may be their character' (Marx, 1959). Society's defence, or more accurately the defence used by members of a society and the State, contains a strong conservative element, for it is directed at the maintenance of the existing social order. In times of revolution it can be used to support new forces against reactionary or non-radical elements, but is conservative none the less, for its function is to maintain whatever social order is uppermost. In Western European-type societies punishment is ultra-conservative, for those societies are politically settled.

Punishment is *for* something and directed *at* someone. The relationship between punisher and punished is, by definition, not a relationship of equals. Suffering is inflicted by someone — perhaps acting as another's agent — against another person invariably against his will. The power resides in those doing the punishment. This is as true of punishment inflicted by the State as of that inflicted by parents. That power is derived not from naked force but from the ability to legislate, the claim to represent the right values, and the right to enforce them. Those being punished are the outsiders or the rule-breakers. It would be the same if the punishment were inflicted by the judiciary as by a trade union or a pedagogue: the hierarchical relationship remains.

All theories of punishment are therefore theories about power, and about the rights and claims to exercise that power. In the exercise of state power the law can be defined as operating or existing when it is externally guaranteed by the probability that coercion exists, either physical or psychological, which will bring about confirmity or avenge violation. Coercion, said Max Weber, will be applied by a staff of people holding themselves ready for that purpose (1954, p. 5). To Weber the link between law and punishment is established by coercion. It matters not that the coercion is supplied by formal rational law, or the non-rational Khadi justice of the Moslem market place or the highly traditional empirical justice to be found in the responses of the rabbis of the Talmud. Once a coercive apparatus exists, law can be said to exist also. With pedagogic punishment the coercive apparatus exists to a different degree, although coercion in some form remains none the less. The relative power of punisher and punished is a reflection of the relative powers of those who make and enforce rules as compared with those who are expected to abide by them.

But power is a variable quality. The parent who makes and enforces rules that children have to obey also has to obey rules made and enforced by others, including those of the State itself: as most adults make and enforce rules for their children, so they have to obey others. Human society is characterized by rules and social life is about social rules. Punishment is one means of securing conformity to those rules. It is not of course the only means, and as a method of securing conformity must be counted as costly. It is hopefully a method to be used in the last resort, when others such as praise, remonstration and perhaps special pleading have failed. Most people obey rules because they believe in their values and accept the authority and power of those whose task it is to make and enforce them — and when they are broken often accept the legitimacy of the punishment. (It has often been a matter of some interest to me why so few prisoners are not politically radical in their outlook, offering in general terms a political view of the world that is essentially conservative and esentially in favour of institutions that enforce rules and punish those who violate rules.) By its very nature human society becomes bound up with the question of punishment even if those punishments are often mild in form.

Punishment is one of the ways in which we can show that rules exist and are broken. It is not the only way, nor is it necessarily the most reliable way. It is also a way in which we can learn about the moral nature of society; for it will show us why we punish and how we punish. Third, it will show which category of persons is exempt from punishment and which is punished less severely. Fourth, it will show us about the ethical claims used to determine the types of punishments, and fifth, it becomes a useful tool for the sociologist attempting to understand the pattern of social relationships within a society. In so far as the sociologist is interested in punishment, the interest surrounds the relationships between punishment and the social order and the ethical claims used to determine those punishments. Punishment also becomes a useful analytical tool for philosophers, because it opens up questions about moral principles and the relationships between those principles and other people. B. M. Barry sums up the position well when he says there is a tradition of thought running from Hobbes to Hume according to which the point of morality is that it offers, in Hobbes's terms, convenient articles of peace. Human beings are sufficiently equal in their capacity to hurt one another, and in their dependence on one another to live well, that it is mutually advantageous to all of them to support an institution designed to give people artificial motives for respecting the interests of others (Barry, 1977, p. 270). This being so, punishment shows how people hurt one another even before they are punished, and why it is necessary to respect the interdependence of others.

I do not think that a great deal can be gained from some of the more strenuous attempts of recent years to believe that we are able to operate a legal system without punishment, or to bring up children without it or to operate organizations and institutions without it. In spite of the prodigious amount of legislation since 1945 — some of which gives the outward impression of attempts to avoid punitive methods for offenders — we cannot break away from punishment. We may have devised different methods of penal treatments, but they remain punishments none the less. We have not yet reached the point where we can confidently live by Spinoza's doctrine that the greatest penalty for having done wrong is simply to have done it; nor shall we ever, as long as human beings make rules for others. Punishment occurs when rules are broken, and as long as rules exist so will punishment.

It seems we must acknowledge that punishment exists and will do in the near and remote future. We shall achieve little by believing it can be mysteriously spirited away by calling it something else. The offender on probation is only too aware of the sanctions and coercion governing his behaviour, as is the child on the care order, the child in school or the member of a trade union or any organization. We need therefore to continue to ask the basic questions that have always bothered philosophers, but sadly not have always bothered criminologists: 'What is the nature of punishment?' and 'How can it be justified?' All other questions are subservient to these.

From what has been said so far it will be clear that, while I have tried to present many competing arguments, I regard rehabilitation as a sad mistake. Sad, because it has always promised to break out of traditional manners of thinking, and promised to do so with a strong humanitarian voice. Its achievements have been many but the humanitarian claims have often been forms of deceit, allowing new and more clandestine tyrannies to develop. This is no hyperbolic statement but one reflecting much of the literature in Britain, North America and elsewhere, and one reflecting the views of many who have been at the receiving end of the rehabilitation process. Rehabilitation is a mistake because its theoretical base is weak and it sees rule-breakers as lacking in dignity, and capable of manipulation. It is a mistake because it attempts to operate away from public scrutiny, and because it has no built-in controls on those acting as the treatment officials.

But if rehabilitation vanished from the penal system, would not that leave the door open to those who rapaciously demand punishment for its own sake or who enjoy the prospect of seeing others suffer? And, what about children? Are they not always to be punished for improvement? Could there ever be a retributive or utilitarian dominance in the juvenile court? Is it really that simple to expect to return to older theoretical arguments that have been shown to be defective?

The answers depend on the aims and assumptions we have about people who break rules. If, as with rehabilitation, we are always looking out for means to improve offenders, then we shall continue to ask different questions and have different aims than if we were to ask about the relationship between the offender and the victim. Rehabilitation becomes a sad mistake because it leads us to believe that penal institutions ought and can improve offenders, be it for social, psychological or moral reasons. We put more and more offenders into the system, devote more and more resources to it and paradoxically produce more and more failures. This leads to new efforts to improve the system; it leads to more and more resources; and we still produce more failures. We then see the failures as ours, and return again to the same theoretical treadmill. Rehabilitationists draw attention to the failure as our failure; we are led to believe that it is society's failure in producing the criminals, and society's failure in being baffled by the solution. But why is it society's failure any more than it is the weakness, meanness or grasping avaricious nature of the offenders? Because, say the rehabilitationists, society has produced them in that way, and we are part of society. We, the society, have condemned the offenders to poor housing, uncertain futures, poor family life, etc., and then they the offenders are condemned to poor-quality penal institutions. How could we ever hope to cure crime in those circumstances? And of course up to a point the argument is well stated. But the flaw lies in the assertion that something *can* be done, not that it *ought* to be done. And a bigger flaw lies in the assumption that it can be done as part of a system of punishments. It is a flaw for two reasons: first, that treatment programmes rarely work; and second, that the theoretical-system on which the arguments are based is faulty. Would it then be possible to have a modified treatment programme? The answer depends on the words 'modified' and 'treatment', and begs the question of what should be its place in any system of punishments.

A modified treatment programme that offered treatment facilities would be acceptable provided that the treatment was entirely voluntary and did not affect the outcome of the sentence in any way. This would be difficult to achieve for treatment officials can be intrusive and persuasive and would rarely be content to offer services without the opportunity to influence decisions. Once part of an organization they would wish to extend their influence and would be restrained from doing so only if they were relegated to the same status as (say) the visiting clergyman. But before even considering that, why not go back to a more basic question, give a closer examination to the nature of treatment, and place the emphasis on the treatment officials by making them justify what they do? This would be no small task. In spite of numerous criticisms of treatment, too numerous to list, there is little or no debate in the reformist literature probing into these questions. The usual defence is to restate the same aims as before and to continue to restate them irrespective of the counter-arguments. It is as if one were opposing a deeply held belief system, almost religious in its structure, and occasionally righteous in its form. A modified treatment programme would need to counter this; hence the demand to place the burden of justification on those doing the treatment.

There still remains the problems of children. Here I think we must recognize the demand for improvement, but meet the argument by defining improvement as training rather than as treatment. We should remember Spinoza's observation that all men are born ignorant, and before they can learn the right way of life and acquire the habit of virtue, the greater part of their life, even if they have been well brought up, has passed away (Spinoza, 1951a, Ch. 16, p. 201). Training becomes a lengthy exercise which for a child is dominating. If as Nowell-Smith says rewards and punishments are means of varying the causal antecedents of actions, so that those we desire will occur and those we wish to prevent will not occur, (1948, p. 59), then this presupposes a form of training. Children require education, and the opportunity to learn social and moral skills, and it becomes the duty of those who act *in loco parentis* to provide those. There is no easy answer to questions about the nature of those skills, or to the methods of providing them, but this should not act as a means of avoiding the discussion. Children in care, and children on supervision, require the same training, if not more than those more fortunate, and they need to be provided with facilities that are not substandard. To fail to live up to those expectations is a failure to see children as children. The essence of this argument is captured in the *Who Cares?* document, where the children themselves claim 'the right to live'. For to live as a child is not to be an object of administrative convenience or of therapeutic manipulation.

If training were substituted for treatment there would be two distinct advantages. First, it would avoid obscurantism. The aims of training programmes, if not entirely clear, would be less muddy than at present, for what was being done to children would permit closer examination and not be allowed to hide behind pseudo-technical language. Second, those responsible for the child would be accountable. The method of transferring children to different institutions and passing them to more and greater 'experts' would be avoided. This, linked to the requirements given in Chapter 4 about the length of sentences to be passed, would produce a more just system of punishments for children. We may not reduce the crime rate as a result, but as argued in Chapter 5 there are limits to what can be done about a crime rate by a penal system anyway.

If treatment is a sad mistake, what then would happen to the other sentences orientated to treatment, such as probation? Quite simply, they could no longer be justified in that form. If treatment is to be voluntary, as I suggest it should be, then offenders should be permitted to see a probation officer if and when they so wish but not as part of a sentence. If however the probation order were to change to one involving close supervision and become a deterrent or retributive sentence, then so be it. The issue would then be the nature of the supervision and what such supervision would entail — for juveniles perhaps part of a training programme; for adults perhaps nothing more than the requirement to report or even perhaps perform a type of community service. Different types or grades of probation could be incorporated into the system.

We are left then with retribution and deterrence. Of the two retribution offers the most possibilities. In saying this no attempt is made to avoid the two major defects of retribution — that men deserve punishment is not by itself a sufficient justification, and that the relationship between the punishment and the crime can never be established. It is the strength of the arguments that are appealing: first, the relationship with guilt; second, the refusal to see punishment as offering promises or advantages; and third, the insistence that people are responsible human beings, capable of acting in ways that may not always be in their best interests yet not met by methods that leave them open to manipulation.

The appeal of retribution is peculiar to the spirit of these times. This is recognized and acknowledged. Yet it is the same appeal that led von Hirsch and his Committee of Friends to argue for 'commensurate deserts', precisely because retribution offers the only possible antidote against rehabilitation. The deterrent doctrine is tainted with 'the promise of advantages' and is too closely allied to rehabilitation to be of value. Its other defects are also plain: it offers possibilities of punishing the innocent; it has a weak link with justice; and it is no less clear than the retributive position as to which acts are to be selected for punishment.

To say that retribution is appealing because it acts as a possible antidote is perhaps not a good enough argument. This too is recognized and acknowledged. It becomes an argument more appropriate to social engineering than to philosophy or criminology. None the less, we ought not to deprecate social engineering too easily, if only because of the large number of offenders who appear at courts each year and who are subject to the engineer's practicalities. Part of the appeal of all philosophies is practical. The deterrent theory also has appeal; we would think less of it if it could be shown to have no empirical deterrent value, as we think little of the rehabilitative theory because it cannot provide practical measures of justice. Social engineering has its place. Inevitably, it has to operate after the details of the arguments have been well sifted over, but is sometimes capable of showing strength and weakness not readily apparent unless put to a sustained practical test. The major strength of retribution is that it has been able to show how weak rehabilitation is once rehabilitation has been allowed an opportunity to prove itself. So, paradoxically, retribution has thrived by showing how weak is the other.

Still, this is not sufficient to give retribution unqualified support. But where else is there to look? To Marx, perhaps, or to some other influential thinker? Marx devoted little attention to crime and even less to punishment. What he said, however, may be a surprise to many, particularly those of a rehabilitationist persuasion. The lengthy quote is worth making:

> Punishment in general has been defended as a means either of ameliorating or of intimidating. Now what right have you to punish me for the amelioration or intimidation of others? And besides there is history — there is such a thing as statistics — which prove with the most complete evidence since Cain the world has been neither intimidated nor ameliorated by punishment. Quite the contrary. From the point of view of abstract right there is only one theory of punishment which recognises human dignity in that abstract, and that is the theory of Kant especially in the more rigid formula given to it by Hegel. [Marx, 1853]

Marx goes on to say that it is necessary to reflect upon and hope to change the system that breeds the crimes instead of glorifying the hangman who executes existing criminals only to make room for new ones. In this at least he remains consistent with his other writings. But he clearly saw the classical retributive theory as something to admire, and in so doing talked of abstract rights and justice in a way that was unusual for him. Perhaps his admiration for retribution was part of his lifelong hostility to utilitarianism (he called Bentham, for example, 'that arch-Philistine, that insipid pedantic leather tongued oracle of the ordinary bourgeois intelligence of the eighteenth century — *Capital,* vol. 1, p. 609), but he may also have been attracted to retribution because of what he called 'human dignity in the abstract'. Retribution at least provides that. Modern Marxists have tended to follow Bonger rather than Marx towards their aims of 'therapeutic justice' rather than 'abstract right.' And in following Bonger they have done little to clarify thinking on punishment.

William Bonger, the great Dutch Marxist criminologist, argued that in a properly designed society all criminality would be a problem for the physician rather than the judge. He hoped we would move towards that society. Many so-called radical penal theorists have adopted Bonger's position; others, perhaps more radical, have hoped for a society where deviance will be not punished but tolerated (Taylor, Walton and Young, 1973).

I cannot take this latter argument seriously, for it seems to depend again on a pious hope akin to the Second Coming. The other argument needs more careful consideration, for it points to a trend in modern thinking that is based on the work of Marx and draws its inspiration from him. Dealing with Bonger, then, his hope that criminality would be eventually a problem for the physician rather than the judge simply will not do. As a theoretician steeped in Marx's doctrine of social class, it is incredible that he was unable to realize that a theory derived from medicine is as class-bound as is punishment. It creates two distinct classes: those in a higher class, whose task it is to treat, and those deemed to be 'ill', who are in the lower class. The latter are there because they have not acquired the right values. In the same way that it takes two parties to punish, so it takes two to treat. Social distance is present in both. Jeffrie Murphy is therefore right when he says the therapeutic state where prisons are called hospitals and jailers are called psychiatrists simply raises again all the old problems about the justification of coercion and its reconciliation with autonomy that exist in discussions about punishment (Murphy, 1973, pp. 242-3). He sees the therapeutic state as capable of producing coercive practices, which in turn become surrounded by a benevolent rhetoric so that it becomes even harder to raise important issues. The move to therapy becomes illusory, says Murphy, a viewpoint that I would share (Bean, 1976).

If not to Marx then where else? We could continue the search for a long time, but the only possible answer must be to some form of retribution or deterrence. These theories do not have to be resurrected in their traditional forms, but the basic structures of the arguments would have to remain. If punishment is to control action, then it involves a set of utilitarian arguments, and if it is to be deserved then it is retributive. And no amount of argument or persuasion can alter those basic positions. To put it crudely, we are stuck with them whether we like it or not.

This does not mean that there will be no experimentation or no new ways of approaching the old problems. But they will be nothing more. They may be grafted on, or become extensions and even developments of existing methods of thinking, but essentially they have to remain the same arguments. Some relatively minor changes are possible; we may, for example, wish to amend the existing methods of court procedure to produce a system that more closely resembles that advocated by Nils Christie, where the victim and the offender operate in more open confrontation (Christie, 1977). Or perhaps we should remember Godwin's arguments about the imperfections of the evidence, about the way the trial is conducted to the detriment of the offender. 'The culprit that escapes, however conscious of innocence, lifts up his hands with astonishment and can scarcely believe his luck having such mighty odds against him' (Godwin, 1971, p. 258). We might wish to amend the court procedure in some way to even up the odds a little. I do not know. The possibilities for change are endless, but they will still exist within the basic philosophical theories.

Nowhere is this more so than in the area of the penal system relating to sentences. The way the debate has neglected to consider punishment is a serious omission producing serious consequences. The 'stagnant lagoon' noted by Nils Christie has dominated thinking yet paradoxically produced an optimism out of all proportion to what can be achieved. We continue to increase the range and number of sentences, each one claiming that it provides a better answer than the ones before, and yet when the final count is made we find it is no better or worse than the successes for any existing sentence. And why should it be? How is it that we have been led to believe that the sentences of the court can improve offenders' lives as a result of a series of short visits to a probation officer, a few Saturday afternoons spent with the police, or a number of hours doing community service? I am sure that some offenders will disagree and some probation officers or police will claim spectacular successes, but even the most optimistic will have to recognize that their efforts have been largely wasted. There may be very good reasons why new sentences should be introduced, but not surely on the grounds that they will provide a significant reduction in the crime rate or improve offenders' wellbeing. The ultimate area of discussion must be the nature and justifications of the punishment.

There is also the prevailing view, noted before, that punishment does not exist, or that if it does we should virtually apologize for it.

Punishment is a poor method of social control, to be used only as a last resort, but when it is used we ought never to try to deceive ourselves and others that we are doing something else. This is why rehabilitation is so shocking, and why it is plainly misguided to question imprisonment on the grounds that it does the offender no good. Prison is used as a punishment. I may not like it, I may even regard it as barbaric, but I should not criticize it on the ground of 'not doing the offender good'. It may not be a good *punishment,* but that is another question. And yet that is the only question that is of value, for to ask if it is a good punishment is to ask about its justification, and to ask about its methods in terms of its justification. There may of course be subsidiary questions that arise relating to other moral issues that require separate analysis (for example, 'Is imprisonment economically justified?' or 'Is imprisonment likely to provide the right sort of medical care?'), but these can only be introduced when the main argument is settled.

There is also a prevailing view that social science has a leading part to play in the debate. Perhaps this is so, but I doubt if it is a leading one. The introduction of social scientists into the penal system, as practitioners and academics, has helped produce that optimism which has led magistrates and judges to believe there are answers to all problems. Where social scientists have fostered this attitude they have done a great disservice to themselves, the courts and most of all to the offenders. The debate is not a technical one, although there are technical features, but the traditional interests of social scientists give the impression that technicalities are important. The debate is a moral one. It is about imposing suffering and about the need to impose it. It is also about the amount of suffering that is required and the methods by which it is imposed.

Although the debate has not been extended into the area of non-legal punishment, the same questions apply there too. We can, and ought to, debate the methods of punishment in our schools, but we should not fall into the same traps we have fallen into for the penal system. The debate about corporal punishment, for example, is a debate about method and must remain so, and it should be placed with the same set of questions about justification, the extent of suffering imposed, etc. Of course, the additional feature is that it takes place on children, so the debate must be extended to include education, training and the levels of the child's responsibility. But the debate is the same none the less, and must ever remain so.

Bibliography

ACTON, H. B. (ed.) (1969) *The Philosophy of Punishment*. Macmillan.
ALLEN, F. A. (1964) *The Borderland of Criminal Justice*. University of Chicago Press.
AMERICAN CORRECTIONAL ASSOCIATION (1972) Development of modern correctional concepts and standards. In R. M. Carter, D. Glaser and L. T. Wilkins (eds) pp. 17-34 *Correctional Institutions*. Lippincott.
AMERICAN FRIENDS SERVICE COMMITTEE (1971) *Struggle for Justice*. Hill and Wang.
ANDENAES, J. (1966) The general preventative effects of punishments. *University of Pennsylvania Law Review*, 114, 949-83.
ANDENAES, J. (1970) The morality of deterrence. *University of Chicago Law Review*, 37, 649-64.
ANDENAES, J. (1971) Deterrence and specific offences. *University of Chicago Law Review*, 38, 537-53.
AQUINAS, St Thomas (1974) *Summa Theologiae*. Latin text and English translation (trans. T. C. O'Brien). Eyre and Spottiswoode.
ARISTOTLE (1925) *Ethica Nicomachea* (trans. W. D. Ross), vol. 9 (especially bk 5). Clarendon Press.
ARMSTRONG, K. G. (1961) The retributivist hits back. *Mind*, 70, 471-90 (also in Acton, 1969, pp. 138-58).
ASSOCIATION OF DIRECTORS OF SOCIAL SERVICES. (1980) Children and young persons legislation in 1980 (mimeo)
AUSTIN, J. (1954) *The Province of Jurisprudence Determined*. Weidenfeld and Nicolson.

BAIER, K. (1955) Is punishment retributive? *Analysis*, 16, 25-32 (also in Acton, 1969, pp. 130-7).
BALDWIN, J. and McCONVILLE, M. (1977) *Negotiated Justice*. Martin Robertson.
BARKER, E. (1952) *Principles of Social and Political Theory*. Clarendon Press.
BARNARD, E. (1976) Parole decision making in Britain. *International Journal of Criminology and Penology*, 4, 145-59.
BARRY, B. M. (1977) Justice between generations. In *Law Morality and Society: Essays in Honour of H. L. Hart*, pp. 268-84. Oxford University Press.

BAXTER, I. F. and EBERTS, M. A. (1978) *The Child and the Courts.* Sweet and Maxwell.

BEAN, P. T. (1974) *The Social Control of Drugs.* Martin Robertson.

BEAN, P. T. (1976) *Rehabilitation and Deviance.* Routledge and Kegan Paul.

BEAN, P. T. (1980) *Compulsory Admissions to Mental Hospitals.* John Wiley and Sons.

BEAN, V. W. (1975) The juvenile court in transition. M. Phil. thesis, University of Nottingham.

BECCARIA, C. (1964) Of crimes and punishments. In A. Manzoni, The *Column of Infamy* (trans. K. Foster and J. Grigson), pp. 11-96, Oxford University Press.

BENN, S. I. (1958) An approach to the problems of punishment. *Philosophy,* 33, 325-341 (also in Feinberg and Gross, 1975, pp. 63-73).

BENN, S. I. and PETERS, R. S. (1959) *Social Principles and the Democratic State.* George Allen and Unwin.

BENTHAM, J. (1948) *An Introduction to the Principles of Morals and Legislation.* Basil Blackwell.

BENTHAM, J. (1962) *Principles of Penal Law* (Part 2. The rationale of punishment. In J. Bentham, *Collected Works* (ed. J. Bowring) especially bk 1, ch. 7, section 7). Russell and Russell.

BENTHAM, J. (1970) Of laws in general. *Collected Works.* (ed. H. L. A. Hart). Athlone Press.

BEYLEVELD, D. (1979a) Deterrence research as a basis for deterrence policies. *Howard Journal,* 18, 135-49.

BEYLEVELD, D. (1979b) Identifying, explaining and predicting deterrence. *British Journal of Criminology.* 19, 205-24.

BOSANQUET, B. (1965) *The Philosophical Theory of the State.* Macmillan.

BOSS, P. (1967) *Social Policy and the Young Delinquent.* Routledge and Kegan Paul.

BOTTOMLEY, A. K. (1973) *Decisions in the Penal Process.* Martin Robertson.

BOTTOMLEY, A. K. (1979) *Criminology in Focus.* Martin Robertson.

BOTTOMS, A. E. (1974) On the decriminalization of the English juvenile court. In R. G. Hood (ed.) *Crime, Criminology and Public Policy,* pp. 319-45. Heinemann.

BOTTOMS, A. E. (1977) The coming crisis in British penology (mimeo).

BOTTOMS, A. E. (1978) Law, order and authority, (mimeo).

BOTTOMS, A. E. and McWILLIAMS, W. (1979) A non-treatment paradigm for probation practice. *British Journal of Social Work,* 9, 159-202.

BRADLEY, F. H. (1927) *Ethical Studies.* Clarendon Press.

BRITISH ASSOCIATION OF SOCIAL WORKERS (1974) Memorandum to the Eleventh Report from the Expenditure Committee (mimeo).

BROMLEY, P. M. (1976) *Family Law* (5th edn). Butterworths.

BUTLER, J. B. (1929) *Sermons* (especially nos. 8 and 9). Clarendon Press.

BUTLER, S. (1960) *Erewhon.* Jonathon Cape.

CAMPBELL, T. D. (1977) Punishment in juvenile justice. *British Journal of Law and Society* 4, 74-86.

CANADIAN MENTAL HEALTH ASSOCIATION (undated) *The Legal Rights of Children.*

CHRISTIE, N. (1974) Utility and social values in court decisions on punishment. In R. G. Hood (ed.) *Crime, Criminology and Public Policy,* pp. 281-96. Heinemann.

CHRISTIE, N. (1977) Conflicts as property. *British Journal of Criminology,* 17, 1-15.

COHEN, S. (1979) Guilt, justice and tolerance. In D. Downes and P. Rock (eds) *Deviant Interpretations,* pp. 17-51. Martin Robertson.

CONRAD, J. P. (1965) *Crime and its Correction.* Tavistock.

COONS, J. E. and MNOOKIN, R. H. (1978) Towards a theory of children's rights. In Baxter and Eberts (1978).

CRETNEY, S. M. (1979) *Principles of Family Law* (3rd edn). Sweet and Maxwell.

CROSS, R. (1975) *The English Sentencing System* (2nd edn). Butterworths.

DEVLIN, P. (1965) *The Enforcement of Morals.* Oxford University Press.

D.H.S.S. (1979a) *Children Referred to Closed Units* (Research Report no. 5).

D.H.S.S. (1979b) *Report of St Charles Youth Centre* (Evaluation Team) 4 October.

DICEY, A. V. (1962) *The Law of Constitution.* Macmillan.

DIXON, K. (1967) Discipline, freedom and the justification of punishments. In L. Stenhouse (ed.) *Discipline in Schools: A Symposium,* pp. 163-92. Pergamon Press.

DOYLE, J. F. (1969) Justice and legal punishment. In Acton (1969), pp. 159-71.

DURKHEIM, E. (1964) *The Division of Labour in Society.* Free Press.

EWING, A. C. (1927) Punishment as a moral agency: an attempt to reconcile the retributive and utilitarian view. *Mind,* 36, 292-305.

EWING, A. C. (1929) *The Morality of Punishment.* Kegan Paul Trench and Trubner.

FARIS, E. (1914) The origin of punishment. *International Journal of Ethics,* 24/5, 54-67.

FEINBERG, J. and GROSS, H. (1975) *Punishment: Selected Readings.* Dickenson.

FICHTE, J. C. (1889) *The Science of Rights.* Trubner.

FLEW, A. (1954) The justification of punishment. *Philosophy,* 29, 291-307 (also in Acton, 1969, pp. 83-104, with postscript).

FLEW, A. (1973) *Crime or Disease.* Macmillan.

FOX, S. (1974) The reform of juvenile justice: children's right to punishment. Address delivered to the New England Juvenile Justice Institute, Williamstown, Massachusetts, 19 April (mimeo) (also in *Juvenile Justice,* vol. 25, August 1974).

FULLER, L. (1964) *The Morality of Law.* Yale University Press.

GIBBS, J. P. (1968) Crime, punishment and deterrence. *Social Sciences Quarterly,* 48, 515-30.
GIBBS, J. P. (1975) *Crime, Punishment and Deterrence.* Elsevier.
GILLER, H. and MORRIS, A. (1976) Children who offend: care, control or confusion. *Criminal Law Review,* November, 656-65.
GODWIN, W. (1971) *Enquiry Concerning Political Justice* (ed. K. C. Carter) Clarendon Press.
GOODMAN, L. (ed.) (1972) *Clarke Hall and Morrison on Children* (8th edn). Butterworths.
GREEN, T. H. (1910) *Principles of Political Obligation* (1888). Longmans. (Relevant sections in *Journal of Criminal Law and Criminology,* 1, 14-43).
GROSS, H. (1979) *A Theory of Criminal Justice.* Oxford University Press.
GUNN, J. (1971) Sentencing — as seen by a psychiatrist. *Medicine, Science and the Law,* 11, 95-103.

HALL-WILLIAMS, E. (1978) Ten years of parole — retrospect and prospect. Paper delivered for the Dennis Carroll Memorial Lecture, University of Nottingham.
HANDLER, J. (1973) *The Coercive Social Worker.* Rand McNally.
HAPGOOD, M. (1979) Issues in juvenile justice: some perceptions of juveniles and parents. PhD thesis, University of Nottingham.
HART, H. L. A. (1951) The ascription of responsibility and rights. In A. Flew (ed.) *Logic and Language,* vol. 1, pp. 145-66. Oxford University Press.
HART, H. L. A. (1953) Justice. *Philosophy,* 28, 348-52.
HART, H. L. A. (1955) Are there any natural rights? *Philosophical Review,* 64, 175-91.
HART, H. L. A. (1963) *Law, Liberty and Morality.* Oxford University Press.
HART, H. L. A. (1967) Intention and punishment. *Oxford Review,* 4, 5-12.
HART, H. L. A. (1968) *Punishment and Responsibility: Essays in the Philosophy of Law.* Clarendon Press.
HAWKINS, K. (1973) Parole procedure: an alternative approach. *British Journal of Criminology,* 13, 6-25.
HEGEL, G. F. (1967) *Philosophy of Right* (trans. T. M. Knox). Clarendon Press.
H.M.S.O. (1927) *Report of the Departmental Committee on the Treatment of Young Offenders* (The Maloney Committee). Cmd 2831.
H.M.S.O. (1953) *Royal Commission on Capital Punishment* (the Gowers Commission). Cmd 8932.
H.M.S.O. (1957) *Report of the Committee on Homosexual Offences and Prostitution* (the Wolfenden Report). Cmd 247.
H.M.S.O. (1959) *Penal Practice in a Changing Society.* Cmnd 645.
H.M.S.O. (1960) *Report of the Committee on Children and Young Persons* (the Ingleby Committee). Cmnd 1191.
H.M.S.O. (1964) *Report of the Committee on Young Persons (Scotland)* (the Kilbrandon Report). Cmnd 2306.

H.M.S.O. (1967) *Report of the Central Advisory Committee for Education (England)* (the Plowden Report), vol. 1.

H.M.S.O. (1968) *Children in Trouble*. Cmnd 3601.

H.M.S.O. (1969a) *The Sentence of the Court.*

H.M.S.O. (1969b) *Minutes of Evidence Taken before the Expenditure Committee* (Children and Young Persons Act.) 6 February 1974.

H.M.S.O. (1974) *Young Adult Offenders. Report of the Advisory Council on the Penal System* (Younger Report).

H.M.S.O. (1975a) *Report of the Committee on Mentally Abnormal Offeners* (the Butler Report). Cmnd 6244.

H.M.S.O. (1975b) *Eleventh Report from the Expenditure Committee* (Session 1974—5). Vol. 1, *The Children and Young Persons Act, 1969.* 30 July.

H.M.S.O. (1977a) *The Length of Prison Sentences. Report of the Advisory Council on the Penal System* (the Serota Report). (interim report).

H.M.S.O. (1977b) *A Review of Criminal Justice Policy (1976)* Home Office Working Paper.

H.M.S.O. (1979) *Report of the Committee of Enquiry into the Actions of the Authorities and Agents Relating to Darryn James Clarke.* Cmnd 7730.

H.M.S.O. (1980) *Young Offenders.* Cmnd 8045.

HERBERT, M. (1978) *Conduct Disorders of Childhood and Adolescence.* John Wiley and Sons.

HENSTON, R. F. (1977) *Salmond on the Law of Torts* (17th edn). Sweet and Maxwell.

von HIRSCH, A. (1976) *Doing Justice.* Hill and Wang.

HOBBES, T. (1973) *Leviathan* (Everyman edn).

HONDERICH, T. (1969) *Punishment: The Supposed Justifications.* Hutchinson.

HOOD, R. G. (1974a) *Tolerançe and the Tariff* NACRO papers and reprints, no. 11.

HOOD, R. G. (1974b) Young adult offenders: comments on the Report of the Advisory Council on the Penal System. *British Journal of Criminology,* 14, 388-95.

HUTCHESON, F. (1971) *Collected Works of George Olms* (especially An Enquiry Concerning Moral Good and Evil).

HYSLOP, J. H. (1894) Freedom, responsibility and punishment. *Mind,* 3, 167-89.

KANT, I. (1897) *Philosophy of Law* (trans. E. T. Hastie). T. and T. Clark.

KANT, I. (1930) *Lectures on Ethics* (trans. L. Infield). Methuen.

KANT, I. (1949) *Critique of Practical Reason* (trans. L. W. Beck). University of Chicago Press.

KANT, I. (1960) *Education* (trans. A. Churton). University of Michigan Press.

KANT, I. (1965) *The Metaphysical Elements of Justice.* Part 1 of *The Metaphysics of Morals* (trans. J. Ladd). Bobbs Merrill.

KAUFMAN, A. S. (1959) Anthony Quinton on punishment. *Analysis,* 20, 10-13.

KLEINIG, J. (1973) *Punishment and Desert.* Martinus Nijhoff.

LEMERT, E. (1971) *Instead of Court.* US Government Printing Office/National Institute for Mental Health.

LEON, J. C. (1978) *Legal Representation of Children in Selected Court Proceedings: The Capacity of Children to Retain Legal Counsel.* University of Toronto (Centre for Urban and Community Studies), December.

LESSNOFF, M. (1971) Two justifications of punishment. *Philosophical Quarterly,* 21 141-8.

LUKES, S. (1973) *Emile Durkheim: His Life and Work.* Allen Lane.

MABBOTT, J. D. (1939) Punishment. *Mind,* 48. 152-67 (also in Acton, 1969, pp. 39-54).

MABBOTT, J. D. (1955) Professor Flew on punishment. *Philosophy,* 30. 256-65 (also in Acton, 1969, pp. 115-29).

MANSER, A. R. (1962) It serves you right. *Philosophy,* 37, 293-306.

MARX, K. (1959) Capital punishment. In L. S. Feuer (ed.) *Basic Writings on Politics and Philosophy: Marx and Engels,* pp. 485-89. Anchor Books.

MATZA, D. (1964) *Delinquency and Drift.* John Wiley and Sons.

McCLOSKEY, H. J. (1957) An examination of restricted utilitarianism. *Philosophical Review,* 66, 466-85.

McCLOSKEY, H. J. (1962) The complexity of the concept of punishment. *Philosophy,* 37, 307-25.

McCLOSKEY, H. J. (1963) A note on utilitarian punishment. *Mind,* 72, 599.

McCLOSKEY, H. J. (1965) A non-utilitarian approach to punishment. *Inquiry,* 8, 249-63.

McPHERSON, T. (1967) Punishment, definition and justification. *Analysis,* 28. 21-7.

McTAGGART, J. E. (1896) Hegel's theory of punishment. *International Journal of Ethics,* 6, 479-502.

McTAGGART, J. E. (1918) *Studies in Hegelian Cosmology.* Cambridge University Press.

MENNINGER, K. (1966) *The Crime of Punishment.* Viking Press.

MILL, J. S. (1865) *An Examination of Sir William Hamilton's Philosophy* (especially ch. 26). Longmans.

MILL, J. S. (1964) *Utilitarianism* (ed. M. Warnock), (especially ch. 5). Collins Fontana.

MOBERLY, W. H. (1925) Some ambiguities in the retributive theory of punishment. *Proceedings of the Aristotelian Society,* 29 June, pp. 289-304.

MOBERLY, Sir W. (1968) *The Ethics of Punishment.* Faber and Faber.

MORGAN, P. (1978) *Delinquent Fantasies.* Temple Smith.

MORGAN, P. (1980) article in *Daily Telegraph,* 22 February.

MORRIS, A. (1974) Scottish juvenile justice: a critique. In R. G. Hood (ed.) *Crime, Criminology and Public Policy,* pp. 347-74. Heinemann.

MORRIS, N. (1974) *The Future of Imprisonment.* University of Chicago Press.

MUNDLE, C. W. (1954) Punishment and Desert. *Philosophical Quarterly,* 4, 216-28 (also in Acton 1969, pp. 65-82, with postscript).
MURPHY, J. G. (1973) Marxism and retribution. *Philosophy and Public Affairs,* 2, 217-43.

NATIONAL CHILDREN'S BUREAU (1977) *Who Cares: Young People in Care Speak Out* (ed. R. Page and G. Clarke).
NOWELL-SMITH, P. (1948) Freewill and responsibility. *Mind,* 62, 45-61.
NOWELL-SMITH, P. (1954) *Ethics.* Penguin.

PACKER, H. L. (1969) *The Limits of the Criminal Sanction.* Stanford University Press.
PARSLOE, P. (1978) *Juvenile Justice in Britain and the United States.* Routledge and Kegan Paul.
de PAULEY, W. C. (1925) Beccaria and punishment. *International Journal of Ethics,* 35, 404-12.
PEASE, K. *et al.* (1980) Report of the penal policy group working party on parole (mimeo).
PETERS, R. S. (1966) *Ethics and Education.* George Allen and Unwin.
PINCOFFS, E. L. (1975) The rationale of punishment. In Feinberg and Gross (1975), pp. 17-25.
PLAMENATZ, J. (1968) *Consent, Freedom and Political Obligation.* Oxford University Press.
PLAMENATZ, J. (1969) Responsibility, blame and punishment. In P. Laslett and W. G. Runciman (eds) *Philosophy, Politics and Society,* (3rd series), pp. 173-93. Basil Blackwell.

QUINTON, A. M. (1954) On punishment. *Analysis,* 14, 133-42 (also in Acton, 1969, pp. 55-64).

RADZINOWICZ, L. (1958) *The Results of Probation.* Macmillan.
RASHDALL, H. (1907) *The theory of good and evil.* Clarendon Press.
RASHDALL, H. (1910) The ethics of forgiveness. *International Journal of Ethics,* 10, 193-206.
RAWLS, J. (1955) Two concepts of rules. *The Philosophical Review,* 64, 3--32 (also in Acton, 1969, pp. 105-14).
ROSEN, A. (1954) Detention of suicidal patients. An example of some limitations of infrequent events. *Journal of Consulting Psychology,* 18, 397-403.
ROSS, A. (1975) *On Guilt, Responsibility and Punishment.* University of California Press.
ROSS, W. D. (1930) *The Right and the Good* (especially Appendix 2, ch. 2, pp. 56-64). Oxford University Press.
ROUSSEAU, J. J. (1930) *The Social Contract* (Everyman edn), (especially ch. 7, bk 1, and chs 5 and 6, bk 2).
ROUSSEAU, J. J. (1969) *Emile* (Everyman edn).
RUSSELL, B. (1946) *A History of Western Philosophy.* George Allen and Unwin.

RYALL, R. (1974) Delinquency: the problem for treatment. *Social Work Today,* 5, 16 May, pp. 98-103.

SALMOND, Lord. (1973) *Crime and Punishment* (the Riddell Lecture). Institute of Legal Executives.
SIDGWICK, H. (1901) *The Methods of Ethics.* Macmillan.
SMART, A. (1969) Mercy. In Acton (1969), pp. 212-28.
SMITH, A. (1808) *The Theory of Moral Sentiments.* Bell and Bradfute.
SMITH, J. C. and HOGAN, B. (1978) *Criminal Law* (4th edn). Butterworths.
SPARKS, R. F. (1969) The depraved are not just deprived. *New Society,* 24 July, pp. 12-15.
SPINOZA, B. de (1951a) *Theologico Politicus* (especially chs 4 and 16). Constable.
SPINOZA, B. de (1951b) *Tractatus Politicus* (especially ch. 3). Constable.
SPRIGGE, T. L. (1965) A utilitarian reply to Dr McCloskey. *Inquiry,* 8, 264-91.
STEPHEN, J. F. (1883) *A History of the Criminal Law in England,* vol. 2. Macmillan (also in Feinberg and Gross, 1975, pp. 45-9).
S.T.O.P.P. (undated) *Abolition Handbook* (ed. P. Newell).
SUMMERS, R. S. (1962) H. L. A. Hart on justice. *Journal of Philosophy,* 59, 497-500.

TAYLOR, I. WALTON, P. and YOUNG, J. (1973) *The New Criminology.* Routledge and Kegan Paul.
TEMPLE, W. (1930) *The ethics of punishment.* Howard League Lecture.
TEMPLE, W. (1934) *The ethics of penal action.* Clarke Hall Lectures Clarke Hall Fellowship, 19 March).
THOMAS, D. A. (1979) *Principles of Sentencing* (2nd edn). Heinemann.

U.S. PRESIDENT'S COMMISSION ON LAW ENFORCEMENT AND THE ADMINISTRATION OF JUSTICE (1967) *The Challenge of Crime in a Free Society,* vol. 81.

del VECCHIO, G. (1952) *Justice.* Edinburgh University Press.

WALKER, N. (1969) *Sentencing in a Rational Society.* Allen Lane.
WALKER, N. (1979) The efficacy and morality of deterrents. *Criminal Law Review,* (March), 129-44.
WALKER, N. (1980) *Punishment, Danger and Stigma.* Basil Blackwell.
WARNOCK, G. J. (1967) *The Object of Morality.* Methuen.
WEBER, M. (1954) *Law in Society.* Harvard University Press.
WEST, D. J. (ed.) (1972) *The Future of Parole.* Duckworth.
WHITELEY, C. H. (1948) Nowell-Smith on retribution and responsibility. *Mind,* 62, 230-1.

WILSON, J. Q. (1975) *Thinking about Crime.* Basic Books.

ZIMRING, F. E. and HAWKINS, G. J. (1973) *Deterrence: the Legal Threat in Crime Control.* University of Chicago Press.

Index

Wilkins, L., 173
Wilson, J.Q., 157, 166, 184, 210

Young Offenders, White Paper on,
  150
Youth Contract Order, 143-4

Youth Treatment Centres, 138,
  142

Zimring, F.E. (and Hawkins, G.J.),
  67, 210